M000266729

BUILDING FILIPINO HAWAI'I

THE ASIAN AMERICAN EXPERIENCE

Series Editors
Eiichiro Azuma
Jigna Desai
Martin F. Manalansan IV
Lisa Sun-Hee Park
David K. Yoo

Roger Daniels, Founding Series Editor

A list of books in the series appears at the end of this book.

BUILDING
FILIPINO HAWAI'I

RODERICK N. LABRADOR

UNIVERSITY OF ILLINOIS PRESS

Urbana, Chicago, and Springfield

Library of Congress Control Number: 2014956525
ISBN 978-0-252-03880-8 (hardcover)
ISBN 978-0-252-08036-4 (pbk.)
ISBN 978-0-252-09676-1 (e-book)

For Miles and Ella,
dakayo makaaramid ti naranraniag a masakbayan

CONTENTS

ILLUSTRATIONS

ACKNOWLEDGMENTS

First and foremost, I want to thank my family, especially Christine Quemuel, my wife, partner, and biggest cheerleader. I am extremely grateful for her unconditional and unwavering love, without which this project could not have been completed. I can always count on her smiles, positivity, and encouragement. I owe her a huge debt of gratitude for spending birthdays and special life events at community activities as part of my fieldwork. To Miles and Ella, my little Pin@ys and JAs in Hawai'i who give me perspective and inspiration, this book is written, in part, to provide you both a broader context for your life experiences yet to come. And to the best mother-in-law, Carolyn Quemuel, I am profoundly thankful for your kindness, understanding, and support.

I want to thank my colleagues in the Department of Ethnic Studies at the University of Hawai'i at Mānoa, who have been extremely supportive as I transitioned from student affairs to academic affairs: Ibrahim Aoude, Noel Kent, Davianna McGregor, Ulla Hasager, Elisa White, Pensri Ho, Lisa Uperesa, Brian Chung, Lee Ann Wang, and Janette Yuasa. I want to express my appreciation to Ty Tengan and Monisha Das Gupta for their continuous nudging and mentorship. Special thanks go to Jonathan Okamura for his careful reading of the manuscript. I want to also acknowledge Dean Alegado for paving the trail for research, teaching, and community work with Filipinos in Hawai'i and Dean Saranillio for blazing new trails and challenging my thinking and writing. I want to express my sincere gratitude to other members of my UH family who have supported me throughout this project: Amy Agbayani, Ruth Mabanglo, Teresita Ramos, Erin Kahunawaika'ala Wright, Kuahiwi Moniz, Christen Sasaki, John Rosa, Precy Espiritu, Julius Soria, Jacinta Galea'i, Trixia Soria, Denise Ah Sue, Chrissy Lam Yuen, Joanne Tang, Erwin Legaspi, Mike Cueva, Jonathan Evangelista (for the awesome photos!), and Ruben Campos (the best GA ever).

A number of colleagues have read and commented on various parts of this project, and I would like to express my thanks to them: Vernadette Gonzalez and Hoku Aikau for organizing the various iterations of the writing hui and Noe Goodyear-Ka'ōpua, Kapā Oliveira, and Njoroge Njoroge from the junior faculty seminar with Chuck Lawrence. I would also like to thank the anonymous reviewers for their comments and insights as well as Robyn Rodriguez for her extensive reviews and advice.

To the growing numbers of Filipina/o American scholars who I have admired from near and afar, thank you for the scholarship that I have used in my classes and the work that has molded and challenged my own thinking about Filipina/os in diaspora. These include Rick Bonus, Martin Manalansan, Rhacel Parreñas, Rick Baldoz, and Joanna Poblete. A special shout out to Theo Gonzalves for initiating our creation of a visually oriented partial view of Filipinos in Hawai'i. This book attempts to add another partial view and contribute to the rich archive of stories in the islands.

I am deeply indebted to the entire University of Illinois Press team. I am extremely grateful to Vijay Shah, with whom I started this project, for seeing the value of centering the experiences of Filipina/os in Hawai'i but also situating the project within the broader Asian American context. I also want to thank Larin McLaughlin, Dawn Durante, and Jennifer Comeau for guiding me through the final stages of the project. It has been wonderful working with you.

This book started as part of my dissertation work in the Department of Anthropology at the University of California, Los Angeles. I would like to thank my committee members who initially helped shape this project: Paul Kroskrity, Mariko Tamanoi, Pauline Agbayani-Siewert, and especially Karen Brodkin for her guidance and unfettered belief in my project. I would also like to thank the dynamic duo of David Kamper and Joanna Brooks for their continued friendship and support that has extended beyond UCLA, as well as Ann Walters, Jason Throop, and particularly Jonathan Jackson for helping me navigate my academic and social lives while in the doctoral program. The Asian American Studies Center and Asian American Studies Department serve as another home at UCLA. Thank you to all who have helped me (and Erin) with developing and sustaining the UCLA Hawai'i Travel Study Program: Enrique De La Cruz, Dennis Arguelles, Meg Thornton, Sefa Aina, Stacey Hirose, Hadyn Dick, Gloria Ruiz-Gonzales, Barrett Korerat, Malcolm Quon, Sergio Broderick-Villa, Emily Moon, Anne Bautista, Jessie Singh, Tricia Fifita, and Keith Camacho.

Finally, a huge mahalo-halo to the various members of Timpuyog and Katipunan as well as the faculty in the Ilokano and Filipino programs at the University of Hawaiʻi at Mānoa and the community members affiliated with the Filipino Community Center who spent time talking with me and allowed me to record them on my cassette tape recorder, microcassette recorder, digital recorder, or my smartphone. I hope this book, at the least, captures some of the multiplicity and complexity of their thoughts and experiences. My apologies to those who helped me along the way but I have failed to mention here. Dios ti agngina and maraming salamat.

BUILDING FILIPINO HAWAI'I

"Why do you want to go to Hawai'i?"

It was a frosty spring in western New York when I was trying to figure out my postcollege plans. I had spent the past four years at a small, private university located near Lake Ontario, and I was looking for some change in terms of weather and demographics. For graduate school, should I go to Hawai'i, or should I return to California, where I had spent much of my youth? I received some advice from a friend's father, a post-1965 Filipino immigrant and a doctor in New Jersey. When I told him that I was leaning toward going to Hawai'i, he responded, "Why do you want to go Hawai'i?" I explained the attraction of the weather and that the archipelago boasted the highest concentration of Filipinos among U.S. states. Even more, the university had a critical mass of scholars whose work focused on Filipinos in the Philippines and in the diaspora. He countered by telling me that there were "different kinds" of Filipinos there and that Filipinos were treated differently there. He explained that unlike the Filipino American communities in the tri-state area (and specifically those in the New York City area), Filipinos in Hawai'i were primarily working class. Because of that, the community was not seen in a particularly good light. His words struck a dissonant chord.

In what ways were Filipinos in Hawai'i different from Filipinos in New York? How were Filipinos treated in Hawai'i? The New York university I attended did not consider Filipinos as a socioeconomic "minority," confirming the community profile of Filipinos in New York suggested by my friend's father. Another friend's Jamaican mother, who worked as a hospital administrator in Manhattan, reaffirmed this understanding and image of Filipinos. She was very familiar with Filipinos, particularly the Filipina nurses she worked with. When I first met her, she recognized right away that I was Filipino (in California most people mistook me for Mexican), and she wondered if my mother was a nurse. She knew many Filipina/os who were occupationally tied to the medical field.[1] I was somewhat disappointed to relay to her that although my mother had started her schooling in the Philippines to work in the medical field, she was mainly employed in low-wage work in the hotel and electronics industries in San Diego.

In his recent study examining the links between educational attainment and socioeconomic status, educator Niki Libarios (2013) uses recent census data to illustrate the stark differences between Filipinos in Hawai'i and their counterparts nationally, especially in New York. Across the United States, 12.6 percent of Filipinos twenty-five years or older had no high school diploma, 33.9 percent held a baccalaureate degree, and 7.8 percent held a graduate degree. In the Hawai'i region, Filipinos composed the highest percentage with no high school diploma (23.9 percent) and the lowest percentage with baccalaureate degrees (14.1 percent) and graduate degrees (2.8 percent) (U.S. Census Bureau, 2003a, 2003b). On the flip side, Filipinos in the New York region had attained the highest educational levels, with only 5.9 percent having no high school diploma, while those with baccalaureate and graduate degrees stood at 51.9 percent and 13.7 percent, respectively. In other words, the national averages for Filipino educational attainment approximately doubled those in Hawai'i, and the number of Filipinos in New York who had baccalaureate and graduate degrees roughly quadrupled those in the islands (Libarios 2013: 35).

According to Libarios's study, the occupational and income profiles follow a similar pattern. Primarily owing to the tourism-driven economy in the islands, the Hawai'i region had the highest percentage of Filipino men (69.8 percent) and second highest percentage of women (45.2 percent) in sales, construction, and service-related jobs, while the national averages for these occupational categories were 47.4 percent for men and 33.4 percent for women. The Washington, D.C., region had the lowest percentage of Filipino men (32.0 percent) and the New York region the lowest percentage of Filipino women (18.5 percent) in these same occupational categories (Libarios 2013: 36). On the other side of the spectrum, for professional and managerial occupations, Filipinos in the Hawai'i region had the lowest percentages for men (30.2 percent) and women (54.9 percent). Nationally, the averages for Filipinos in these occupations were higher—52.5 percent for men and 68.3 percent for women. The Washington, D.C., region had the highest percentage of Filipino men (68.0 percent) and the New York region the highest percentage of Filipino women (81.1 percent) in these same occupational categories (Libarios 2013: 37). For per-capita income, Filipinos in the Hawai'i region had the lowest, at $14,545, with the national average about one-fourth higher at $19,259. Filipinos in the New York region nearly doubled the per-capita income of Filipinos in Hawai'i at $26,587 (Libarios 2013: 38).

I began with my two experiences and the demographic profiles not just to highlight the differences between Filipino communities in Hawai'i and New York but also to help frame *Building Filipino Hawai'i* and to underscore the interrelatedness of identity, power, and representation discussed throughout the book. These stories draw attention to the heterogeneity of Filipino communities in Hawai'i and the United States and highlight the markers often used by Filipinos and non-Filipinos to draw distinctions. We often use place and the accompanying histories of these locations as points of differentiation, but in this book I also want to include class and language to explore representational dynamics. We readily acknowledge that Filipinos in California, Illinois, Texas, Washington, New Jersey, New York, Nevada, Florida, and Virginia[2] are different from one another, depending on their community's particular histories—for example, whether they are former and/or current navy towns, formed primarily from post-1965 immigration, or trace their genealogies to pensionados, farmworkers, or cannery workers. In this book, I focus on the Filipino community in Hawai'i to reveal how they are similar to and different from Filipino communities elsewhere in the United States, but I also explore differences within the community.

Within this context, the book starts with two basic and interrelated questions: What does it mean to be "Filipino," and what are the contexts and consequences of how the identity category is defined? Although I focus on the Filipino community in Hawai'i, this book is concerned with broader processes of identity making and the politics of representation among immigrant communities in the contemporary era of globalization and transnationalism. In essence, the volume contends that minority immigrant populations politicize identity as part of their efforts to resist marginalization where they employ identity as an organizing principle in struggles for community empowerment. Following Espiritu's work on Filipinos in San Diego (2003), this book examines how the Filipino "ethnic community" (Tintiangco-Cubales 2009) in Hawai'i configures, negotiates, and enacts their sense of Filipinoness in their constructions of "home" and "homeland." In addition, *Building Filipino Hawai'i* highlights the ways language and class shape the contours of immigrant imaginations of "home" and "homeland."

Studying Filipinos in Hawai'i

Because of its central location in the Pacific (geographically, culturally, politically, and militarily), its links to the Asia-Pacific region, and its incorporation as part of the "American Tropics" (Isaac 2006), Hawai'i's border islands are sites of multiple intercultural and political exchanges that transgress geographic and national boundaries. In addition, Hawai'i reflects the population trends suggested by recent demographic changes in the United States. According to the 2010 U.S. Census the majority of residents in Hawai'i are nonwhite, and Asian Americans and Pacific Islanders constitute roughly 70 percent of the total population. Whites are numerically the largest individual racial/ethnic group, and Filipinos are the second most populous group and are now the largest Asian ancestry group in Hawai'i, comprising 14.5 percent (single race) and approximately one-quarter (single and mixed race) of the total population. As such, Hawai'i is an ideal site for interrogating issues related to race, ethnicity, culture, place, and immigration. *Building Filipino Hawai'i* examines the construction of Filipino identities in a place where a politics of representation and a politics of location are already integral parts of immigrant and indigenous struggles against American hegemony and the legacies of U.S. colonialism.

The typical image of Hawai'i[3] is that of the commoditized touristic scene of white sandy beaches, swaying palm trees, picture-perfect sunsets, and highly sexualized hula girls and surfer boys. In large part, the political, economic, and ideological machinery of global tourism produces and heavily markets this image of Hawai'i as "tropical paradise," a tourist playground for rest and relaxation with warm and inviting "natives" who "hang loose" and happily welcome and serve visitors. A complementary image of Hawai'i depends on its much-celebrated multiculturalism and perceived racial/ethnic harmony, and of the idea of Hawai'i as "racial paradise" and "the most notable instance of a melting-pot of the modern world" (Park 1938, xiv).[4] This image of groups harmoniously coexisting stems partially from the fact that there is no numerical majority among the various racial/ethnic groups who have settled the islands. Because there is no numerical majority, there exists a widely held misperception that "everyone is a minority," which serves as "living proof" (Grant and Ogawa 1993) of racial tolerance and cultural intermixture where "peoples of different races and creeds can live together, enriching each other, in harmony and democracy" (Fuchs 1961, 449). In other words, there is a general perception that the various groups have "mixed" and that no single racial/ethnic group is politically and economically dominant despite evidence to the contrary—namely, the history of U.S. colonialism and foreign domination; the displacement, dispossession, and population collapse of Native Hawaiians; the exploitation of Asian workers as sources of cheap labor that facilitated the development of U.S. capitalism in Hawai'i and investment in Asia; and the racial and ethnic stratification that positions whites, Japanese, and Chinese as elites, and Native Hawaiians, Filipinos, and Samoans as subordinate (Okamura 1990). Hawai'i as "racial paradise" is also constructed through the widespread promotion of the "Hawai'i Multicultural Model" (see Okamura 1998) and its endorsement of Local,[5] a racialized identity category that indexes a sociopolitically constructed pan-ethnic formation, as the unmarked normative order (Hill 1998) and the mainstream principle for collective identification. The elevation of the Local as the mainstream disguises differential access to wealth and power and frames multiculturalism not merely as a political symbol or ideal but also as the ideological underpinning of everyday social, cultural, political, and economic realities and contemporary settler colonialism.

Questions about Filipino identity and the politics around identity formation have been key components in my social, educational, and professional experiences in the islands. When I first arrived in Honolulu as a graduate student at the University of Hawai'i at Mānoa in the summer of 1994, a university-sponsored public humanities institute called "Filipino Culture: Reclaiming a Heritage" had recently concluded. The two-week summer session included a cultural fair, a film series, and a program of lectures, art exhibits, and music and dance concerts. The institute brought together Philippine and Filipino American scholars, artists, writers, students, and community leaders to discuss issues regarding the experiences of Filipinos in the Philippines, in Hawai'i and in the continental United States (particularly those related to language, literature, education, identity, and cultural values and acculturation). More interestingly, the institute posed the question, "What is 'Filipino'?" Many expressed concern that local Filipino youth, especially those born and raised in Hawai'i, were neglecting Filipino history, culture, tradition, and language and were denying their heritage. The organizers felt that Hawai'i-born Filipinos did not have a positive image or definition of "Filipino" and, as a result, they were disregarding or denying their cultural roots and not self-identifying as Filipino. Instead, Hawai'i-born Filipinos identified themselves as "Local,"[6] a pan-ethnic category with roots in plantation society. As suggested in the summer institute guide, the question "What is 'Filipino'?" was particularly relevant because "the [Filipino] tradition was being forgotten by younger generations of Filipino Americans" (Ward 1994: 2). Through the institute, the question could be answered, and in the process they could "help Hawai'i's Filipino-American youth and the community in general gain a better understanding of Filipino culture through the humanities" (ibid.: 4). In effect, by participating in the institute, Filipino youth could more sufficiently understand Filipino culture, and in this way they would be able to reclaim their heritage and identify as "Filipino."

Although at that time I was new to Hawai'i, I was a bit surprised to see that in a place containing such a high concentration of Filipinos and a long history in the islands, there was a compelling need to ask, "What is 'Filipino'?" Should they not already have an idea of what it means to be Filipino? Why were Filipino youth not identifying themselves as "Filipino"? And why did community and university leaders care so much about this issue? From this initial encounter, it was clear that the dynamics and character of Hawai'i's Filipino community was quite different from both the largely military and low-income community that shaped my upbringing in San Diego and the high-income Filipino American community I encountered during my undergraduate education in New York. At the time, Hawai'i was on the verge of electing the first Filipino American governor in the United States, and as a result, the Filipino community was receiving a lot of media coverage.[7] But perhaps more relevant to the "Filipino Culture" institute was the continuing media attention, both in the two mainstream dailies and in the two local Filipino community newspapers, on Filipino youth gangs and their involvement in crime, drugs, and violence.[8] As Maria Torres-Kitamura suggested in one of the Filipino community newspapers, in addition to the anxieties and nervousness that normally accompanies the beginning of a school year, it was also "[the] season for Filipinos to cringe as their children are described by the media as typical members of youth gangs" (Torres-Kitamura 1993: 6). Torres-Kitamura also wondered if these young Filipinos were part of "A Generation Lost?"

In addition to the highly publicized Filipino youth gang issue, another "Filipino problem" was the persistent low performance, low achievement, and lack of success among Filipino students at Hawai'i K–12 public schools, which contributed to the idea of Filipinos as the islands' "immigrant menace."[9] At the University of Hawai'i, with pending budget cuts and tuition increases, there arose increased interest in issues of access, equity, and diversity and the underrepresentation of Filipino students, staff, and faculty in the University of Hawai'i system.[10] Many hoped that the Filipino Culture Institute could find the "lost" generation of Filipino youth, gang member and non–gang member alike, and address the inequities in the public educational system. Such an approach could set Filipino youth on the path to success, and their futures would no longer be in jeopardy. As such, Filipinos could take their place as valued contributors in Hawai'i society.

In 1996, two years after "Filipino Culture: Reclaiming A Heritage," I helped organize another university-community event, "Pagdiriwang '96" (the term "pagdiriwang" means "celebration" in Tagalog). Unlike the two-week "Filipino Culture" institute, Pagdiriwang '96 was a year-long series of events and activities that commemorated and celebrated the one-hundredth anniversary of the Philippine Revolution, the ninetieth anniversary of the first Filipino plantation workers' arrival to the islands, the fiftieth anniversary of Philippine independence from the United States, and the fiftieth anniversary of the last recruitment of Filipino plantation workers. Pagdiriwang '96 was largely university-driven but enjoyed active and strong support from the community. Monthly community forums were a central component of the celebrations. The community forums involved a humanities scholar (usually a university professor) and other panelists who discussed a range of relevant issues, which included identity construction, stereotyping, discrimination in education and employment, and the need for more involvement in business and electoral politics. Pagdiriwang '96 also produced a publication (see Okamura and Labrador, 1996) addressing the issues discussed in the monthly forums. This publication was distributed to high schools, colleges and universities (in Hawai'i and on the continent), and the broader community.

Pagdiriwang '96 had two primary interlocking objectives. First, the celebrations allowed the Filipino community to think about its past, present, and future. In the words of the organizers, they sought "to celebrate the achievements of the past and present generations, and to discuss and articulate the problems and aspirations of present and future generations" (Andaya and Ayson, 1996: vi). Furthermore, the community forums provided the opportunity "to discuss how far Filipino Americans have progressed and what still needs to be done for them to take their place as equals in multicultural Hawai'i and the U.S." (ibid.: vi). Second, Pagdiriwang '96 was an opportunity to unite the community and address the issue of community factionalism and division that, according to many of the community forum panelists and speakers, stemmed from intragroup rivalry and regionalism (an expression of persistent loyalties and ties people have to their home provinces and languages in the Philippines), which always seemed to crop up in discussions about what it means to be Filipino and what it would take for the community to become "equals in multicultural Hawai'i and the U.S." Through its various events and activities, Pagdiriwang '96 allowed participants to take stock of the past, examine the present, and create a vision for their collective future.

Pagdiriwang '96 came at a time when community and university discussions centered on the racist stereotypes used in Hawai'i ethnic humor, namely the comedy of Frank De Lima,[11] who I discuss more in-depth in chapter 2, and the negative representations depicted in the literary works of Hawai'i-born writer Lois-Ann Yamanaka.[12] According to Quemuel (1996), in addition to media misrepresentations of Filipinos as "sex danger," criminally inclined, and prone to violence, in Hawai'i ethnic humor also stereotypes

Filipinos as dog eaters, the perpetual immigrant or JOJ (Just Off the Jet), and speaking with an accent (which implies stupidity or lack of intelligence). Okamura traces the historical emergence and contemporary relevance of such representations:

> The stereotypes are an unfortunate historical burden of the plantation period of labor recruitment when unattached young males with little formal education dominated the Filipino population. . . . Once the damage was done, it has been extremely difficult for Filipino Americans to undo, even with a Filipino as a governor, and the anti-Filipino jokes should be seen as perpetuating this historical stigmatizing. Thus it is not surprising that young Filipino Americans continue to speak about feeling 'ashamed' being Filipino because of how society has denigrated that identity which should be reclaimed and redefined on their own terms (Okamura 1996: 3).

Like the "Filipino Culture" institute, Pagdiriwang '96 was central in community and university discourse on Filipino identity in Hawai'i, and, similar to its predecessor, it attempted to reclaim "Filipino." Even further, it sought a redefinition and reconstruction of the identity category.

Although the year-long Pagdiriwang '96 was a huge undertaking, it was not the first of its kind. In 1977, the Hawai'i State Legislature passed Enabling Act 181, which created the Filipino 75th Anniversary Commemoration Commission[13] to oversee the events surrounding the celebrations of the seventy-fifth anniversary of the first sakadas' arrival in Hawai'i. The seventy-fifth anniversary celebrations included cultural events and community forums, and two books were published in 1981: *Filipinos in Hawaii . . . The First 75 Years* and *Out of This Struggle: The Filipinos in Hawaii*. The celebrations questioned why Filipinos were at the bottom of the socioeconomic ladder while their fellow plantation workers, primarily the Japanese and Chinese, were able to leave the sugarcane fields and enter the middle class. Why had Filipinos not experienced the same type of upward socioeconomic mobility like their Japanese and Chinese counterparts? At the time and continuing into the present, Filipinos were and continue to be heavily concentrated in the less prestigious and lower-paying service and retail occupations. More than fifty years ago, Filipinos were the largest labor force in the plantation fields. Presently, Filipinos dominate the low-status work in the new plantations (that is, the hotels and resorts of the tourism industry) toiling as chambermaids, janitors, and gardeners. Popular explanations of Filipino low status and low educational achievement wrongly assume "that neither history, prevailing social circumstances, nor discriminatory practices based on stereotyping matter; that the fault is entirely that of Filipinos themselves. If they are generally poorly educated and poorly paid, and engaged in the least prestigious occupations, it is because this is what they want—these are the limits of their aspirations" (Teodoro 1981: 26). In one respect, as a contrast to cultural deficit thinking and popular mythology in Hawai'i that explained the low socioeconomic status of Filipinos in terms of "low levels of aspiration," Teodoro's analysis attempted to shift attention to the impact of government policies, racist institutional practices, and the Hawai'i political economy, especially the patterns of stratification and inequality that run along ethnic lines.[14]

Like similar events that followed, the celebrations also posed the question, "What is 'Filipino'?" Then, as was the case twenty-five years later, it seemed that Filipinos were not identifying themselves as Filipino: "Filipinos as a whole have indeed tended to either deny their cultural heritage, or to see it merely as a means of distinguishing themselves from the many other cultural groups in Hawaii" (Teodoro 1981: 54). For example, the "Overcoming Stereotypes" chapter in *Out of This Struggle* included a now oft-used political cartoon by Corky Trinidad in which one of the characters is asked, "Are you Filipino?" The character responds in two quote bubbles, the first of which reads, "Course not! I'm Spanish-Chinese-British-Irish-French-Indian-Finnish-Thai-Mexican-Hawaiian." The second bubble reads, "But my, uh . . . parents are er, Filipino."[15] In addition, the seventy-fifth anniversary celebrations occurred at a time when there was a series of violent clashes between local and immigrant Filipinos at several Hawai'i high schools (Chang 1996; Teodoro 1981; Okamura 1980). This violence highlighted a growing Local/immigrant Filipino split that continues today.

Filipino American scholar Steffi San Buenaventura has suggested that Filipino identity making in Hawai'i takes place along a Local/non-Local continuum, represented by those who are Hawai'i-born on one side, and on the other, those whose birthplace and upbringing are located outside the islands: "Fundamental to understanding Hawai'i is to know the meaning and nuances of 'local' identity and the continuous contradistinctions that are made between the local and the 'non-local' other" (1996a: 38, emphasis in original). Here, following common usage, I understand "Local" as a relational identity category that marks loyalty and attachment to the peoples, cultures, and lands of Hawai'i; it is the popular designation of choice of those residents who claim a natural and rightful belonging to Hawai'i. The most salient "non-Local" categories include "immigrant," "mainland," "haole" ("foreigner" in Hawaiian, but refers to "white" in its more racialized contemporary usage), and "Native Hawaiian" (the categories of "tourist" and "military" should also be added to this list, although I do not directly address these in this book). For Filipino identity making, "immigrant," referring to those born in the Philippines, is the most salient non-Local category, although with the increased movement of Filipinos from the continental United States to Hawai'i, a Local Filipino/mainland Filipino polarity has also emerged. Nevertheless, the questions "What is 'Filipino'?" and "Who is Filipino?" are posed primarily within the context of the Local-immigrant-mainland spectrum. In other words, the "Filipino" identity category is relationally produced using the triangulation of immigrant, Local, and mainland.[16] As San Buenaventura notes, the relational construction of the Local/non-Local binary has its roots in plantation society and in the arrival of the 1946 sakadas, the last and largest group of Filipino laborers imported by the HSPA to work on the plantations (San Buenaventura 1996). The Local/non-Local dichotomy further crystallized with the change in immigration legislation in 1965.

The more recent Filipino immigration to Hawai'i and the continental United States has been conditioned by changes in United States immigration legislation as well as sociopolitical and economic circumstances in the Philippines. The Immigration and Naturalization Act of 1965 formally ended the national-origins quotas, allowing entrance into the United States based on family reunification or occupational preferences. This act had a tremendous impact on the numbers of Asian immigrants and especially Filipinos, who comprised almost one-quarter of the total Asian immigration (Espiritu 1995). San Buenaventura observes the dual impact of the changes in immigration law: "Post-1965 immigration has had an empowering, replenishing effect on the Filipino American community, providing the numerical strength needed to push for minority rights. However, the dual chain migration has also begun to highlight the diversity of the Filipino community, reflecting conflicting values and concerns based on the differing perspectives and interests of the American-born and the immigrant Filipinos" (San Buenaventura 1995: 452). With roughly 3,500 immigrants arriving in Hawai'i annually since the 1970s, the post-1965 immigration has had a numerically revitalizing effect. The constant flow of new immigrants increased the size of the community, drawing attention to the possibility of collective social action and political power. The changes in U.S. immigration law also coincided with Hawai'i's transition from an agriculture-based economy to the development of the tourism industry and construction of resorts and hotels, as well as service contracts with the U.S. military (defense industry), which firmly established Hawai'i as tourist destination and military colony. This shift has corresponded with the arrival of new immigrants not directly connected to the plantations, particularly post-1965 professionals and other workers, referred to as "postwar Filipinos" (Teodoro 1981), "new breed" Filipinos

(Alcantara in Dionisio 1981), or according to some of my interviewees, "the educated Filipinos." As a result of the continuing influx of new immigrants, there exists the juxtaposition of old and new definitions of Filipino identity. Thus in recent years, Filipino labor history and the plantation experience no longer serve as the primary marker of Filipino identity in Hawai'i; it is only one of the available resources in the repertoire of identification.[17]

In addition, the post-1965 immigrants, particularly those who entered the United States under the sixth preference (the employment provision) and came from urban centers in the Philippines, brought a different understanding and alternative image of what it meant to be Filipino, effectively changing the character and dynamics of the Filipino community in Hawai'i. As San Buenaventura states, the entry of "the post-1965 immigrants drew attention in the community, not just to immigrant issues (relating to public education, employment, social services) but also to the immigrant image ('bright clothes,' 'strong accent,' 'provincial,' 'clannish')" (1996a: 38). The influx of new immigrants and the shift from issues to images or stereotypes led to the development of ostensibly different and competing constructions of Filipino identity. The constructions fall along generational and class differences between old-timers and newcomers, working-class local Filipinos and middle-class immigrant Filipinos. Post-1965 immigrants were and are stereotyped by local Filipinos as "uppity," "pushy," "know-it-all," and "materialistic," while post-1965 immigrants perceive local Filipinos as "passive," "lacking in class," "uncultured," and "lacking in depth" (Teodoro 1981: 58). Furthermore, there is a rural/urban divide that correlates to a linguistic distinction and constructs a relational alterity. As Teodoro notes, "Bakya, a Tagalog term referring to wooden slippers worn by peasants in the rural areas, is another term commonly used to describe local Filipinos. By extension, bakya means country bumpkin, crude, low-class, lacking in manners . . . non-Ilokano Filipinos tend to use the term mostly in connection with local Filipinos who are mostly Ilokanos from the rural areas of the Philippines" (Teodoro 1981: 58). For the new Tagalog immigrants, Ilokanos are understood as rural and provincial (read: not only in the sense of coming from the provinces, but also simple, less educated, poorer, and unsophisticated), whereas Tagalogs are perceived to embody the opposite characteristics (that is, more cosmopolitan, more advanced, more educated, wealthier, and more refined), and Visayans are characterized as fun-loving and laid back.[18] The difference of post-1965 immigrants is also marked by their speech practices. Speaking Filipino English, talking "English with an accent," and not the local lingua franca of Hawai'i Creole English, or Pidgin, assumes another point of difference. According to Teodoro, "for many local Filipinos speaking English that is not pidgin is interpreted as wanting to be considered better than the locals; speaking with a nonpidgin Filipino accent means that a person is a 'noninsider Filipino' " (Teodoro 1981: 58).

Generation, culture, class, and language are the primary loci of differentiation in the Local/non-Local binary that are played out in public discourse and in everyday social life. Deep-seated stereotypes and assumptions based on these loci of differentiation have shaped and served as the basis for (mis)understanding and interacting with one another. Evidence of the rift between locals and immigrants can be seen in the conflicts in schools that began in the 1970s and continue today (which sometimes escalated to violence and is part of the partial explanation of the proliferation of gang involvement): "Not only do local Filipinos distance themselves from immigrant Filipinos, they also persecute them for being immigrants. . . . Immigrant Filipinos will say that they hate local Filipinos because the locals were the ones who were the most notorious for harassing the immigrants in school" (Revilla 1996b: 10).

The constant flow of Filipino immigrants since 1965 has led local Filipinos to dissociate themselves from their immigrant counterparts, drawing attention to their "Local" rather than a "Filipino" identity. As a result, Local Filipinos have undergone what is commonly interpreted as a process of cultural and ethnic disidentification, a denial of their heritage. With respect to this phenomenon, Leonard Andaya, a University of Hawai'i at Mānoa professor and second-generation Local Filipino, frames his experiences growing up in a plantation community in the following way:

> As children of immigrants, we believed in the American dream and welcomed the opportunities which beckoned. Those aspects of my identity linked to Hawai'i and America were ones that I believed to offer future promise because they were my home. Filipino culture, on the other hand, I saw as the culture of my parents and their friends. While I participated in Filipino activities, I did so mechanically mainly to please my parents. It was not because of any conscious effort to reject my Filipino heritage, but it was only because it appeared to be so foreign and irrelevant compared to the vibrance and promise which characterized Hawai'i and America to the young (Andaya 1996: 6).

Like other Locals, Andaya draws an evaluative distinction between the Philippines and Hawai'i/America (as well as the gloss of Hawai'i as America). He sees the Philippines as a place that lacks opportunities, which has propelled the immigration of his parents. The Philippines is the place of his parents, while he claims Hawai'i as his "home." Participation in things Filipino was a mechanical filial obligation, a duty performed by a good Filipino son for his parents. "Filipino heritage" is understood from an instrumentalist perspective. Moreover, because "Filipino heritage" was foreign, it was irrelevant and inconceivable that it could be useful in fulfilling the idealized dream, vibrancy, and promise of opportunity that Hawai'i/America represented. As such, for Andaya (and other Locals) to succeed and achieve in Hawai'i, the logical choice was Localization, an assimilation and acculturation process grounded in the rejection, denial, or suppression of "Filipino heritage" and the making of Hawai'i as "home." It is this assimilation process that university and community leaders often find as the problematic source of an "identity crisis." By discussing who and what is "Filipino" this process potentially can be reversed, which in turn can set into motion other processes that attend to the lack of collective political and economic power among Filipinos in Hawai'i.

Toward a Filipino Cultural Politics of Representation

The process of Localization, of becoming Local, among Hawai'i-born Filipinos and the continuous immigration from the Philippines (as well as the movement of Filipinos and Filipino Americans from the continental United States) has created multiple competing definitions of Filipino identities, based on differing symbols, images, and narratives. Filipino-ness is constantly being negotiated and renegotiated, validated and invalidated. The multiplicity of Filipino identities has led to a development of what some have called an "identity crisis" among Filipino Americans (Revilla 1997; Cordova 1973, 1983). For example, Filipino American scholar Linda Revilla (1997) writes that there has been a persistent "identity crisis" among Filipino Americans, particularly among youth both in Hawai'i and the continental United States. Evidence of this "identity crisis" can be found in the numerous events and community forums similar to those I discussed earlier in the chapter. More specifically, Revilla cites the feelings of embarrassment and shame that young Filipinos have about being Filipino, as well as the ongoing denial or rejection of their cultural heritage that I also found among my interviewees. Indeed, many of my interviewees talked about being "shame to be Filipino" or that growing up they wanted to be "anything but Filipino" (which I take up more fully in chapter 3).

Revilla argues that the "identity crisis" is part of the legacies of Spanish and American colonialism, resulting in a "colonial mentality" that regards all things Filipino inferior to that of their colonial masters, especially toward Americans. Similarly, Espiritu writes that the U.S.-Philippine colonial relationship "has produced a pervasive cultural Americanization of the population, exhorting Filipinos to regard the American culture, political system, and way of life as superior to their own" (Espiritu 1985: 19). According to Revilla, the "identity crisis" can be transcended by "reconciling issues of self-love and self-respect" (1997: 96) and her diagnosis also includes a focus on a re-presentation of identity that incorporates what Strobel (1991) calls indigenization and multiculturality. For Strobel, indigenization is the process of rediscovering "native" Philippine oral traditions, folklore, beliefs, and values as well as returning to a Filipino language as a medium of communication. Multiculturality calls attention to the need for cultural awareness, primarily in the form of learning about Philippine and Filipino American history and culture. For Revilla and Strobel, the focus on traditional Philippine songs, dances, stories, and myths are ways in which Filipinos in the United States can assert, avow, and transmit their culture and heritage. Thus, indigenization and multiculturality are seen as strategies to reclaim a cultural identity thought to be lost in the process of immigration and assimilation or repressed by United States colonialism and contemporary American racism.

The attempts to transcend this "identity crisis" through strategies of indigenization and multiculturality are often understood as efforts to construct a Filipino identity amid multiplicity and hybridity. In Hawai'i (as elsewhere), there is no unified "Filipino" identity; it is a fundamentally contested identity category. Because Filipinos have come from different parts of the Philippines and arrived in Hawai'i under different sociohistorical circumstances, there are multiple, competing, and discrepant histories among Filipinos in Hawai'i. In addition, indigenization and multiculturality can prove difficult because for many Filipinos in Hawai'i, there is a sense of ambivalence toward the Philippine homeland. As is the case with Local Filipinos, the desire is not to return to the "homeland" but to belong to Hawai'i, the new "home." For Local Filipinos, the Philippines functions more as a spiritual homeland, the center from which "authentic Filipino culture" emanates, but it also a place they associate with recently arrived immigrants and to which they feel disconnected. This is quite clear in the cultural productions performed at the University of Hawai'i at Mānoa in which students attempt to establish historical and cultural links to the Philippines and in the process, "rediscover" their Filipino identities. I take this up more fully in chapter 3.

Attempts to construct a Filipino identity also often involve competing myths of origin and essentialist claims to cultural purity. Declarations of cultural authenticity and purity are principally fought over the nature of "home," that is to say, what and where is "home" and what is the relationship to the "homeland." In Hawai'i, there are three primary responses to these questions. The first response is a more geographically particular notion of "home" that symbolizes belonging to Hawai'i society. This corresponds to those who identify as "Local" Filipino, those born and raised in Hawai'i. The second response invokes a nationalistic notion of ethnic identity, one that indexes membership in the Philippine homeland. This corresponds to those categorized as "immigrant" Filipinos, those born and raised in the Philippines who are recent arrivals to Hawai'i. The third response draws attention to a diasporic and transnational Filipino community and corresponds to those categorized as "mainland" Filipinos, recent arrivals to the islands from the continental United States. The adjective that precedes "Filipino"—Local, immigrant, or mainland—indexes specific identities and triggers a chain of cultural associations, its social manifestations a type of identity-play in different cultural fields. This identity-play and play of symbols draws attention to the idea that constructing "Filipino" involves "home" making that relies on notions of authenticity and validation. As I suggest above, Filipino identity-play and the play of symbols and narratives point to within-group differences that are understood as detrimental intragroup division and disunity that inhibit collective political action.

Consequently, Filipinos are collectively diagnosed with a self-image problem that can be transcended with self-knowledge and cultural awareness, which is often understood as a necessary first step toward collective action and political empowerment. In contrast, I argue that rather than using an "identity crisis" explanation, "What is 'Filipino'?" and "Who is Filipino?" can be better understood as political questions. In this book, I suggest a "cultural politics of representation" (Rattansi 1995; see also Hall 1996 [1992]) framework, where these questions are recontextualized by emphasizing the structures of inequality and the systems of power that underscore the lived experiences of Filipinos and the discourses of Filipino identity. Central to the tension around the multiple constructions of "Filipino" is the dual meaning of representation. On one hand, representation is a question about who can legitimately speak for whom, which points to issues of contestation and hegemony between and within racial/ethnic groups and the importance of narratives, images, and symbols in the articulation and formation of collective identities. For Filipinos in Hawai'i, this is an issue of who belongs to the "Filipino" category, meaning who are legitimate members of the group and what criteria are used to determine membership. Moreover, what does membership mean and why does it matter? In this sense, representation refers to "issues of authority and accountability in the articulation of communal views and 'interests' " (Rattansi 1992: 257–58) and points to the social, political, and economic stakes for members and leaders of the community. On the other hand, representation also refers to "a voice in the allocation and redistribution of resources, often from local and national state agencies" (1992: 258). This second meaning points to the degree of participation in the political and economic distribution system (that is, the amount of relative power a group has with respect to other groups and the state). *Building Filipino Hawai'i* demonstrates ways that struggles over how Filipino identity is to be represented, in terms of which symbols, images, and narratives are legitimated, authenticated, and disseminated, are intimately tied to issues of sociopolitical power and involvement in the state distribution system. The construction of Filipino identities is part of struggles for a larger share of decision making and to participate in the power structure, not only as passive participants but as active decision makers. The construction of Filipino identities directly challenges the effects of colonialism, opposes racism, and confronts their collective marginalization, while demanding complete participation in Hawai'i society. Thus, working through matters of Filipino identity in Hawai'i is to contest Filipino subordination in the contemporary racial/ethnic and class hierarchy in hopes of eventually taking "their place as equals in multicultural Hawai'i and the U.S." Understanding the various constructions of Filipino identity through a "cultural politics of representation" frame shifts the focus from community psychoanalysis and pathology toward looking at how the group engages the social, political, and economic system and structures in which it participates, including an engagement with indigeneity.

A Filipino conducting research in Filipino Hawai'i

This book is partly inspired by my own travel experience and my engagement with Filipino American diversity. Prior to arriving in O'ahu, I had heard that unlike many Filipinos in the continental United States, most Filipinos in Hawai'i were speakers of Ilokano, one of the numerous regional languages in the Philippines and the third most commonly spoken language (behind Cebuano and Tagalog). This was of particular personal interest to me as a native speaker of Ilokano and as a 1.5-generation Filipino American. I was born in the Philippines and when I was six years old, my family immigrated to the United States. As part of my upbringing in southeast San Diego, the majority of Filipinos my family interacted with spoke Tagalog, formerly the national language of the Philippines and the language often said to be the lingua franca of Filipinos throughout the world. I thought that going to Hawai'i would be more or less a cultural and linguistic homecoming, yet on several occasions my positionality as a "Filipino" and my authenticity as an insider were called into question. I also discovered that although intellectually I recognized the heterogeneity of Filipinos, working through the sociocultural and political diversity of the group on the ground proved more challenging than I expected.

During the heart of my fieldwork, the same issues I initially encountered in the mid-1990s were still highly relevant, especially questions around identity and what it meant to be Filipino. These issues were particularly stark and insightful in my interviews and interactions with Cliff Galvante, one of my key research participants. Cliff, like many of my other research participants, identified three primary Filipino types that are constructed along a Local-immigrant-mainland spectrum. At the time, Cliff was in his midtwenties and self-identified primarily as "Local" (he told me he was "born and raised" in Hawai'i). He is a second-generation immigrant and both of his parents are from Ilocos Norte, an Ilokano-speaking province in the northern Philippines. I spent more than nine months interviewing him and getting to know his family and friends. In one of my early interviews, I asked him about his educational experiences. In a matter-of-fact way, he told me he went to an elementary school that was, "you know, the one by the prison" and that he went to the middle school where "you know, the one by the gym where they box." Further, mainly using Hawai'i Creole English (or Pidgin) he told me he graduated from a local high school "where they get plenty Filipinos, you know, the one by KFC. The one wit' the swimming pool that no work." Initially, Cliff thought that I was an insider, assuming that I grew up in the islands and that my upbringing was similar to his. My facial expressions and body language suggested otherwise, that I did not understand his references. I asked him to further describe the schools he attended and then he exclaimed, "Where you wen grad? You Filipino, ya?" In asking which high school I graduated from and whether or not I was Filipino, Cliff positioned me as an outsider to the local Filipino community. In his mind, as someone who is Filipino, I should know the geographical markers he used and should be familiar with the seemingly common-sense landmarks in his descriptions (that is, the elementary school near the state prison, the middle school known for its after-school boxing program, and the high school with the nonfunctioning swimming pool). Why did he need to further explain these places in the Filipino neighborhood he grew up in? In essence, he was questioning the type of Filipino I was because I was unfamiliar with these local references. We shared Filipino ethnic identity, but we were different types of Filipinos. I was an insider because I was Filipino, but I was now positioned as an outsider because I was from the continental United States, or in his terms, "the mainland." Although he accepted that I looked like I could be Local, where I was born, where I grew up, and my language (that is, he spoke mainly in Pidgin and classified my speech as "straight English") marked me as an outsider. These identity dynamics demonstrate the problematics of "insider" research, depicting more what I would consider inside/out ethnography[19]—who is in/out is not always clear cut, and researchers and research participants navigate and co-construct the fluidities of who is considered an insider and/or outsider. In other words, what makes a researcher an insider/outsider is not solely an academic exercise but is actively and continually negotiated in the field among and between the researcher and research participants.

Cel De Guzman is Cliff's cousin. He was a recent immigrant from Ilocos Norte. Cel immigrated to Hawai'i when he was twelve and was now in his early twenties. Cliff had suggested that I talk with Cel to get an immigrant perspective about Filipino identity. Cliff described his cousin as "buk."[20] Although Cel and Cliff attended the same middle school and high school, there were differences in their social and educational experiences that highlighted a Local/immigrant binary. During our introductory meeting (which involved the three of us), Cel told me that he was from the town of Bacarra, and in response I shared that I was born in Zambales but my grandparents were from Laoag, Ilocos Norte. Cel nodded, acknowledging the geographical proximity of the two towns (Laoag is actually a few towns south of Bacarra) and the possibility of ethnolinguistic similarity. During this greeting where Cel and I "placed" each other, Cliff did not understand the geographical references and asked where Laoag was, because he had never been to the Philippines. Cel admonished Cliff and exclaimed, "What? You don't know where that is? You Filipino, ya?" Cel's use of "You Filipino, ya?" is both an affirmation and rejection of Cliff's Filipino-ness. Cel recognized that Cliff is indeed Filipino, but sees him as a different type of Filipino, perhaps one too "Americanized" and possessing very little knowledge of and experience in the Philippines. Like in the previous interaction, Filipino-ness is being negotiated, but in this scenario, it is Cliff who is positioned as an outsider, as an "inauthentic" Filipino.

Several months later, Cliff and I attended the annual Filipino Fiesta and Parade in Waikiki and Kapi'olani Park. There we met Cedric Surio, who was in his late twenties and had recently moved to Honolulu from northern California. Cedric represents someone who Cliff usually categorized as "mainland" Filipino. Cliff and I introduced ourselves, and Cedric told us that he had moved to the islands not more than a year ago, and then proudly informed us that he was from Daly City, California. I nodded, knowing that Daly City is in the Bay Area and, like Honolulu, has a high concentration of Filipino residents, albeit with a different socioeconomic profile.[21] Cliff did not know the geographic reference so he asked politely, "Where is that?"

Cedric told Cliff directly and expressively, "Come on, man! Daly City is the Filipino capital! You're Filipino, right?"

As illustrated in the interactions above, methodologically, *Building Filipino Hawai'i* relies on data that came mainly from participant observation, formal and informal interviews, person-centered ethnography, and archival research. The study combines the traditional anthropological focus on everyday lived experiences, sociolinguistic analysis, and examinations of public cultural performances to analyze discursive constructions of Filipino immigrant subjectivity. Over the course of ten years (1998–2008), I conducted formal and informal interviews with more than one hundred Filipinos who were students, staff, and faculty at the University of Hawai'i at Mānoa, teachers and administrators at two local high schools, community leaders, and board members and staff at the Filipino Community Center. Although I wanted to get a wide range of interviewees in terms of language, class, gender, immigrant generation, and age, the information for this book depends on a "snowball" purposeful sampling. Throughout the book, I have given fictitious names to the research participants to maintain confidentiality and protect their privacy. However, in the book I use the person's real name if I rely on data that appears in the community newspaper or was from a public event. I regularly read the two main Filipino community newspapers (the *Fil-Am Courier* and the *Hawaii Filipino Chronicle*) as well as combed the two Honolulu dailies (the *Star-Bulletin* and *Honolulu Advertiser*, which have since merged into the *Star-Advertiser*) for stories on Filipinos.

The interviews were tape recorded in English, Hawai'i Creole English or Pidgin, Ilokano, and Tagalog (the two Philippine languages that I understand and can speak conversationally), depending on the interviewee's and my comfort level in using the language; the sessions usually involved code-switching. The interviews varied in time (usually one to three hours, although the person-centered ethnographies were conducted weekly over a six-month period), location (coffee shops, tables at malls, restaurants, offices, and homes), and process (some required the strict use of an interview guide and others were more open and free-flowing). The interviews covered several general areas: Filipino identity primarily framed in terms of language and class, the images and stereotypes of Filipinos in Hawai'i, issues related to community politics and empowerment, and individuals' relationships to Hawai'i, the United States, and the Philippines. Although the majority of my interviewees were multilingual, many of them were able to speak some combination of the standard variety of English, Hawai'i Creole English or Pidgin, Ilokano, Tagalog, and Cebuano (or Visayan), many chose to speak to me in "standard English," often self-correcting when they would "slip" into Pidgin or a Philippine language during tape-recorded interviews. When I asked some of them why they chose "standard English," several responded by saying they did not think that I understood Pidgin or the Philippine language because I was from the "mainland." Others talked about how they felt like they had to speak in a particular way to be understood by readers of my research project. For example, one interviewee suggested that I would need to translate his Pidgin. I must also note that there were a handful of interviewees who insisted on speaking Pidgin, arguing that my project's readers and I needed to learn their language. More often than not, these interviewees were those who strongly self-identified as Local.

I attended more than thirty meetings held by different community and student organizations and I went to dozens of events and activities sponsored by these organizations, including the university student-sponsored theatrical cultural performances held every semester. I observed the grand opening of the Filipino Community Center (which I describe in greater detail in chapter 4) as well as the numerous events associated with the opening (which began a few weeks prior to the official opening of the center). Lastly, during the fieldwork period I attended the Filipino Fiesta and Parade, held annually in the spring at Kapiʻolani Park in Waikīkī.

Overview of the book

This book comes at the heels of a relatively recent surge in books relating to Filipina/os in the United States and in diaspora, like Rick Bonus's *Locating Filipino Americans: Ethnicity and the Cultural Politics of Space* (2000), Martin Manalansan's *Global Divas: Filipino Gay Men in the Diaspora* (2003), Emily Ignacio's *Building Diaspora: Filipino Cultural Community Formation on the Internet* (2005); Filipina/o migration and global capitalism, like Robyn Rodriguez's *Migrants for Export: How the Philippine State Brokers Labor to the World* (2010), Kale Fajardo's *Filipino Crosscurrents: Oceanographies of Seafaring, Masculinities and Globalization* (2011), and Rhacel Parrenas's various works, including *Servants of Globalization: Women, Migration and Domestic Work* (2001), *Children of Global Migration: Transnational Families and Gendered Woes* (2005), *The Force of Domesticity: Filipina Migrants and Globalization* (2008), and *Illicit Flirtations: Labor, Migration and Sex Trafficking in Tokyo* (2011); colonialism and empire, like Catherine Choy's *Empire of Care: Nursing and Migration in Filipino American History* (2003), Augusto Espiritu's *Five Faces of Exile: The Nation and Filipino American Intellectuals* (2005), and Tiongson et al.'s *Positively No Filipinos Allowed: Building Communities and Discourse* (2006); community histories, like Yen Espiritu's *Home Bound: Filipino American Lives across Cultures, Communities, and Countries* (2003) and *Filipino American Lives* (1995) and Dawn Mabalon's *Little Manila is in the Heart: The Making of the Filipina/o American Community in Stockton, California* (2013).

A set of recently published books on Filipino Americans addresses topics and concerns similar to *Building Filipino Hawai'i*. For example, Joaquin Jay Gonzalez's *Filipino American Faith in Action: Immigration, Religion, and Civic Engagement* (2009) and Benito Vergara's *Pinoy Capital: The Filipino Nation in Daly City* (2009) both use the San Francisco Bay Area to depict the story of Filipina/o migration to the United States. Gonzales uses an adaptationist framework to depict the Filipina/o "sociocultural integration experience," focusing on the faith-inspired community formation and community action activities of Filipina/o migrants, their influences on and contributions to the Bay Area (and the broader American society), and their affirmation and maintenance of transnational ties to their homeland. Vergara's ethnographic study, on the other hand, explores the feelings of ambivalence many Filipino immigrants have toward the Philippines and the United States, manifesting in conflicted obligations to their new homes and the homeland they left behind. Vergara also examines the consequences of large-scale policies, like NAFTA and U.S. immigration legislation, in the everyday social lives of Filipino migrants and the politics and poetics of belonging and citizenship. From a more historical perspective, Rick Baldoz's *The Third Asiatic Invasion: Empire and Migration in Filipino America, 1898–1946* (2011) uses archival resources to create a narrative that illuminates the significant role Filipinos have played in the politics of race, immigration, and nationality in the United States, particularly in the first half of the twentieth century. Lastly, Theodore Gonzalves's *The Day the Dancers Stayed: Performing in the Filipino/American Diaspora* (2009) and Sarita See's *The Decolonized Eye: Filipino American Art and Performance* (2009) probe the connection between performance, identity, and history. Gonzalves examines the relationship between the invention of a performance repertoire (that is, Pilipino Cultural Nights or PCNs) and the development of diasporic identification, while See analyzes the work of artists of Filipino descent in the United States to expose the unexpected legacies of U.S. empire in the Philippines. *Building Filipino Hawai'i* is more akin to Dylan Rodriguez's *Suspended Apocalypse: White Supremacy, Genocide, and the Filipino Condition* in its critique of Filipino American identity processes and politics and Tony Tiongson's *Filipinos Represent: DJs, Racial Authenticity, and the Hip-hop Nation* in its focus on second-generation immigrants and the negotiation of identities.

Unlike these other publications but similar to Bonus's *Locating Filipino Americans*, *Building Filipino Hawai'i* also incorporates a spatial discourse in its analytical framework. The book suggests that im/migrants continue to insist on territorializing identity as they make homes in the diaspora while politicizing identity in struggles for power and inclusion. Bonus's focus on public space and community formation highlights the possibilities of "alternative spaces of collective action," particularly Filipino American *palengke* politics that take place in community centers, or "doing politics Filipino-style" reminiscent of the ordered chaos in Philippine marketplaces. He suggests, "Filipino American styles of politics are principally geared toward creating and maintaining spaces where Filipinos can actively engage each other in the pursuit of shared interests in local political representation, in the protection of their civil rights, and in the improvement of their well-being" (94). Furthermore, Filipino American politics occur where they have "no representation in mainstream politics and no access to it" and are spatially "constituted in and through maps of historical memories of immigration and settlement, of links between original homeland and new destination, of mainstream and informal/alternative political practice, and of 'Filipinoness' and 'Americanness.' " (94). Here is where this book departs from Bonus's work, especially because in Hawai'i, Filipinos are well-represented in mainstream island politics. However, this representation has not translated to group power. This is reflected in what several of my interviewees suggested to me: Filipinos are in political office but do not wield collective political power. In addition, the construction of "Filipino" in the islands occurs in the spatial triangulation of the Philippines, Hawai'i, and the continental United States. "Hawai'i" is further inflected with the local politics of indigeneity, Localness, and nonLocalness (usually associated with recent immigrants, tourists, the military, and haoles) that is not reflected in Bonus's ethnography of Los Angeles and San Diego. *Building Filipino Hawai'i* explores these points of difference and what they mean for identity formation and cultural politics in Filipino Hawai'i, particularly the ways they speak to in-group diversity based on immigrant generation, language, class, and culture.

Like Emily Ignacio's *Building Diaspora*, this book explores how Filipinos construct and maintain racial, ethnic, and national identities among themselves to create connections and a sense of unity, regardless of how tenuous or ephemeral. By focusing on cyber communities, Ignacio illustrates the ways space gets territorialized when "home" is detached from specific geographic places. Similar to her analysis of language in identity and community formation, *Building Filipino Hawai'i* also asks where language and class enter in contemporary politics of belonging and answers this question through an examination of specific place-based identity territorializations or community-building processes and practices, namely linguistic performances among students at the University of Hawai'i at Mānoa and the construction of the Filipino Community Center. Methodologically, *Building Filipino Hawai'i* differs in its focus on place and its use of the anthropological emphasis on everyday lived realities while connecting them to larger social, cultural, political, economic, and historical processes.

Building Filipino Hawai'i is also situated in the wake of significant demographic shifts in the United States that show minorities are quickly becoming the numerical majority, owing in large part to continuing waves of immigration from Asia and Mexico. Despite these demographic changes, immigrant communities continue to occupy the margins of U.S. society and they often use identity to build community and challenge their minority status. These changing demographics and their social, cultural, political, and economic implications invoke an analytical need to investigate the dynamics of identity making and struggles for community empowerment among immigrant groups. This book arrives at a moment when scholars, policy makers at the national and state levels, and local communities are discussing the politics of immigration along the axes of place and belonging. These discussions often revolve around the question of who rightfully belongs to the nation, which assumes a narrow congruence of people, identity, and territory. This book introduces another important consideration in these discussions: the ways immigrants themselves infuse discourses on language and class in these narratives about nation, citizenship, migration, and belonging and the claims they make to place.

Building Filipino Hawai'i follows contemporary Filipino immigrants' struggles to physically and figuratively build community, where they enact a politics of incorporation built on race, ethnicity, class, culture, and language. The title is intended to reflect the doubleness of "building," the active metaphorical and material construction and reconstruction of individual and collective selves. "Filipino" is continuously being re/defined and Filipinos build selves that sometimes contest in other times (sometimes simultaneously) reinforce the existing social order and unequal structures of power. The volume focuses on two sites of building and representation, the University of Hawai'i at Mānoa and the Filipino Community Center in Waipahu. At these two sites, the book focuses on the narratives and discourses about "home" and "homeland." In particular, I ask how immigrants talk about their relationships to the place(s) they left and the place(s) to which they have settled and, consequently, how these discourses shape their identities and politics.[22]

The first chapter, "Overlapping Architectures," serves as a history of Filipino migration to Hawai'i and uses the Filipino Community Center as the primary analytical site for looking at class as an anchor for identity territorializations. I suggest that through the physical building, the Filipino Community Center discursively constructs identity territorializations that frame Filipino labor history and struggles for incorporation as a development-based settler narrative underscored by a multiculturalist ideology. The chapter explores the ways in which the Filipino Community Center represents overlapping architectures, a type of historical and political economic layering whereby the contemporary late capitalist, transnational world that is anchored to a multiculturalist ideology is built on top of the industrial plantation-based agricultural system dependent on the racialization of its workers, which itself is constructed on top of an indigenous, communal land rights–based mode of production. Espiritu (2003) has maintained the need to historically contextualize the ways Filipinos construct the identities and communities in the cultural, economic, and political relationships between the Philippines and the United States. This chapter suggests that analysis of Filipino identity and community formation in Hawai'i needs to also account for the colonial relationship between Hawai'i and the United States.

The second chapter, "What's so p/funny?" examines the broader local racializing discourses, particularly comedy performances, that position immigrant Filipinos specifically, and Filipinos in general, as a cultural and linguistic other, signifying their outsider status and their subordinate position in the social hierarchy and order. Specifically, I argue that linguistic practices in Filipino jokes and comedy performances are identity acts that help to produce and disseminate ideas about language, culture, and identity that normalize the Local pan-ethnic identity category and reinforce Hawai'i's mainstream multiculturalist ideology.

The third chapter, "Anything but . . .", explores the relationship between language, identity, and politics and Filipino responses to broader racializing discourses. Where do language and identity fit in Filipino identity territorializations? How do Filipinos present themselves to each other and how do they present themselves to a society that sees them as somewhat familiar but primarily assigns them a cultural and linguistic otherness? Using the Katipunan Club at the university, this chapter analyzes events that employ a nationalist ideology of language and identity that equates one language, "Filipino/Tagalog," with one nation-state, "the Philippines," to create one people, "Filipino." In short, language serves a critical role in shaping identity territorializations in terms of how the boundaries of the social group are defined and what political interests are deemed meaningful and important.

The fourth chapter, "The Center is not just for Filipinos, but for all of Hawai'i nei," argues that the Filipino Community Center represents a "class project" (Ortner 2003) that not only reveals a repertoire of Filipino identities but also an active confrontation with the group's ethnoracially assigned identity and its political, economic, and social consequences. In my analysis of the grand opening ceremonies of the Filipino Community Center, I suggest that as a middle class project (with the Filipino Chamber of Commerce a central stakeholder), it emphasizes self-help entrepreneurship and the elevation of business-related "ethnic heroes" as part of the never-ending pursuit of the "American Dream" in a "Land of Immigrants." The chapter investigates several interrelated issues, namely how those in the middle class shape subjectivity in a community that has intensely been defined and defined itself as impoverished and subaltern and the various ways Filipinos think about and perform class (via the images, symbols, and ideologies they use) to construct competing visions of "Filipino."

The Conclusion, "Unsettling Hawai'i," revisits the idea of identity territorializations and their use in immigrant struggles for community empowerment. This asks what happens when "home"-making processes and practices occur in someone else's "homeland." Specifically, I examine how Filipino identity territorializations directly and indirectly engage indigeneity and local struggles for indigenous rights. Are Filipinos in Hawai'i one of the Asian settlers participating in the double colonialism of Hawai'i (Saranillio 2006; Fujikane 2008)? How does engaging indigeneity shift our understandings of people, place, identity, and empowerment? What are the relationships between indigenous rights and immigrant rights? This Conclusion participates in broader conversations about settler colonialism (Razack 2002; Wolfe 2006; Jacobs 2009; Ford 2010) but is also involved in more general discussions about the relationship between people, place, identity, and politics.

* PResentation ES 333
12ᵉ‐1⁴⁵ₚₘ
(Ch.#1 pg.#27-48)
* m 2.22.2016
may use powerpoint

OLD DATE

Changed DATE

CHAPTER I

OVERLAPPING ARCHITECTURES

There are several neighborhoods in Oʻahu that most local people identify as "Filipino neighborhoods." One of my interviewees, Antonio Buan, who was taking an Ilokano language class at the University of Hawaiʻi at Mānoa and self-identified as Local, summed up his "Filipino" upbringing in the following way: "I went [to] elementary in Kalihi but middle school and high school in Waipahu. How much more Filipino can you get?" For many people on Oʻahu, Kalihi and Waipahu are the prototypical "Filipino" neighborhoods, and from this perspective and given his residential history, Antonio grew up very Filipino. However, the naming and categorizing of Kalihi and Waipahu as "Filipino neighborhoods" perform the staking of a metaphorical and material claim to place. In this chapter, I examine the physical structure of the Filipino Community Center in Waipahu to provide a broad history of Filipino migration to the islands, which is dependent on two interrelated U.S. colonizations that occurred at roughly the same time, that of the Philippines and Hawaiʻi.

Waipahu is usually known first and foremost as a former plantation community that is currently a semirural, semisuburban neighborhood with residents who range from low-income to middle class. The presence of the old Waipahu plantation sugar mill smokestack is a continuing reminder of this plantation heritage, exhibiting a type of adaptive reuse—it is now the site of a YMCA. Waipahu is also a Filipino ethnic enclave. During the 2011 school year Filipino students comprised 67.6 percent of the nearly twenty-five hundred students at Waipahu High School. According to many of my interviewees, the neighborhood is lined with "Filipino houses," which can be characterized by their landscaping/vegetation (that is, they usually have marunggay[1] trees in their yards) and architecture. That is, they are usually large, two-story, brightly colored homes often extending to the edges of

Figure 1. View of the three stories of the Filipino Community Center from Waipahu Street, photo courtesy of Took HNLA.

the property line and include tile roofs, stucco walls, wrought iron fences, and features that are reminiscent of the Philippine bahay na bato[2] style popularized during Spanish colonization. This style also reflects the more contemporary homes of wealthier families in the Ilocos region, particularly those with relatives who work abroad—two-story concrete residences with balustrades and often having six or more bedrooms. The Filipino Community Center, although not for exclusive use by Filipinos, is perceived as a type of "big Filipino house." As I discuss in a subsequent chapter, the Filipino Community Center reflects the community desire to be seen as equal (socially, politically, and economically) to the other plantation-based ethnic groups in the islands, namely the Japanese, Chinese, and Okinawans. Each of these communities has their own community centers, and with the completion of the Filipino Community Center in 2002, Filipinos could claim equality with their local Asian counterparts. In this chapter I use the Filipino Community Center as my primary analytical site to suggest that through the physical building itself, Filipinos discursively construct identity territorializations that map out a collective sense of place and a sense of self along political economic and ideological coordinates. The Filipino Community Center represents overlapping architectures, a type of historical

Historical

and political economic layering whereby the contemporary late capitalist, transnational world anchored to a multiculturalist ideology is built on top of the industrial plantation-based agri-capitalist system dependent on the racialization of its workers, which itself is constructed on top of an indigenous, communal land rights–based mode of production. In other words, the Filipino Community Center depends on what Ruben Alcantara calls "the sakada story," a narrative of development that positions indigeneity (represented as the Hawaiian past), racialization (depicted as the exploitation of Asian and Hawaiian labor during the plantation era), and multiculturalism (portrayed as the contemporary period of liberal inclusion in which the various racial and ethnic groups share power) in a linear historical progression that corresponds with changes in Hawai'i's political economy and modes of production.[3] In this way, the completion of the Filipino Community Center embodies a settler Filipino developmental narrative in which Waipahu (and by extension, Hawai'i) is constructed and claimed as a Filipino "home."

According to Fujikane, narratives of development create a historical record that "can be used either to maintain existing structures of power or help us envision alternative forms of political organization" (1997: 43). In

Historical Record

Figure 2. View of key architectural elements—square pillars, columns, stuccoed walls, and arched corridors—of the Filipino Community Center, photo courtesy of Took HNLA.

this way, narratives of development can challenge, conceal, and reproduce relations, structures, and institutions of power. Although Fujikane examines narratives and ideologies of development in relation to Local identity and Native Hawaiian struggles for sovereignty and self-determination, in this chapter I am interested in the ways developmental narratives are employed by Filipinos in Hawai'i to make claims about themselves in relation to broader structures and institutions of power in the islands, and in relation to other groups: whites, Japanese, Chinese, and Native Hawaiians, in particular. Developmental narratives construct a particular historical trajectory in the islands: "Many historians employ a developmental narrative that begins with the colonization of Hawaiians and ends with multicultural democracy in Hawai'i. The story of multiethnic diversity is thus cast as the triumphant 'resolution' to Hawai'i's colonial 'past'" (Fujikane 2008: 3). Narratives of development dovetail with assimilationist narratives, which function to reinscribe the broader, settler colonial structures and institutions but also reorganize them to allow for the incorporation of previously oppressed populations. In other words, the developmental narrative in Hawai'i works as a story of settler dominance that integrates populations who were historically oppressed and marginalized into the current structures of power. Along these lines, the Filipino Community Center envisions the full social, cultural, political, and economic participation of Filipinos in Hawai'i society, where they are no longer on the margins and through this logic of incorporation, and in so doing this narrative upholds the multicultural, settler order and hierarchy. Here, I use incorporation to capture the assimilationist narrative and developmental historicization and to point to the ways business (and entrepreneurship, in particular) is often the preferred path to upward mobility (re: assimilation). To extend the in/corporation metaphor, the building of the FilCom Center functions as a charter that grants or recognizes Filipino rights and privileges to fully participate in the settler colony, to take their place "in multicultural Hawai'i" albeit in the service of maintaining the superiority of the settler state. The charter (that is, the building) confirms the validity of Filipino existence and governance. The erection of the building is the staking of a settler claim, the metaphorical and material marking of Filipino territory.)

The Filipino Community Center is a huge and beautiful building. The grand opening of the Filipino Community Center occurred in June 2002 and since then, it is often advertised as the largest Filipino community center outside the Philippines. The Center is a three-story Spanish mission–style structure reminiscent of colonial Intramuros,[4] the "walled city"

[Handwritten margin notes: "SITE: Imagined as a site of Pol./Econ. Power in the islands" with "EX." circled]

Figure 3. View of the Waipahu Street entrance, with the José Rizal statue on the left, photo courtesy of Took HNLA.

within Manila that was a complex of houses, churches, and a fortress and served as the seat of government during Spanish colonialism. In effect, the Filipino Community Center is imagined as a site of political and economic power in the islands. The Center exhibits many of the basic and common elements that characterize Spanish mission–style architecture.[5] Usually there is a courtyard lined with potted plants with a large fountain near the entrance of the building. There are solid and massive walls, large square pillars, long arcades (these are the arched corridors that flank the interior and exterior walls), pedimented gables,[6] wide, projecting eaves, broad, undecorated and stuccoed wall surfaces, and tile roofs. The belfry above the Casamina-Flores Ballroom suggests that the ballroom is the "chapel" usually found in mission complexes. Several of my interviewees remarked how the Spanish mission–style building reminded them of the large houses of "wealthy Filipinos" in the Philippines places like Vigan, in Ilocos Sur. In the Philippines, these types of structures are usually the homes of the elite; they are signs of status, wealth, and privilege.

The Filipino Community Center occupies fifty thousand square feet on the grounds of a two-acre site near the former location of the Oahu Sugar

[Handwritten margin note: "Occupies 50,000 sq ft. on 2 acre site"]

Figure 4. View of the Consuelo Zobel Alger Courtyard and the Casamina-Flores Ballroom from the third floor, photo courtesy of Took HNLA.

Company's administrative offices. The Filipino Community Center is on historic ground. Plantation history is literally beneath the Center; the Waipahu plantation is the site of toil and resistance, specifically the 1909 strike by Japanese workers and 1920 strike that involved Japanese and Filipino workers. This is also, reportedly, the site where the first fifteen sakadas, or Filipino plantation workers, signed their labor contracts in 1906. These first fifteen sakadas eventually went to the Olaa planation on Hawai'i island. The "sakada story" is literally buried underneath the Center. The Filipino Community Center pays tribute to the sakadas and the plantation history it is built upon. There are statues, plaques, and a mural dedicated to the sakada generation, celebrating and honoring this heritage. Ironically, it is this same legacy that has structured the contemporary social, political, and economic conditions that position Filipinos at the margins of Hawai'i society. Having the Filipino Community Center on the grounds of the Waipahu sugar plantation can be understood as a type of symbolic subversion of power (that is, the Filipinos, who represent the agricultural workers, are now on top) of the plantation past. But there is a layer that is buried deep down and is often missed: indigeneity and the native dispossession that serve as the conditions the possibility of agri-industrial plantations. Indigeneity in

Figure 5. View of the entrance from the parking lot. The tympanum above the front entrance pediment is decorated with seventeen rays of half a sun with a blue background, reminiscent of the sun in the Philippine flag, photo courtesy of Took HNLA.

Hawai'i is often literally and figuratively interred, submerged beneath the plantation past (usually understood as the beginnings of "modern Hawai'i" and the multicultural present). Yet, it is the displacement and dispossession of Native Hawaiians that pave the paths toward a capitalism built on agricultural plantations. The Filipino Community Center embodies this tiered set of overlapping architectures; the building is a celebratory appeal to a multicultural Hawai'i that sits atop the racial and class oppression of the plantation era, which in turn rests upon native dispossession.[8]

The old Waipahu sugar mill smokestack, the most recognizable community landmark, is only a few hundred yards away from the Filipino Community Center. Although the sugar mill closed in 1995, it continues to loom in the background. The Oahu Sugar Company began its operations in Waipahu in 1897, turning the community into a large sugarcane-processing area until the demise of the sugar industry with the last harvest in 1995. The company initially hired workers from Hawai'i, Portugal, Japan, Spain, Puerto Rico, Philippines, and China to clear the land of rocks, plants, and other vegetation in preparation for the planting of sugarcane. Filipinos were first imported as workers in 1906, at a time when Hawai'i was firmly entrenched in supporting U.S. capitalist development. As Miriam Sharma suggests, "The migration of Filipino workers to Hawaii, from 1906 to 1946, took place within the context of an ever-increasing capitalist penetration of the islands and Hawaii's concomitant absorption into the world capitalist economy" (Sharma 1984: 579)

According to Native Hawaiian scholar Kapā Oliveira, "only by understanding the ties shared between various places and their names can we truly understand the meaning of individual place names and the collective story that they tell. Hawaiian place names also serve as mnemonic devices in their oral maps." Traditional Hawaiian place names could point to significant events, natural features of the terrain, or resources available in a particular area (Oliveira 2009: 104) The area of what is now called Waipahu traditionally covers the ahupua'a[9] of Hoaeae to the west, and Waikele and Waipio to the east, but it was not administratively considered a separate outlying community until 1930 (Yamamoto et al. 2005: 7) Waipahu is in the Ewa district of leeward (or western) O'ahu, at the intersection of the West and Middle Lochs of Pu'uloa (or what is now known as Pearl Harbor) and is south of what is now called Schofield Plateau. Prior to the industrial plantations, the area was home to at least twenty-seven fish ponds and was known for its freshwater springs. In the Hawaiian language, Waipahu is derived from two words: wai, meaning freshwater, and pahū, meaning "to burst or gush forth."[10] Waipahu then means something like "the land of gushing or bursting freshwater." At one time, Waipahu was considered to be the capital of O'ahu, with the Hawaiian ruling class establishing residences in the area where they would gather and enjoy the water from the nearby artesian springs (Munro 1983; Nedbalek 1984; Yamamoto et al. 2005; Moniz 2007) It was these springs that sugar planters eventually tapped, creating artesian wells that were used to irrigate the cane fields of the usually dry leeward area.

Waipahu also housed kalo (or taro) fields for the agriculture-based subsistence economy of Native Hawaiians that depended on a communal land tenure system. Marion Kelly explains the Native Hawaiian mode of production in the following way: "Although the land was controlled by the chiefs (ali'i) who expropriated food and labor from the cultivators of the soil, the commoners (maka'ainana), everyone had rights of access and use to the resources of the land and sea. Parcels of land (ahupua'a, 'ili) were divided into small units (kuleana) cultivated by families and larger units used in common. The people were sustained by a tradition of sharing and common use" (Kelly 1980: 57). This tradition of exchange and hospitality are important themes in mo'olelo (or stories) associated with the area.

According to J. Kuahiwi Moniz,[12] a Native Hawaiian educator and cultural specialist whose work and expertise focuses on the Waiʻanae coast, there are numerous moʻolelo from the Waipahu area that involve the shark goddess, Kaʻahupahau, and her brother Kahiʻuka, who were guardians of waters along Puʻuloa. Although there are other stories (that involve an eel boy and oysters), perhaps the most well-known story associated with the area involves a kapa-maker from Kahuku. Moniz relayed the story to me in the following way:

> There once was a woman from Kahuku, which is in the northern part of the island on other side of the Koʻolau mountain range, who was known for the kapa[13] she made. One day while pounding kapa near a stream, she lost her beloved kapa board, or kapa kua. The stream took her kapa kua and it floated in the underwater springs that connect the windward and leeward sides of Oʻahu. Using the natural elements and animals as her guide, the woman set out on a journey to find her beloved kapa kua. She traveled far and wide but was unable to find her kapa board. One day, right before she was ready to go back home to Kahuku, she heard the sound of her kapa kua while it was being struck by someone else. She looked for the source of the sound and found a woman, near the spring in Waikele, who was using her kapa kua. She tells the woman from Waikele about her journey to find her kapa kua and once she finished her tale, the kapa board was returned. The Waikele woman then asked her new friend to rest and spend the night before departing for her long journey back home to Kahuku. The next morning, the two friends walked together and stopped briefly near a cliff which overlooked the spring where they met. This area became known as Keʻone Kuilima Laula o ʻEwa, which means "the land of joining hands in ʻEwa."

For Moniz, the story exemplifies the Native Hawaiian values of aloha[14] (here, read as "welcoming," "hospitality," "love," and "sharing") and kuilima (or "working together" or "cooperation"). What is also particularly interesting is that the cliff where the two women stood arm-in-arm was the site eventually chosen by the Oahu Sugar Company to construct the Waipahu mill in 1897 (Munro 1983). In addition, the Filipino Community Center uses a similar narrative, one that replaces the two women with two men, Roland Casamina and Eddie Flores Jr., who use the parallel Filipino cultural value of bayanihan (or "cooperation") to successfully construct the Center, which is near Keʻone Kuilima Laula o ʻEwa.

The contemporary telling of Waipahu's history does not usually take into account a Native Hawaiian, preplantation past. For example, 1897 is usually marked as the year of Waipahu's birth, when the Oahu Sugar Company was incorporated. In fact, the State of Hawaiʻi held Waipahu's centennial celebrations in 1997. In this regard, Saranillio has remarked:

While Asian American history usually begins with Western colonialism/imperialism's displacement of peoples from Asia, or at the point of entry to the Americas or the Pacific, Asian American histories are seldom placed in relation to an indigenous history of dispossession by the United States. Though the effects of land dispossession and genocide against Native Americans and Hawaiians are acknowledged, indigenous histories are often written in past tense, as memorialized moments that are rarely used to interpret relations of force in the present (2011: 465).

According to the various materials related to the Waipahu centennial celebrations, the plantation heritage is characterized as the parent while the contemporary community, one that is undergoing an economic transition, is depicted as the child. Native Hawaiians do not officially appear in the narrative (not even as a grandparent or ancestor).

Similarly, for the Filipino Community Center, the Oahu Sugar Company and the Waipahu plantation are central to the setting of Filipino history in the islands, and the sakadas are central characters. In his seminal study, *Sakada: Filipino Adaptation in Hawai'i,* Ruben Alcantara states that "the sakada story is the basic historical foundation of Filipino life in Hawaii today" (Alcantara 1981: ix). For Alcantara the story of the sakadas, or Filipino plantation workers, is the fundamental basis of Filipino history in Hawai'i and underpins their contemporary social, political, and economic realities. The term *sakada* comes from the Spanish word *sacada,* which refers to laborers who are imported from an external geographic area and are paid lower wages than local workers. In general, sakadas can be defined as cheap, foreign or immigrant laborers, and in the context of Hawai'i the term specifically refers to the more than 125,000 Filipino plantation labor migrants who came to work on sugar and pineapple plantations between 1906 and 1946. The sakadas came to Hawai'i to take advantage of plantation wage employment in hopes of earning and saving enough money to return to the Philippines, where they could live comfortably off their earnings.

Alcantara also explains that the term *sakada* has a second meaning that points to "the process of recruiting for temporary labor migration; among Hawaii Filipinos, the term serves as the focus of distinct identity among those who came during the years of labor recruitment between 1906 and 1946" (1981: ix). In this second sense, the term *sakada* and the sociohistorical formation it implies serves as an important marker of Filipino identity in Hawai'i. In other words, Filipino identity in Hawai'i can be traced to the plantation labor history and is based on the formation of a working-class consciousness. In this chapter, I present a brief overview of "the sakada

story," the history of Filipino workers in Hawai'i, by focusing on the ways the capitalist world economy and U.S. immigration policy and legislation have shaped Filipino immigration to the islands. In this sense, I explore what Stuart Hall (1996a [1986]) calls the "race/class question" (the relationship between race and capitalism). By focusing on the race/class question, my analysis moves beyond the problematic acculturation/cultural assimilation paradigm (San Juan 1998) and adaptationist approaches (Okamura 1991; Gonzales 2010) that have underscored scholarship investigating the social, cultural, economic, and political situation of Filipinos in the United States, and particularly in Hawai'i.

Following Espiritu (1995, 2003) and San Buenaventura (1995)[15] I suggest that the "sakada story" (beginning with large-scale immigration in the early twentieth century enabled by American annexation of the Philippines) can be better interpreted from a colonial and postcolonial framework, one that focuses on the social, political, and economic relationship between the United States and the Philippines. From a somewhat different angle (from a more push/pull perspective), Luis Teodoro (1981) understands the migration of Filipino laborers to Hawai'i within the context of Philippine culture and history, particularly the cleavage between the Filipino peasantry and elite that emerged from the Spanish colonial period and magnified during American colonialism. He sees out-migration as an expression of "peasant dissatisfaction," noting that between 1916 and 1928, there were more than twenty-three thousand labor recruits to Hawai'i from Ilocos Norte, a large agricultural province, and only 129 from Manila, an urban center. However, the out-migration phenomenon, particularly to Hawai'i, must also be understood within the context of capitalist expansion in the United States and the development of U.S. agribusiness interests in the Philippines that effectively stifled the growth of Philippine agricultural production and industrialization.

Extending Espiritu and San Buenaventura's colonial framework and echoing Cheng and Bonacich (1984) and Sharma (1984), the history of Filipino immigration and experience in the United States and in Hawai'i, in particular, must also be understood within the context of the development of United States capitalism and the absorption of Hawai'i and the Philippines into the world capitalist system. As Miriam Sharma suggests, "The migration of Filipino workers to Hawaii, from 1906 to 1946, took place within the context of an ever-increasing capitalist penetration of the islands and Hawaii's concomitant absorption into the world capitalist economy" (1984: 579). In other words, Filipino history in Hawai'i must account for two colonizations: U.S. colonialism in the Philippines and in Hawai'i.

Most historical accounts of Filipinos in Hawai'i begin in 1906, with the arrival of the first sakadas. Other studies, especially those that apply a colonial framework, begin in 1898, the year in which the Philippines and Hawai'i were annexed by the United States. However, I take as my starting point 1778, the year in which Captain James Cook "discovered" Hawai'i (then named the Sandwich Islands after the Earl of Sandwich). Cook's "discovery" not only put the islands on newly drawn world maps, it also opened Hawai'i's ports to foreign traders and businesspeople, signaling the entry of external political and economic interests (particularly American and British), the incorporation of Hawai'i into the world economy, and the emergence of settler colonial relations. Two years prior to Cook's arrival, the American Revolution and subsequent independence from Britain cut off American maritime commercial interests from British-controlled ports. This obstacle led Americans to seek new markets to replace those they could not access or those they deemed unprofitable (Liu 1984). The "discovery" of Hawai'i provided a new market for American commercial interests, and the opening of Hawaiian ports also paved the way for American entrance into the rest of the Pacific and Asia.

Supplying visiting ships and engaging in trade with foreigners brought significant social, economic, and political changes in Hawai'i. Prior to Cook's "discovery," the traditional mode of production was an agriculture-centered subsistence economy based on reciprocal social and economic relations. With the arrival of visiting ships, the ali'i, or chiefs, and the maka'ainana, or commoners, were introduced to European concepts of wealth and exchange values. In this new system, the ali'i were converted into conspicuous consumers and the maka'ainana, usually farmers or craftspeople, were transformed into laborers employed by the ali'i to provide provisions and supplies for visiting vessels (Beechert 1985). Beechert explains this shift in the following way: "From a class of people accustomed to producing for themselves, their immediate family, and the kinship group (expressed as the chief), the Hawaiian commoners were being converted into taxpaying producers for the accumulation of wealth and extravagant consumption of the chiefly class" (Beechert 1985: 12). Traditional communal use and intrafamilial exchange gave way to commodity exchange and a market mechanism that controlled the satisfaction of economic needs.

Cook's "discovery" and the subsequent absorption of Hawai'i into the capitalist world-economy coincided with the expansion of European and American maritime commerce. Western mercantile expansion facilitated the transformation of the subjugated populations "into providers of coerced surplus labor" (ibid.: 381). In Hawai'i, capitalism seized on preexisting distinctions, reinforcing and ordering the divisions among the workers in racial and ethnic ways. The kanaka ("humans"), particularly the maka'ainana, became "Hawaiian" and later served as the initial core of the Hawai'i agribusiness workforce.[16] The "Hawaiian" classification differentiated the maka'ainana from the white merchant/missionary class and signaled a change in the maka'ainana relationship to the means of production: "Henceforth the Hawaiian, whether farmer or worker, was to be measured by his ability to amass money. No longer would his contribution to the 'ohana and the 'ahupua'a express his worth in the community"[17] (Beechert 1985: 29).

Visiting ships and trade also led to the creation of Western settlements in the islands (Liu 1984). In these settlements merchants established businesses, foreign governments set up consulates, and starting in 1820 missionaries began efforts to Christianize the population. By 1850, the power and influence of American missionaries were firmly established in the islands, representing the convergence of theological and economic interests. American missionaries served as political advisors to Hawaiian monarchs and teachers to the nobility and maka'ainana (Liu 1984).

In addition to bringing about changes in the political economy, trade with foreigners and western settlements brought diseases that depleted the population. Western diseases to which Native Hawaiians had no resistance, like venereal diseases, tuberculosis, and measles, led to a population collapse. Estimates of the Native Hawaiian population range from 300,000 to one million at the time of Cook's arrival, but by 1850 there were roughly only seventy thousand Native Hawaiians. This population collapse was crucial to the development of the sugar industry and the ensuing changes in the racial and ethnic landscape in the islands. Because the sugar plantations required large supplies of cheap and controllable labor, the dramatic decline in the Native Hawaiian population forced the fledgling sugar industry to look elsewhere for workers.

The development of the sugar industry and the emergence of the "industrial plantation" (Beechert 1985) coincided with Americans gaining military, political, and economic control of the islands and the dispossession and disfranchisement of Native Hawaiians. Numerous key events set the stage for the shift from Native Hawaiian agriculture-based subsistence economy and communal society to maritime commerce and trade to a U.S-controlled capitalist economy participating in the world economic system. Early efforts to produce sugar were hampered by three primary factors: (1) the traditional land tenure system that was not conducive to large-scale agribusiness; (2) Hawaiians' refusal to work on the plantations (they had the option to work in other industries, and plantation work did not match traditional economic behavior and activity), and the collapse of the indigenous population (which hindered the development of labor-intensive industry); and (3) the absence of viable markets and long-term investors (Beechert 1985: 21). The traditional Hawaiian land tenure system was the first factor to be addressed by the sugar planters.

Perhaps the most significant event that paved the way for the industrial plantations was the Mahele, or Land Division or Redistribution, in 1848 (Kameleʻihiwa 1992). The Mahele reallocated the lands of the Kingdom of Hawaiʻi among three primary groups: the king (at the time, Kamehameha III), the aliʻi, and the Hawaiian government. However, there were small parcels (or kuleana) that could be held in fee simple by purchase or grant. In a sense, in contrast to the traditional land tenure system, land became private property and thus, a commodity. As Beechert notes, the consequences of the Mahele extended beyond simple redistribution of land: "The net effect of the Great Mahele was therefore a momentous shift in value systems which was to speed up the process of converting the makaʻainana into a western-style labor force, or, at best, into a group of farmers dependent on market conditions for their existence" (Beechert 1985: 34). Two years later in 1850, the Hawaiian government passed the Kuleana Act, which allowed foreigners and noncitizens to buy land. As a result of the Great Mahele and the Kuleana Act, land was separated into tracts and parcels that makaʻainana and foreigners could own, which essentially opened the path to private ownership of land and foreign capital investment, thereby abolishing the traditional land tenure system. Besides changing the traditional land tenure system, these two events facilitated the acquisition and control of large tracts of land by a small group of New England missionaries/businessmen that were needed for sugar production and the development of the plantation agricultural system. These missionaries/businessmen later consolidated into five major sources of capital investment: the "Big Five" (Alexander and Baldwin, Inc., Castle and Cooke Inc., H. Hackfeld and Company, which later became American Factors Inc., Theo H. Davies and Company Ltd., and C. Brewer and Company Ltd.). The "Big Five" were the primary agents for the sugar industry and had almost total political and economic control of Hawaiʻi beginning in the late-nineteenth century to the middle of the twentieth century; their demands were high priorities in government policy.

Although between 1835 and 1876 Native Hawaiians comprised the majority of plantation workers, their mobility, the disjuncture between traditional economic behavior (the makaʻainana usually performed only enough work to satisfy their own needs and their obligations to the aliʻi) and the plantation wage-work system, and the collapse of the population forced planters to look for workers elsewhere. In 1850, the Hawaiian government passed the Masters and Servants Act, which initiated the penal contract labor system. In an attempt to supplement the rapidly diminishing Hawaiian workforce, the Masters and Servants Act permitted the importation of foreign laborers to Hawai'i for contract work on the sugar plantations. The contract work system that emerged from the act also served to control laborers and prevent their organization and collective political action. In 1852, because of Western imperial penetration into Asia, Asia's geographical proximity to Hawai'i (and thus, cheaper transportation costs), and Asian workers' experience with extensive cultivation and manufacture of cash crops, particularly sugar, Hawai'i sugar planters began to import Chinese contract labor (Liu 1984). Thus began the steady stream of Asian contract workers formally recruited by the Hawai'i sugar industry, a movement of laborers that would last until 1946.

The illegal U.S. overthrow of the Kingdom of Hawai'i in 1893, the subsequent annexation of Hawai'i in 1898, and the Organic Act of 1900, which coincided with U.S. imperial expansion, changed the dynamics of labor importation and immigration. Hawai'i, as an American possession, had the same tariff protection and privileges as sugar growers on the continent, which encouraged further capital investment and opened up more areas for production. This in turn created more demand for plantation workers. However, the annexation of Hawai'i complicated the labor needs of the plantations. Annexation made U.S. laws applicable to Hawai'i, including the end of the penal contract system and the Chinese Exclusion Acts. Anderson explains the net effect of the United States taking possession of Hawai'i: "The American annexation of Hawaii in 1898 brought the virtual guarantee of a rich, protected market for sugar, but it also caused labor problems for the planters, because legislation and diplomatic agreements had by 1908 effectively prevented further immigration from Japan, China, and Korea" (Anderson et al 1984: 1).

Because of the continuing need for cheap labor and the restrictions on importing workers from East Asia, the Hawaiian Sugar Planters Association (HSPA)[18] turned to other sources, namely, the Philippines and Puerto Rico, both American territories with large rural communities from which to extract workers. Owing to their political status as "U.S. nationals"—they were neither foreign nationals nor American citizens but political dependents and colonial subjects of the United States—Filipinos and Puerto Ricans were able to migrate freely to (and between) the United States and its territories. However, as "aliens ineligible for citizenship" Filipinos were also in a particularly difficult and vulnerable position: "They were colonial subjects of the United States who never had a spokesman for their interests either in the Philippines or in Washington. They could not effectively participate in the political activity of their homeland. Neither was there a place for political participation in Hawai'i as they were not citizens" (Sharma 1980: 101).[19]

By 1909 Puerto Rico and the Philippines became the primary sources of cheap labor for the sugar industry. However, the Philippines had an advantage: "The expense of transporting recruits from the Philippines was lesser; thus, after 1909 the Philippines became the primary source of laborers for Hawaii's main industry" (Alcantara 1981: 3). San Buenaventura explains more fully: "The HSPA persisted in its efforts to entice Filipinos to come because they represented an ideal source of cheap and stable labor. The Filipinos came from an agrarian background and had experience in sugar production; they were also perceived to be docile and willing workers. With the U.S. annexation of both Hawaii and the Philippines, the diplomatic and legal barriers to recruiting Filipinos were non-existent or greatly minimized, particularly the immigration hurdle. It was also beneficial to the HSPA at this time to bring in a new national group to counter its predominantly Japanese workforce, which had begun to press for higher wages and reforms" (San Buenaventura 1995: 444). Not only was it cheaper for the HSPA to bring in Filipino workers, these new workers could also be used to offset the unionizing efforts by Japanese workers that began to take root in the early 1900s.

The HSPA began recruiting in the Philippines after annexation and brought over the first sakadas in 1906. There were early attempts by the HSPA to recruit in urban areas near Manila (and other Tagalog-speaking regions) and Cebu City in the Visayas (in the Cebuano-speaking central Philippines), but by the 1920s HSPA recruiters turned to the Ilocos region, which had a high population density, diminishing natural resources (there was land scarcity and intense competition, and farming was difficult with low yields), and curtailed industries owing to U.S. colonial policy.[20] The region had a tradition of out-migration and provided a large pool of available and mobile agricultural workers. Even before the arrival of HSPA recruiters, Ilokanos participated in an intranational labor migrant circuit: "Filipinos typically left home so they could save enough money to buy land and achieved higher social status when they returned" (Anderson et al. 1984: 4). Filipinos saw themselves as migratory sojourners, understanding their movement as simply a "temporary absence from the barrio" (San Buenaventura 1996: 36). For the sakadas, travel to Hawai'i extended this tradition of out-migration and "temporary absence" into the international sphere, and transformed them into an agri-industrial proletariat.

Between 1906 and 1946, more than 125,000 Filipino laborers were re-cruited to work for Hawai'i's plantations. To attract workers, the HSPA employed a recruitment strategy that involved returning sakadas, "who managed to bring back their savings and those [workers] who wrote home and sent money orders and positive news about working in Hawaii" (San Buenaventura 1995: 444). The sakadas who were able to return to the Phil-ippines, with their newly acquired riches, sold the idea that "Kasla Glorya Ti Haway" (Hawai'i Is Like Paradise). According to Anderson et al., "some laborers returned to the Philippines with what appeared to be pockets full of money, people began to see Hawaii as a place to get rich" (Anderson et al. 1984: 4). Despite counterstories of hardships and oppressive conditions on the plantations, the lure of work in Hawai'i was so great that after 1925, HSPA recruiters no longer needed to provide transportation costs to enlist workers; they volunteered in large number to come to the islands. From 1911 to 1920, there were almost three thousand sakadas, nearly all men, arriving annually. From 1921 to 1931, the number of sakadas arriving an-nually more than doubled, to almost eight thousand (again, mostly men). In 1932, owing to the Great Depression, Filipino recruitment was halted and more than seven thousand sakadas repatriated. In 1934, the United States passed the Tydings-McDuffie Act. The act created the Commonwealth of the Philippines and stipulated that the Philippines would be given independence in ten years. The Tydings-McDuffie Act also limited Filipino immigration to the United States to fifty persons per year, although there was a special exemption for the Territory of Hawai'i (that was invoked in 1946). The Tydings-McDuffie Act along with the Philippine Repatriation Act of 1935 essentially ended the large-scale immigration of Filipinos to Hawai'i and the United States. However, by this time, Filipinos workers had replaced the Japanese as the largest ethnic group on the plantations. By 1940, there were more than fifty thousand Filipinos in Hawai'i. Within a decade, the sakadas and their descendants begin dreaming of a collective home, a Fili-pino community center, to call their own.

The recruitment and importation of the 1946 (or '46) sakadas, which was the last and largest wave of Filipino plantation laborers, occurred when there was an impending interethnic and islandwide strike organized by the newly established ILWU. As part of its traditional strategy of importing strikebreak-ers, in the previous year the HSPA sent recruitment representatives to the Philippines, who were able to enlist more than six thousand laborers and their families, comprised of more than fifteen hundred women and children (San Buenaventura 1996a). The ILWU was split in its stance toward the im-portation of these Filipino workers, and their union's Japanese and Filipino members were the most vocal opponents of the importation. They argued that the new Filipino workers would upset the "racial harmony" of the island community, and for the Filipinos in particular, they claimed that the new immigrant recruits would damage the image of Filipinos (San Buenaventura 1996a). This led to tension between members of the different racial/ethnic groups (Filipinos, Japanese, and whites) and also created friction between older and newer members of the same ethnic group (Filipinos) that ran along the line of "old-timer" versus "new arrival" or "Local" versus "immigrant." However, even before the 1946 sakadas set foot on the islands, ILWU representatives found their way onto their ships and recruited them for the union, denying the HSPA of its strikebreakers and surplus labor supply. Although there was initial friction between the older and new Filipino workers, the 1946 sakadas were instrumental in developing a "Local" Filipino identity.

The prewar and 1946 sakadas endured different political and economic realities in Hawai'i. On the plantations prior to World War II, the workers faced a tremendous lack of opportunities for economic advancement, racial discrimination (in terms of differential pay for the same work), and exploitation by their employers. And as political dependents of the United States, the Filipino laborers had no real representation from the Philippine or the United States government. Because of the harsh working and living conditions, many Filipinos were forced to return home to the Philippines or move to the continental United States to supply U.S. agribusiness with cheap labor on the West Coast: "Most Filipinos during this phase of their history in Hawaii regarded themselves as temporary residents. Even those with Hawaii-born children still thought of returning to their homeland. By 1940, half of those who had come in the first wave had left Hawaii; of these, two-thirds had gone back to the Philippines and the rest to the mainland. . . . Only a small nucleus of a business and semiprofessional class, which wished to establish a successful community in Hawaii, had developed by the '30s" (Teodoro 1981: 21). However, for the 1946 Sakadas cohort, there were two significant differences in the sociopolitical conditions in postwar Hawai'i. First, the HSPA, which was crucial to the recruitment and importation of more than 125,000 Filipino workers since 1906, and which had monitored, disciplined, and regimented their lives as plantation laborers, was now challenged by organized labor, the ILWU, which fought on their behalf to negotiate better working and living conditions. Second, there was a boom in the postwar Hawai'i economy and, according to San Buenaventura, the 1946 sakadas were "a new breed of postwar immigrant workers" who were better equipped to take advantage of the new sociopolitical circumstances. Unlike their predecessors they were better educated, they attended high school, and a number were college-educated. As a result, "With the mechanization of industry and the stipulations negotiated in the labor contract, many who worked the fields moved up to skilled and clerical positions. Encouraged by the opportunities of a booming postwar economy and the spirit of re-building which permeated the time, they made Hawai'i their home" (1996b: 86).

The sheer numbers of the 1946 sakadas, particularly the higher proportion of women and children compared to previous waves of immigrants, had a stabilizing effect on the Filipino community. Despite the large numbers of prewar Filipino immigrants, the community was mostly composed of single men; it was a "bachelor society."[21] At the height of Filipino immigration to Hawai'i, the male to female ratio was 3 to 1 in 1923 and 9 to 1 in 1927 (San Buenaventura 1995). During the first wave of labor importation, from 1906 to 1919, approximately thirty-thousand Filipinos arrived in Hawai'i (twenty-five thousand men, three thousand women, and two thousand children). During the second wave, between 1920 and 1929, there were roughly seventy-five thousand Filipinos brought to Hawai'i, of whom sixty-six thousand were men, six thousand were women, and three thousand were children. During the third wave of labor recruitment, from 1930 to 1934, fifteen thousand Filipino workers were imported, of whom fourteen thousand were men, five hundred were women, and six hundred were children. Unlike previous waves of labor importation, the last wave of recruitment in 1946 had higher proportions of women and children (of the seventy-five hundred total immigrants, fifteen hundred were women and children). Because they brought families or formed families upon arrival in Hawai'i, the 1946 sakadas helped to stabilize the composition of the Filipino community. Even before the post-1965 immigration phenomenon, the postwar labor immigrants were able to bring the families (nuclear and extended) into Hawai'i and initiate the process of family chain migration (particularly among Ilokanos) that would intensify with the subsequent changes in immigration legislation (San Buenaventura 1996b). The arrival of the 1946 sakadas was a significant turning point in Filipino immigration to Hawai'i. Not only did it signal the end of organized labor importation from the Philippines, it also contributed to "the development of a more integrated Filipino community in Hawaii and to the dynamics of post-1965 immigration" (San Buenaventura 1995: 445). In effect, the 1946 sakadas, along with those who stayed in Hawai'i and endured the long work hours, low wages, and bad living conditions, transitioned from "temporary residents" to permanent settlers, embracing Hawai'i as their home and claiming it as their own (Alegado 1996; Revilla 1996). "Local" identity in general has its roots in this transformation from sojourner to settler, indicating the move from "Filipino" to "Local Filipino." The "sakada story" is the foundation upon which a viable "Local Filipino" community is built.

The post–World War II period in Hawai'i had four key historical developments that helped to shape the character of contemporary Hawai'i and the Filipino community, providing the conditions for imagining and striving for community empowerment and collective upward mobility. First, this period marked the development and growing political strength of organized labor in the islands, namely the ILWU. Before World War II, the number of Filipino laborers did not begin to grow dramatically until 1915 and thus, they did not begin to actively organize until the late 1910s. Teodoro outlines the importance of Filipino labor organizing: "[the] efforts of Filipinos at labor organizing during the 1920s and the 1940s are probably their greatest contribution to the history of Hawaii's diverse peoples, because those efforts were exerted under the most difficult conditions, resulting in significant gains for workers of all races and leading to the enlargement of democratic life in Hawaii" (Teodoro 1981: 19). The most prominent figure in the development of Filipino unions was Pablo Manlapit.[22] In 1919 Manlapit organized the Filipino Federation of Labor and in 1920, Manlapit's organization, along with the Japanese Federation of Labor, arguably staged the first interethnic strike in Hawai'i (Takaki 1983).[23] Despite the collective effort of the unions, the planters were able to break the strike by creating division and distrust among the leadership of both unions. In addition, planters enlisted Hawaiians, Portuguese, and Koreans as strikebreakers as well as continuing to import more Filipino laborers from the Philippines (mainly Ilokanos), which created a division between the new and old workers. In 1924, Manlapit's Filipino Federation of Labor organized the Higher Wages Movement. Like the 1920 strike, the Filipino workers were defeated when the Hawaiian Sugar Planter's Association brought in strikebreakers from the Philippines. The 1924 strike was particularly notable because it involved the "Hanapepe Massacre" in which sixteen Filipino strikers and four policemen were killed. In addition, after the strike ended Manlapit was convicted and sentenced to four years in prison. He was subsequently paroled to California, only to return to the islands in 1932 to form another union with the assistance of Antonio Fagel and Epifanio Taok. In 1934, Manlapit was again arrested and deported to the Philippines. That same year, Taok was jailed, but Fagel continued and formed the organization Vibora Luviminda. In 1937 Vibora Luviminda called a strike at four plantations on Maui, demanding higher wages and the dismissal of five foremen. After nearly three months, the planters agreed to a 15 percent pay increase. This was especially significant in that it marked one of the first victories for the union forces, the first time sugar planters negotiated a settlement. The 1937 Vibora Luviminda strike was also the last of the racially or ethnically exclusive strikes, paving the way for organized labor and the emergence of the International Longshoremen's and Warehousemen's Union (ILWU).

Because of their numbers in the workforce, Filipinos were critical in the development and growth of the ILWU. According to Teodoro, "The greatest impact of Filipinos on Hawaii during this period was in the building of the ILWU. Perhaps no other group was more aware of the necessity for building a strong labor organization that could challenge the power of the plantation oligarchy than the Filipino workers. Although they were not in the leadership of the labor movement, the Filipinos were the main force in the struggle to establish the ILWU in Hawaii—and therefore the ones who made the greatest sacrifices" (Teodoro 1981: 24–25). However, in contrast to Teodoro's claim, Filipinos were indeed in leadership roles,[24] but as a whole this did not translate to collective political and economic power, and they were not in positions to participate in the newly arranged power structure and achieve group upward mobility. Regardless, their roles and histories in labor organizing have been key components in configuring a Local Filipino identity.

The other post–World War II developments involved class, organized labor, electoral politics, and statehood. Shortly after the war, a new middle class emerged in Hawai'i, with the local Japanese and Chinese as the primary forces. For Trask (1998) this marks the Local Asian ascendancy to power, signaling the emergence of Asian settler colonialism in the islands. The third development points to the established alliance between organized labor and the emergent middle class. This alliance gave rise to a political force paving the way for the "democratic revolution" of 1954 (which took political control away from Republicans and initiated the dominance of the Democratic Party in Hawai'i politics that continues today, despite the election of a Republican governor in 2002). For Saranillio, this is a key event in the development of a settler, multicultural order in the islands: "The so-called Democratic Revolution is often narrated as the moment when liberal multiculturalism displaced a white racial dictatorship in Hawai'i" (2010a: 463). Lastly, Hawai'i statehood in 1959 solidified the political power of the labor movement and the growing middle class. In this regard, Saranillio has also suggested that statehood illustrates a representational tension in which settler and Native histories collide (2010).[25]

The completion of the Filipino Community Center occurred at a time when the idealization of Hawai'i as multicultural or "racial paradise" was firmly in place. The "racial paradise" paradigm depends on a development narrative that glosses over struggles for Native Hawaiian self-determination

Figure 6. The Center's entryway to the Consuelo Zobel Alger Courtyard. The metal gates also incorporate key Philippine symbols, like the sun from the flag, photo courtesy of Took HNLA.

and positions Kanaka Maoli as anachronistic, belonging to the past or merely serving as a contemporary cultural backdrop for the hegemonic multiculturalist ideology. The dominant multiculturalist ideology often delegitimizes indigenous claims to place and belonging, resulting in competing and "colliding histories" that situate settler struggles for empowerment against indigenous self-determination. There is a plaque at the Filipino Community Center that outlines the history of Filipinos in Hawai'i. It reads:

> Filipino-Americans have made significant contributions to Hawai'i's modern history and culture since the arrival of the first "sakadas" (laborers) in 1906. In 2002, Filipinos made up more than fifteen percent of Hawai'i's population and have developed a powerful identity in the community through culture, education, business, and politics. The Filipino Community Center, Inc., known as the FilCom Center, is the symbol of Filipinos' achievements, as a place that can be called their own.

In this way, the Filipino Community Center is a place local Filipinos can claim as their own, a "Filipino home" in Waipahu/Hawai'i, effectively burying the indigenous and plantation pasts beneath its foundations.

CHAPTER 2

"What's so p/funny?"

Sherry Ann is anxious and excited to tell me a story about "being Filipino in Hawai'i." She describes herself as a "Local Filipino" but is quick to add, "but I didn't really grow up Filipino." When I first asked to interview her, she was reluctant. She asked me, "Why do you want to interview me for your project? I'm so not Filipino!" Both of her parents immigrated to the islands from the Philippines but unlike most Filipinos in Hawai'i, she grew up in a predominantly white, Japanese and Chinese high-income neighborhood where, as she puts it, "there were only a handful of Filipinos." For elementary, middle, and high school Sherry Ann attended an elite private school, where she states again, "there were only a handful of Filipinos" who went to school with her. Now, as a student at the University of Hawai'i at Mānoa she is no longer one of the "handful of Filipinos" on campus, especially in the first-level Tagalog class, but she has become exposed to a type of Filipino visibility that has been both jarring and eye-opening for her personally. She tells me, "I grew up Local. Growing up, I didn't have to confront being Filipino but I heard all the Filipino jokes. I just didn't think they applied to me." She then relays a story about a recent birthday party where her friends (who were mostly from high school and non-Filipino) decided to surprise her with a cake in the shape of a black dog. To a roar of laughter and cheers, her friends exclaimed, "Now we can all eat black dog!" Sherry then asks me somewhat rhetorically, "What's so funny? What was so funny?" Her questions lingered.

Fast forward a year and it is now December 2007 and two maintenance workers at the Moanalua Golf Course (on O'ahu) were recently arrested for allegedly stealing, butchering, and eating a dog (while its owner was playing a round of golf). Before their club meeting, a group of Filipino students, all of whom self-identified as Local, from the Timpuyog Organization were having a lively discussion about the situation and the local news coverage. One student loudly proclaimed, "They gotta be Filipino. Guaranteed!" There was a mixture of laughter and private dread. Another student countered, "Why they gotta be Filipino? Other cultures eat dog." And another student quietly pleaded, "I hope they're not Filipino." When the names and mug shots of Nelson Domingo and Saturnino Palting were released, they confirmed the suspicions and fears of the students. The two men, who were recent immigrants to Hawai'i and lived in the Filipino ethnic enclave of Kalihi, were subsequently charged and convicted of felony animal cruelty. Both were eventually sentenced to three years' probation. Domingo was also fined $500 and ordered to complete four hundred hours of community service, while Palting was required to perform three hundred hours. They were also both ordered to spend a year in prison as a condition of their probation (Palting's whole term was suspended, while Domingo served three months). At the next meeting, the students greeted me with wry smiles and head nods of "I told you so" and looks of quiet disappointment. With a slight shake of her head, Sherry Ann faintly said to me, "They had to be Filipino."

In this chapter I situate Sherry Ann's experience and the other students' conversation as part of my critique of the idea of Hawai'i as "multicultural paradise" and the production of Local by examining the popular practice of ethnic humor. I argue that Hawai'i ethnic humor is a space for the production of "Local knowledge(s)" (Chang 1996) and ideologies where identities are constructed and social order and racial hierarchy enacted. While others have focused on the construction of Local as a nonwhite pan-ethnic formation (Okamura 1994; Takaki 1983) and as a sociopolitical identity set in opposition to Native Hawaiians (Fujikane 2000; Trask 2000), I draw attention to the production of Local as a nonimmigrant identity, especially the ways in which Local comedians appropriate the voice of immigrant Filipinos through the use of Mock Filipino (or speaking English with a "Filipino accent"). Mock Filipino is a strategy often employed by Local comedians to differentiate the speakers of Philippine languages from speakers of Pidgin, or what most linguists call Hawai'i Creole English, the lingua franca of Local residents. Audience members and comedians do not necessarily speak or understand Philippine languages, yet many often recognize individual Filipino words and the shift into Mock Filipino. Although there are approximately one hundred Philippine languages and the national language of the Philippines is officially called "Filipino," the language variety mocked by Local comedians is more of an amalgamation of Ilokano and Tagalog, two of the most commonly spoken Philippine languages in Hawai'i. Similar to the effects of Mock Spanish (Hill 1993, 1995, 1998) and Mock Asian

(Chun 2009), Mock Filipino produces stigmatizing discourses of immigrant Filipinos, which in turn work to stigmatize Locals as immigrants. Like Mock Asian, public utterances of Mock Filipino in the continental United States are rather rare outside the comedy performances of Filipino American comics like Rex Navarrete and Kevin Camia.[1] In Hawai'i, Mock Filipino seems to have more resonance, where Filipinos and non-Filipinos are more likely to publicly voice a cautionary "Halla," an exasperated "Ay sus!" or front a "Filipino accent" in everyday linguistic practice.[2] These public utterances simultaneously reinforce discourses of tolerance, inclusivity, and acceptance that reinscribe Hawai'i's mainstream "multiculturalist ideology" (San Juan 2002) and the marking of immigrant Filipino otherness.

In this chapter, I examine the linguistic practices in the comedy performances of Frank De Lima as well as excerpts from *Buckaloose: Shmall Keed Time* (Small Kid Time), a comedy CD by Da Braddahs, a contemporary and tremendously popular comedy duo in Hawai'i. De Lima, who self-identifies as Portuguese, Hawaiian, Chinese, English, Spanish, Scottish, Irish, and French, is a pillar of the local comedy scene and is commonly referred to as the "king of ethnic humor in Hawaii" (Coleman 2003).[3] Da Braddahs comprises two Hawai'i-born and -reared comics, James Roaché, who is Filipino and Italian, and Tony Silva, who is Hawaiian, Chinese, Portuguese, and Irish. In *Buckaloose: Shmall Keed Time*, Da Braddahs follows the template of local comedy established by the pioneering comedy team of Booga Booga[4] in the 1970s and 1980s, who performed jokes based on racial/ethnic stereotypes familiar to Hawai'i audiences (for example, cheap Chinese, dumb Portuguese), used Pidgin as the primary medium of communication, and included song parodies and character sketches involving wild costumes, racial/ethnic caricatures, and overstated accents. In addition to their comedy CD, Da Braddahs have four self-produced videos and four DVDs, a thirty-minute-long television show (called "Da Braddahs and Friends") that airs on local cable television six nights per week, and they host a live weekly comedy show that depicts "the comic underside of contemporary local living" (Berger 2002, D1). Da Braddahs' character sketches play off long-standing racial/ethnic stereotypes, and a review of *Buckaloose: Shmall Keed Time* notes that the "Chinese, Filipino, 'haole,'[5] and other characters here are staple types" where "the characters and situations are almost all basic Booga/Rap bits that have been used and abused by almost all local comics for the past 20 years" (Berger 1998, D5). Although there are other problematic characters in the videos and on the television show, like Keoki and Kakio who play on the image of the gay male kumu hula[6] and his alaka'i,[7] Bush and Bully (the mindless Samoan tree trimmers), and

Pocho and Tanda (two Local boys), I focus on the Filipino character, Tata Cayatmo, who has a more prominent role in the CD, and his interactions with the Local character, Joe.[8] Da Braddahs' Tata Cayatmo functions as the stereotypical elderly male Filipino immigrant whose linguistic incompetence is positioned against Joe's Pidgin, drawing attention to the use of language in the othering of immigrant Filipinos.

The use of Mock Filipino in Hawai'i ethnic humor is part of broader racializing and stigmatizing discourses. Although media depictions often criminalize and misrepresent Filipinos as prone to violence (Quemuel 1996) as well as focus on "Filipino male sexual violence" (Fujikane 2000), I focus on discourses that highlight immigrant Filipino linguistic and cultural difference. Local comedians use Mock Filipino as a "strategy of pejoration" (Hill 1993) to construct discourses that place immigrant Filipinos as cultural and linguistic Others, signifying their subordinate position in the social hierarchy and order. Through Mock Filipino, Local comedians construct the linguistic incompetence and subordinate identity of immigrant Filipinos. Although understood as "innocent" and "harmless" joking in which "we can laugh at ourselves," Hawai'i ethnic humor in general and Mock Filipino in particular simultaneously produce racially demeaning or "racially interested" discourses (Hill 1995) that uphold the positive self-image of Locals, especially their membership in Hawai'i's "racial paradise," while lowering that of immigrant Filipinos. It is important to note that I do not argue that Local humor is simply about marginalizing Filipinos. Instead, the everyday practice and public performance of racial and ethnic joking in the islands help to construct the buk buk identity category, a highly public and visible negative label of a particular type of Filipino, the immigrant Filipino or FOB (Fresh Off the Boat). The linguistic practice in the comedy performances are thus identity acts that normalize Local and reinforce Hawai'i's myth of multiculturalism while disseminating hierarchical ideas about language, culture, and identity.

Local and Multiculturalism

The idea of Local is crucial for understanding ethnic humor and the politics of identity in Hawai'i. Although Local operates in a field of ongoing relational oppositions that form a Local/non-Local binary, it is a racialized identity category composed primarily of the various nonwhite groups that usually trace their entrance into the islands to the plantation era—namely those of Chinese, Portuguese, Japanese, Okinawan, Filipino, and Korean descent. Local is the label for those who are usually classified as "Asian American" or "Asian Pacific American" in the continental United States. For many Hawai'i residents, particularly those of Asian ancestry, Local is the most salient category for political and cultural identification. Various scholars have focused on the cultural (Grant and Ogawa 1993; Ogawa 1978, 1981; Takaki 1983, 1993), structural (Okamura 1980, 1994, 1998, 2008), and political (Fujikane and Okamura 2008; Fujikane 2000; Trask 2000) to examine the nature and dynamics of Local. A common feature among these various approaches is that each locates the emergence and development of Local in Hawai'i's labor history (preceded by the entry of European and American capital investment and the shift from mercantilism to large-scale agricultural production) and the shared experiences among the mainly Asian plantation workers.

A key aspect of the emergence of Local is the development of Pidgin or Hawai'i Creole English (or HCE), the language that now serves as the lingua franca of those who identify themselves as Local and is often used as the primary marker of Local-ness. Ronald Takaki (1983) argues that Pidgin was the shared language among the nonwhite plantation workers and facilitated their shift from "sojourners to settlers" and from individual ethnic groups to an overarching panethnic consolidation. Although "standard English," or mainstream U.S. English, continues to be the language of power and prestige, Pidgin has come to function as the language of Locals, enjoying "covert prestige" as a "badge of honor" (Da Pidgin Coup 1999; see also Lum 1998). It is the primary medium of communication for Local comedians. In addition, Pidgin has come to symbolize Hawai'i's multiculturalism and the ideologies of mixing, acceptance, equality, and assimilation. Pidgin is depicted as a reflection of the islands' history of interracial harmony: "Pidgin is inclusive, a reflection of our historical attitudes and the value placed on getting along and trying to find common ground. It is non-hierarchical, and puts people on an even footing" (Da Pidgin Coup 1999). The language exemplifies the "common ground" on which Locals stand, with both feet firmly and equally planted; it illustrates that everyone can indeed get along. Pidgin is also causally linked to the formation of the panethnic Local: "It is a language that has brought people together in spite of their differences in ancestral culture and language and has created a 'local' culture which blends ideas and flavors. It has taught us to be not just tolerant but accepting. It has allowed immigrants to begin new shoots without losing old roots" (Da Pidgin Coup 1999). Pidgin epitomizes the "blending process" associated with the development of Local identity and culture. In this way, Pidgin and

Local are inseparable, constituting the symbolic, cultural, and linguistic aspect of multiculturalism in Hawai'i. As Local comedian Frank De Lima puts it: "Hawaii is local. Hawaii is Pidgin" (quoted in Coleman 2003, C4).

The "blending process" is not only linguistic but involves a type of cultural assimilation, resulting in various "points of commonality" (Grant and Ogawa 1993), an inventory of cultural traits and characteristics. Included among these cultural points of commonality are shared food preferences (represented by the "mixed plate," which includes different culinary items from the various plantation groups), social customs and traditions (for example, taking off shoes before entering a home), application of the Native Hawaiian concept of 'ohana (or "family") as part of extended family networks, folk beliefs (for example, the prevalence of ghost stories), and ethnic joke telling. These "points of commonality" have served as the bases for the seemingly low-keyed social interactions and smooth interpersonal relationships among Hawai'i residents. This understanding of the Local highlights the atmosphere of mutual respect, consideration, generosity, friendliness, tolerance, and harmony in the islands (Okamura 1980; Grant and Ogawa 1993); characteristics often associated with the appropriation and celebration of aloha.

However, from a political perspective that highlights the islands' history of Native subordination and settler domination, Local also points to sources of division and opposition. According to Trask, Hawai'i's history of colonization is "a twice-told tale, first of discovery and settlement by European and American businessmen and missionaries, then of the plantation Japanese, Chinese, and eventually Filipino rise to dominance in the islands" (2000: 2–3). The development of Local is part and parcel of the "twice-told tale" and the formation of Hawai'i's settler society. For Trask, Local is the name that children of Asian settlers call themselves, which feeds the American ethnic myth of success and helps to justify immigrant hegemony:

> In truth, "local" ideology tells a familiar, and false, tale of success: Asians came as poor plantation workers and triumphed decades later as the new, democratically-elected ruling class. Not coincidentally, the responsibility for continued Hawaiian dispossession falls to imperialist haole and incapacitated Natives, that is, not to Asians. Thus do these settlers deny their ascendancy was made possible by the continued national oppression of Hawaiians, particularly the theft of our lands and the crushing of our independence (Trask 2000: 4).

Thus, the use of Local locates Asians outside the white and "settler" category and elides Asian participation in U.S. colonial domination and Native Hawaiian subjugation. For Trask, Local equals Asian but not Native Hawaiian. Thus the development of Local obscures the history of Hawai'i's indigenous people while staking a settler claim. In this sense, Local challenges Native Hawaiian indigeneity while asserting a competing claim of rightful belonging to the islands. The idea of Local espouses a "land of immigrants" rhetoric that depends on a multiculturalist ideology and purports an ethos of racial diversity, heterogeneity, tolerance, and harmony while masking the islands' settler history of foreign domination and Native subordination.

Political and economic changes in Hawai'i since the mid-1960s, including the Native Hawaiian sovereignty movement, have enhanced the continuing salience of Local. According to Okamura, these structural factors are the backdrop for the field of relational oppositions in which Local identity is constructed:

> [L]ocal identity is based on the categorical opposition between groups considered Local and those considered non-Local, including haole, immigrants, the military, tourists, and foreign investors. Local is essentially a relative category; groups and individuals are viewed or view themselves as local in relation to others who are not so perceived. From this perspective, local identity is very exclusive rather than all inclusive and serves to create and maintain social boundaries between groups (Okamura 1994: 165).

In this sense, Local is both inclusive and exclusive, involving processes of self- and other-definition. Okamura points to the slipperiness of Local and observes that the policing of boundaries are situationally dependent on structural oppositions. The historical formulation and formation of Local involves a nested hierarchy of relational alterities, in which a dominant node indexes a working class background, the subordinate position of plantation workers in opposition to the dominant white planter and merchant oligarchy. In this dominant form, Local is defined as a nonwhite, primarily Asian Pacific Islander working-class identity. However, in this chapter I foreground the relationality and situatedness of Local. Depending on the sociohistorical context and actors involved, Local can index racialized bodies ("look Local"), sociocultural identities ("act Local"), linguistic affiliations ("talk Local"), place ("born here not flown here"), and political positionings. In this way, the boundaries of Local are constantly changing and continuously policed through processes of self-definition and othering. In the sections that follow, I examine the ways in which racializing imagery and language practices in Local comedy are used to construct Locals and non-Locals.

Constructing Filipinos as "Buk Buk"

Hawai'i ethnic humor is an important site for the practice and performance of Local identity and culture. The history of "Local comedy" can be traced to the 1950s and 1960s when Sterling Mossman, Lucky Luck, and Kent Bowman, aka perpetual senatorial candidate K. K. Ka'umanua (pronounced like "cow manure"), were popular comedic performers (Tonouchi 1999). Mossman, dubbed "Hawai'i's First Comedic Entertainer," was a bandleader who combined singing and telling jokes in his comedy routines. Lucky Luck, known as "Hawai'i's Prince of Comedy," was a popular radio personality with his own variety show and children's television show. Bowman, known as "The King of Pidgin English," recorded a half dozen albums that included his stand-up routines and children's stories told in Pidgin. Arguably, the heyday of Hawai'i ethnic humor was the late 1970s and 1980s. During this period, Andy Bumatai, Mel Cabang, and Booga Booga, the pioneering comedy group of James Kawika Piimauna "Rap" Reiplinger, James Grant Benton, and Ed Ka'ahea, set the stage for subsequent local comedians and established the template for contemporary Hawai'i ethnic humor, often referred to as "Kanaka[9] comedy." Race and ethnicity and the production of Local were crucial to the popularity of Booga Booga. Their comedy sketches played up familiar racial/ethnic stereotypes: "Ethnic identity is the key to their ability to generate material which is universally appealing to local audiences: Ka'ahea as the laid back 'token Hawaiian,' Benton the reserved 'Kabuki type,' Reiplinger more indefinably as the hustler—the 'token Portagee,'[10] perhaps" (Smith 1977, 20–21, in Tonouchi 1999). As Naomi Sodetani observes,

> [t]heir whole act was nothing but ethnic jokes and stereotypes: families bickering at home; Hawaiian musicians, busboys, hotel workers having fun while aspiring to be more. They made visible and celebrated a sense of "us-ness" onstage. All spoken in pidgin, not school-mandated 'good English grammar.' (Sodetani 2001, 6)

Booga Booga's "kanaka comedy" poked fun at social life in Hawai'i, resonating with the everyday realities of their Local audiences. Although based on problematic racial and ethnic stereotypes, "kanaka comedy" and its use of Pidgin, not "school-mandated" English, is integral in the discursive construction of Local and the creation of an "us-ness" particularly among Hawai'i's working-class people. In addition, the comedy group's rise to prominence coincided with the growing legitimization of Pidgin in academic and popular discourse during the 1980s, despite the Hawai'i Department of Education's policies against the use of Pidgin in schools. Furthermore, as Lee Tonouchi suggests, the rise of "kanaka comedy" corresponded with the racial/ethnic consciousness raising of the late 1960s and 1970s and the emergence of "Local nationalism" (Fujikane 1994): "Booga Booga's substan-

FilipinO/a = Seen As Cooks/Bakers/Busboys/Hotel workers = Service Industry workers

tial popularity stems in part from being able to capitalize on dis movement creating separate ethnic identities as well as positing one collective Local identity against da mainland continent" (Tonouchi 1999, 24). The racial/ethnic awareness of this period helped to establish the idea of Local, especially as an identity positioned against "da mainland," producing a Hawai'i/continental U.S. dichotomy. Although the 1990s experienced a lull in the development of "kanaka comedy," there has been a recent resurgence with the rise of the next generation of Local comedians, like Augie T, Lanai, Paul Ogata, Greg Hammer, and Da Braddahs, among others.

Filipino jokes are part of the broader "ethnic humor" widely circulated in Local comedy. Filipinos are by no means the only targets of ethnic jokes, but some argue that they bear a disproportionate burden (Quemuel 1996; Revilla 1996). The following poem by Pizo illustrates the prevalence of Filipino jokes:

> Beloved Frank de Limas,
> Willy Ks,
> everytime you meet me
> on the narrow streets of
> Waipahu or Ewa or Kalihi,
> in wedding celebrations
> or birthday parties,
> in the mortuaries
> or pharmacies,
> in the supermarkets
> or churches,
> even in the schools
> or cinema houses,
> you never failed to ask me
> about that Black Dog.
> —Elmer Omar Pizo, "Black Dog [pinoy style]"[11]

Using surveys conducted by Keesing in the 1930s and Cariaga (1974), Okamura (2008) has argued that the stereotypes used for Filipino jokes have been in circulation since at least the 1930s. The continuing prevalence of Filipino jokes is often understood as a source of "shame of being Filipino" (Revilla 1996) and a basis for local Filipino cultural disidentification and "defensive othering" (Eisen 2011). Eisen's recent study suggests that these stereotypes and jokes persist and often lead to the internalization of the negative imagery. As one of my second-generation female student interviewees told me: "In high school, I used a lot of ethnic jokes and teased the other

Filipinos. I didn't want to be teased. I wanted to be known as the local girl who danced hula and Tahitian, just so I wouldn't get teased for being Filipino." Another second-generation female student, who is mixed race, talked about the benefits of being a product of intermarriage: "I was looking for acceptance when I was a teenager. I didn't want to be picked on. Because I'm mixed, and I don't look Filipino, not being Filipino was beneficial."

Although there is a wide variety of Filipino jokes, there appear to be two primary types: those that focus on "Filipino vocabulary" (which depend on Mock Filipino) and "Filipino culinary tastes" (specifically dog eating). The Filipino dog-eating jokes are especially prevalent. The following examples are taken from *Frank De Lima's Joke Book* (1991, 68–70):[12]

> Did you hear about the new Filipino cookbook?
> 101 Ways to Wok Your Dog
> What do Filipinos call a dogcatcher's truck?
> Meals on Wheels
> What's a Filipino's favorite meal?
> Mutt loaf.
> What do you call a Filipino family without a dog?
> Vegetarians.
> What do you call a Filipino family with one dog?
> A family that doesn't know where its next meal is coming from.
> What do you call a Filipino family with five dogs?
> Ranchers.

As demonstrated in the excerpt from the Pizo poem, "Black Dog [pinoy style]," Filipino dog-eating jokes are widely disseminated, in public and in private. They greet the poet "everytime you meet me" in the Filipino neighborhoods of Oʻahu. The Black Dog follows him even outside the Filipino residential enclaves, illustrating the pervasiveness of Filipino dog-eating jokes in the media and entertainment industry (particularly in the references to Local comedian Frank De Lima and Local singer Willie K.). Sherry Ann's story, mentioned at the beginning of the chapter, reflects the realities of Pizo's poem, suggesting the persistence of Filipino dog-eating jokes at the interpersonal level, as private jokes "among friends." As standards in Local comedy routines (Quemuel 1996), Filipino dog-eating jokes move from light talk in private spheres to public joking (Hill 1993) that is both entertainment and the enactment of social hierarchy and order.

In Local comedy, a dominant Filipino character type is the manong,[13] the elderly male immigrant who is Fresh Off the Boat (or FOB) or Just Off the Jet (JOJ), eats dog and goats, speaks with a "heavy Filipino accent," and holds multiple low-wage and low-prestige jobs.[14] The manong often stumbles over his words, uses awkward expressions, has long pauses when he talks, and has problems with English pronunciation (that is, phonological and morphological exaggerations and general linguistic incompetence). What is usually belittled in Filipino jokes is the fresh-off-the-boatness and the linguistic, cultural, social, and ideological characteristics associated with recent immigrants, particularly their perceived "heavy Filipino accent," affinity for bright clothes, foreign culinary tastes, and their general cultural incompatibility and incompetence. De Lima's "Filipino Purple Danube,"[15] a song parody of "The Blue Danube" using a waltz tempo that mimics the music for the tinikling, a traditional Filipino folk dance that uses two bamboo poles, is exemplary. De Lima begins the song with the Ilokano greeting "Kumustakayo" ('How are you all?') and immediately jumps into Mock Filipino nonsensical sounds that transform into clucking sounds. The lyrics for the song are as follows:

"FILIPINO PURPLE DANUBE"

01 what's purple and brown, buk buk, buk buk
02 what squats on the ground, buk buk, buk buk
03 hold knife to your throat, buk buk, buk buk
04 and eats billy goat, buk buk, buk buk
05 who dance with two poles, buk buk, buk buk
06 has hairs on his moles, buk buk, buk buk
07 who eats bagoong,[16] all day long
08 you are right, it's the manong
09 who drives Cadillac, buk buk, manong
10 light show on the back, manong, manong
11 who wears silver pants, manong, manong
12 goes out disco dance, manong, manong
13 who greases his hair, manong, manong
14 who perfumes the air, manong, manong
15 who mixes opai[17] with fish eye
16 you are right, it's the P.I.[18]
17 you are right, salamat[19]

In the Silva Anniversary version of the song above, De Lima substitutes "who greases his hair / who perfumes the air" (lines 13–14) for "who works on Lanai[20] / whose wife is hapai"[21] and leaves out the entire third verse that appears in his Joke Book. The missing verse is more of the same, referring to Filipinos as "Flips" who participate in cockfighting and wear orange socks to go with their purple shirt and silver pants.[22] "Filipino Purple Danube" helps construct the identity category of "buk buk"[23] /bUkbUk /, which is synonymous with immigrant Filipinos and is the primary marker of Filipino linguistic and cultural otherness. De Lima's "Danube" constructs the stereotypical buk buk who is dangerous (holds knife to your throat), hypersexualized (whose wife is hapai), wears bright-colored clothes (purple shirt, silver pants, orange socks), conspicuously showy or flashy (the entire second verse), and maintains Philippine ethnic signs, primarily culinary tastes (billy goat, bagoong, and opae with fish eye), cultural behaviors ("squats on the ground"), and traditions ("dance with two poles").[24] This stereotypical image can also be found in Local greeting cards. For instance, a belated birthday card has a picture of a "Filipino" man wearing a bright purple shirt who is accompanied by a black dog, goat, and chicken. The "Filipino" man, aghast, has his hands on his face and the caption exclaims "Ay Sus!" The inside of the card reads, "I porgot yo' bertdey." In order to get the joke in the card, the reader must find both the racialized images as well as the Mock Filipino "funny."

De Lima's stereotypical buk buk reappears in the comedy of Da Braddahs. In *Shmall Keed Time*, the Filipino character is Tata Cayatmo. The choice of the name is particularly interesting. In Ilokano, tata is a term of address that is used for a male parent or uncle, one generation above the speaker. The word "cayat" or "kayat"[25] can mean "to want, like, wish, desire, [or] be willing" (Rubino 2000, 267) and mo is a second-person informal singular genitive possessive enclitic. The words combined, cayatmo, means "do you want like, wish, desire, or are you willing?" Thus, the name "Tata Cayatmo" can mean "old man do you like/want," and with the sexual connotations, it can mean something like "dirty old man."[26] By all means, Da Braddahs' Tata Cayatmo is buk buk and in the context of Filipino representation in Hawai'i, he is an extension of the criminally inclined and sexually predatory men in the Filipino "bachelor societies" of the sugar plantations.[27]

In *Shmall Keed Time*, Tata Cayatmo takes center stage in the song, "We Are Filipino," which is sung with a "Filipino accent." The song is the second track in a two-track sequence involving two characters, Joe and Tata Cayatmo. Throughout the CD, the character Joe is the Local "hero," the protagonist in the sketch who meets up with various ethnic characters. Tata Cayatmo is the Filipino character, an older immigrant Filipino man in his fifties. Tata Cayatmo's status as an immigrant is crucial for the setup of the joke. The song is a form of speech play that heavily depends on Mock Filipino for its humor:

"WE ARE FILIPINO"

01 ahhhh. I would like to dedicate dis song
02 to all of my fellow countryman
03 from the Filifeens
04 and flease mister DJ
05 can you flease gib me da good reburb
06 like da one on ahhh Hawai'i Stars[28]
07 cause I like to be like da good kadugo[29]
08 everybody put your hand together
09 and sing wit me the song of my countryman
10 Jim Shapper, gib me the tunes, boy
11 who do you think we are
12 we have to trabel so dam par
13 do you understand my accent?
14 excuse me sir, your change is ahh, fifty cent.
15 hoy barok,[30] will you like to try some really fresh kalamunggay?[31]
16 barok, naimas kayatmo?[32]
    ((The sound of chickens crowing in the background))
17 everyday my fighting chicken is getting i-stronger
18 (Joe: Tata, Tata, put the chicken down)

    Chorus:
19 we are Filifino
20 we come from the Filifeens
21 we are Filifino
22 trabeling with our pamily
23 we are Filifino
24 my family name is Tangunan
25 we are Filifino
26 my grandfader's your cleaning man
27 we are a buk buk, a suksok[33]
28 we are a buk buk, a suksok
29 boy, listen
30 nataraki la unay dayta, nataraki la unay dayta
31 haan nga babait, haan nga babait na babai dayta, nataraki la unay dayta[34]
32 excuse me, Kalihi[35]
33 everyday my pants are getting i-higher

Chorus:

34   we are Filifino
35   we come from the Filifeens
36   we are Filifino
37   trabeling with more pamily
38   we are Filifino
39   we all squeeze in dat pink house
40   we are Filifino
41   I go PI[36] for one more spouse
42   we are a buk buk, a suksok
43   we are a buk buk, a suksok
44   ahhh, my hair does not moob all day
45   because I use goat pomade
46   working at da bus stop
47   we buy our clothes from the Body Shop[37]
48   working 27 more year
49   so I can retarded[38] here
50   da PI channel[39] is da one por me
51   so I can watch it on da big TV
52   everyday my pants are getting i-higher
        ((leafblower sound))
53   (Joe: Tata, get out of the tree. Tata, come down from the tree)

Chorus:

54   we are Filifino
55   we come from the Filifeens
56   we are Filifino (song fades out . . .)

Like De Lima's "Danube," "We Are Filipino" tells the listeners what it means to be Filipino in Hawai'i. For those unfamiliar with Filipinos in Hawai'i, the song serves as a brief primer on Filipino speech, culture, history, and socioeconomic status. For example, the song illustrates how Filipinos continue to be heavily concentrated in the more readily available, less prestigious, and lower-paying occupations. When Tata Cayatmo says, "Excuse me sir, your change is, ahh fifty cent" and later, "my grandfader's your cleaning man," he refers to the fact that Filipinos are occupationally concentrated in the new plantations, the hotels and resorts of the tourism industry, as chambermaids, janitors, and gardeners, as well as workers in the retail and service industries. Thus, it is not surprising to find older Filipinos working at fast-food restaurants or as groundskeepers (that is, "yardman"), Tata *stereotypes cont.*

Cayatmo's occupation. Even though the audience may not understand all of the words in the song, they are familiar with the racialized and classed imagery.

Similar to De Lima's use of hapai in "Filipino Purple Danube," Da Braddahs also highlight that Filipinos are suksok, a sexually laden Ilokano word that means to insert (or stab, like with a knife)[40] or penetrate (with a phallus). This portrayal of Filipinos continues a tradition of media representations that have depicted Filipinos as a "sex danger," criminally inclined, and prone to violence, which have their origins in the plantation era. In the plantation camps, the image of the Filipino was that of an uncontrollable, dangerous, and sexually predatory male:

> A well-educated professional of Japanese ancestry . . . remembered the stern warning of his parents that children should not wander too close to the Filipino camps lest something awful should befall them. He also recalled that young girls were told to avoid Filipino men because their mere gaze was said to be sufficient to cause pregnancy. (Teodoro 1981, 55–56)

Myth Tales

In the song, the character of Tata Cayatmo takes us back to plantation imagery. The reference to the disreputable woman uttered in Ilokano, "haan nga babait, haan nga babait. nataraki la unay dayta/she's not virtuous, she's not virtuous, she's very flashy," and the line, "I go PI for one more spouse" only heightens the sexualization and deviation of Tata Cayatmo and the normalization of Joe.

We also find out in the chorus of the song that Filipinos are largely an immigrant community: "we are Filifino, we come from the Filifeens, we are Filifino, trabeling with more pamily." Since the 1970s Filipinos have constituted the majority of immigrants who arrive annually in Hawai'i. The focus on Filipino immigrants in Local comedy helps to create a social cleavage between Locals and immigrants: "One effect [of these negative stereotypes and jokes] is that we have young Filipinos who are ashamed of being Filipino. Local Filipinos socially and culturally distance themselves from immigrant Filipinos because many of the jokes and stereotypes are based upon immigrant Filipino behaviors, like the accent" (Revilla 1996: 9). In this way, the constant flow of Filipino immigrants and their highly marked visibility, reproduced in ethnic humor, have led many Local Filipinos to dissociate themselves from their immigrant counterparts, drawing attention to their Local rather than "Philippine" identity (Revilla 1997). Da Braddahs' song elicits laughter because the imagery resonates with their largely Local audience. As Roache notes, "[P]eople can relate to us and say . . . 'I have a cousin who's like that' " (in Coleon 2001: F5). In this particular case, "like that" refers to a cousin who is "buk buk." The assertion "I have a cousin who's like that" also makes the evaluative claim that "I'm not like my cousin," thereby creating a Local/immigrant dichotomy and constructing immigrant Filipinos as Others.

Mocking Filipinos

An important feature in Local comedy is the use of exaggerated accents to differentiate the speech of Locals and non-Locals. Exaggerated accents are a form of speech play that rely on "the manipulation of elements and components of language in relation to one another, in relation to the social and cultural contexts of language use, and against the backdrop of other verbal possibilities in which it is not foregrounded" (Sherzer 2002: 1). In Local comedy, Mock Filipino depends on the intentional disjunctive use of puns, miscommunication, and the manipulation of sound patterns in the formulation of perceived linguistic differences. Furthermore, Mock Filipino and "Filipino vocabulary" jokes (like the example above) depend on phonological and prosodic differences between pidgin (or "standard English," as is the case above) and Tagalog and Ilokano and the ensuing communicative confusion for the jokes to be perceived as humorous.[41] Take for example the following joke from Frank De Lima:

> Eduardo went to UH[42] to learn English. First, he learned vocabulary. The teacher said, "Please use 'tenacious' in a sentence."
> Eduardo thought for a minute, scratched his head. Then he said, "Ebery morning, before I go to school, I bend down and tie my ten-ay-shoos."
> The teacher next asked Eduardo to use the word "window" in a sentence.
> Eduardo got that right away and said, "Win do we eat?"
> Finally, the teacher said, "Please use the following four words in a sentence: 'deduct . . . defense . . . defeat . . . and detail.' "
> Eduardo was quiet for a long time and finally he said, "De duck jumped ober de fence, de feet before de tail."[43]

For the above joke to work, Eduardo's speech must issue in Mock Filipino style. In other words Eduardo, who is typified as an immigrant Filipino, must speak with a "Filipino accent"; he must "sound" buk buk. This "accent" is indicated by certain phonological substitutions: the bilabialization of labiodentals /v/ → /b/ (<every> /Ev´ri/ → /Eb´ri/; <over> /ov´r/ → /ob´r/) and the alveolarization of interdentals /D/ → /d/ (<the> /D√/ → /d√/). In addition, Eduardo confuses syllable stress: <tenacious> /t´»neS´s/ → /»tE»ne»Sus/ ('tennis shoes'); <window> /»wIndo/ → /»wIn»do/ ('when do'); <deduct> /

d´»dʌ̆kt/ → /»di»dʌ̆k/ ('the duck'); <defense> /»difEns/ → /»di»fEns/ ('the fence'); <defeat> /d´»fit/ → /»di»fit/ ('the feet'); and <detail> /»ditel/ → /»di»tel/ ('the tail'). In many "Filipino vocabulary" jokes, the punch line or what elicits laughter is not so much what is said but how it is said (that is, the pronunciation); that is to say "Filipino" linguistic practices and the speakers associated with them are the objects of derision.

In Local comedy, what is considered humorous about Filipino jokes is that they highlight the different linguistic practices of Locals and immigrant Filipinos and the communicative misunderstandings that arise. In the following excerpts from *Buckaloose: Shmall Keed Time*, mispronunciation leads to linguistic mix-ups and miscommunication between Joe and Tata Cayatmo. Throughout the CD, Joe is authenticated as the pidgin speaker, and it is his linguistic practices that are privileged. The first excerpt centers on the differences between the words "retired" and "retarded."

"RETARDED/RETIRED"[44]

01	TC:	Imagine dis one kadugu, twenty sheben more year.
		Imagine this, my friend. Twenty seven more years.
02	J:	Rait, rait.
		Right, right.
03	TC:	I'm to going to be retarded.
		I'm going to be retarded.
04	J:	Nou nou nou nou nou. Yu min ritai:ad.
		No, no, no, no, no. You mean retired.
05	TC:	It is to be working poreber. [No? What are you sfeaking tired?
		I'll be working forever. [No! *What are you talking about, tired?*
06	J:	[NO:::U(h) Not- Ho?
		[No! Not. What?
07	TC:	My pamily is working two hundred shebenty sheben hours a week
		My family works two hundred seventy-seven hours a week
08	J:	Tu handred seventi seven?
		Two hundred seventy-seven?

((lines 9–19 are omitted))

20	J:	Hau old yu Tawtaw Kayats.
		How old are you Tata Kayats?
21	TC:	Nga in January I'm going to be making fifty-seven.
		Ahh, in January I'm going to be fifty-seven
22	J:	Lem mi si. lem mi si. Faiv seven tu, kaeri da wan
		Lemme see. Lemme see. Five, seven, two, carry the one.
23	TC:	Yas.

         Yes.

24   J: Ho- HOU

          Ho!

25   TC: Das da good one. Eighty-pour

          That's the good one. Eighty-four

26   J: Das eiti for wen u ritaia. E daes nuts maen.

          That's eighty-four when you retire. Hey, that's nuts, man.

27   TC: Eighty-pour. Ay, dat age is ferfect to be ritarted.

          Eighty-four. Hey, that age is perfect to be retarded.

28   J: Ritaiad. Tawtaw. Ritaiad.

          Retired, Tata. Retired.

Here, Joe and Tata Cayatmo are talking about Cayatmo's age, the type and amount of work he does, and when he plans on retiring. In Cayatmo's first turn, Joe acknowledges mutual intelligibility when he says, "right, right" (line 2). In addition to Cayatmo's phonological substitutions (alveolarization of interdentals /DIs/ → /dIs/, and alveo-palatalization of alveolars and bilabialization of labiodentals /sEv′n/ → /Seb′n/ in line 1) what is perceived to be humorous arises in Cayatmo's second turn. He tells Joe that he plans to retire in twenty-seven years when he is eighty-four years old, but instead of saying that he is going to be retired, he says "I'm to going to be retarded" in line 3 and again in line 27, "dat age is ferfect to be ritarted." In much the same way that Eduardo's "deduct" becomes "the duck," Cayatmo is not "retired," he's "retarded." Both times Joe picks up on the mispronunciation and corrects Cayatmo (line 4 and line 28), a correction done in pidgin. In line 4 Joe says, "Nou nou nou nou nou. yu min ritai:ad/No, no, no, no, no. You mean retired." Rather than using standard English, Joe uses the r-less pidgin form, "ritaiad." Even with Joe's correction, miscommunication still occurs as Cayatmo misconstrues Joe's "ritaiad" for "tired" and is offended by the insinuation that he is lazy and not hard-working (line 5). Joe repeats this correction in line 28 in a more definitive and emphatic way: "Ritaiad. Tawtaw. Ritaiad. / Retired, Tata. Retired."

Tata Cayatmo's inability to differentiate between "retired" and "retarded" points to his linguistic incompetence, which becomes an explicit point of communicative confusion. Is Cayatmo "retired" or "retarded"? Joe's corrections in line 4 and line 28 help to position Cayatmo as linguistically inferior and Pidgin as the linguistic norm; he speaks neither the overtly prominent "Standard English" nor the covertly prestigious Pidgin. Joe's corrections and Cayatmo's inability to pick up on them suggest that perhaps Cayatmo is indeed "retarded," at least linguistically.

In the next excerpt, Cayatmo's linguistic ineptitude is the unambiguous site of misunderstanding. The confusion is over the inconsistency of the phonological substitutions /f/ → /p/ and /p/ → /f/ as Joe wants to clarify who is "fat" and who is "Pat."

"SO HARD TO UNDERSTAND"

01   J: Yur bradas waif Paet Imelda
               Your brother's wife Pat Imelda

02   TC: Yah, she sure is
               Yes, she sure is.

03   J: Shis wat, Paet or Imelda
               She's what, Pat or Imelda?

04   TC: She's Imelda
               She's Imelda.

05   J: Den hus Paet?
               Then who's Pat?

06   TC: Imelda. Imelda is Pat.
               Imelda. Imelda is Pat

07   J: Ou fae:t? Imelda is fae:t. (hhhh)
               Oh, fat. Imelda is fat. ((laughs))

08   TC: Yes Imelda Fat Josefina Kabina Cayatmo. But not now because they are diborced.
               Yes, Imelda Fat Josefina Kabina Kayatmo. But not now because they are divorced.

09   J: Sou hawd fo andastaend. I get om, I get om. Okei okei. Sou yur pis awr efs aend yur efs awr pis end yur bis awr vis aend yur vis awr bis.
               So hard to understand. I get 'em. I get 'em. Okay, okay. So your Ps are Fs and your Fs are Ps and your Bs are Vs and your Vs are Bs.

10:    TC: Pinally, you pigure out my boice.
               Finally, you figure out my voice.

In their first three turns, Joe and Tata Cayatmo are confused over who exactly is "Pat" and who is "fat." Although Joe and Tata Cayatmo arrive at some type of communicative resolution in lines 7–9, Joe expresses his frustration in line 9 when he says, "Sou hawd fo andastaend/So hard to understand." More specifically, for the Pidgin speaker, Philippine languages are "sou hawd fo andastaend/so hard to understand" because the phonological substitutions make it difficult to figure out if Imelda is named "Pat" or if she is "fat." Joe's frustrated "sou hawd fo andastaend/so hard to understand" is an "active distancing" (Hill 1993) from Tata Cayatmo and speakers of Philippine languages. Joe's arrival at some phonological clarity in line 9 illustrates common linguistic practices of native Filipino speakers who are second-language learners of English, namely the substitution of consonant sounds (Ramos n.d.): bilabialization of labiodentals /f/ → /p/ (/fQt/ → /pQt/); /v/ → /b/ (/vçjs/ → /bçjs/); and the labiodentalization of bilabials /p/ → /f/ (/pQt/ → /fQt/) and /b/ → /v/.[45] Cayatmo affirms Joe's understanding of his pronunciation miscues and phonological substitutions in line 10: "Pinally, you pigure out my boice / Finally, you figure out my voice." In the end, the interactions between Joe and Tata Cayatmo in the excerpts, "retarded / retired" and "sou hawd fo andastaend / so hard to understand," establish the following sets of oppositions: Local/immigrant, Local/"Filipino," Pidgin/ Mock Filipino, and insider/outsider. Joe is the young, cool Local while Tata Cayatmo is the flip side (pun intended), the elderly Filipino immigrant who is linguistically and culturally the object of ridicule.[46]

"We can laugh at ourselves"

Hawai'i ethnic humor depends on a shared set of assumptions and ideologies about linguistic practice, cultural identity, and Hawai'i society. These "ideologies of legitimacy" (Chun 2007) hinge on pluralist ideals of racial harmony and the notion that "we can laugh at ourselves." Local comedian Augie T[47] explains why people from Hawai'i are able to laugh at themselves: On the Mainland, you can't do ethnic jokes, people get all offended. . . . But us local people, we live on an island, we real open, we share everything. We can look at all the dumbness of our lives and talk about it. And that's the beauty of Hawai'i. We can laugh at ourselves.

The "we can laugh at ourselves" ideology is understood as a celebration of the islands' racial diversity and cultural differences ("all the dumbness of our lives") and positions the "uniqueness" of Hawai'i against the volatile race relations on the "mainland." Hawai'i is understood as having gone beyond the "melting pot" and "salad bowl" models of race/ethnic relations and is instead an Asian-inspired "chop suey nation." As De Lima explains:

> Here in Hawaii, we laugh at ourselves more than most people do in other places. Hawaii is a chop suey nation—Portagee, Pake, Buddha Head, Sole, Yobo, Kanaka, Haole,[48] all mixed up. Nobody is the majority here. We are all part of at least one minority group. Some of us are part of several minority groups. And we all laugh at ourselves. This is healthy. (De Lima 1991: v)

The "chop suey nation" that De Lima imagines perpetuates the illusion of Hawai'i as a racial paradise (Okamura 1998) where "nobody is the majority," everyone is racially/ethnically "all mixed up," and "we all laugh at

ourselves." In this vision of Hawai'i no one can be really racist or discriminatory because everyone is considered to be equal and everyone is understood
to be a minority. Ogawa (1978) suggests that the ability to "laugh at each
other" and "poke fun at each other" was a key aspect in the development
of Local identity and culture:

> One thing each ethnic group in Hawaii had to learn was a healthy sense of hu-
> mor so that they would be able to laugh at each other and not take themselves
> too seriously. Living on a series of small islands requires a high degree of open
> friendliness. Therefore, Hawaii's people are not reluctant to poke fun at each
> other and at themselves using words which from the mainland standpoint seem
> derogatory but from the Island perspective seem descriptive or simply funny.
> 'Buddhahead,' 'Pake,' 'Kanaka,' 'Haole Crab,' 'Bok-bok,' 'Porogee Mouth,' are
> just a small sampling of the words which ethnic groups often use in reference
> to themselves; these words are essential parts of the local Island culture (Ogawa
> 1978: 155–56).

But who is the "we" that is laughing and who is being laughed at? When
"we laugh at ourselves" do "we" acquiesce to the extant structures and
systems of white and Local domination while reducing ethnic groups to
stigmatizing stereotypes? Or is "laughing at ourselves" a way to maintain the
zones of intimacy and friendliness that were initially developed in response
to haole domination?

In November 2000, Lee Cataluna, a local playwright, comedian, former
local news anchor, and columnist for one of the Honolulu daily newspapers
created a spirited public debate when she criticized the "grand Hawai'i tradition" of race- and ethnicity-based humor.[49] In particular, she was severely
critical of the prevalence of "Portagee jokes," the negative portrayals of
Portuguese as "stupid, loud, and obnoxious." She noted that "Portuguese
jokes are racist and cruel and nobody seems to give a rip" (Cataluna 2000a).
In addition, Cataluna singled out Frank De Lima, who for nearly two and
a half decades has based his comedy routine on Hawai'i's racial/ethnic and
cultural diversity, as exemplary of the widely accepted but highly problematic brand of humor. Through his work with the Frank De Lima Student
Enrichment Program, which is sponsored in part by the Hawai'i Department
of Education, De Lima also does presentations for schoolchildren on building self-esteem and valuing multiculturalism, encouraging them to "study
hard, stay drug-free, [and] maintain comedy as an equalizer" (Harada 2000).
Despite the positive message of the importance of staying in school and
valuing diversity, and teaching students to laugh at themselves, Cataluna
argued that De Lima's humor has a different effect: "De Lima's defense is

that he's teaching kids the value of diversity and teaching them to laugh at themselves. In reality, he's teaching kids to laugh while others insult them" (Cataluna 2000a: B1).

It is December 2000, and on campus there is talk about the prevalence of ethnic jokes in the local Filipino community (in light of Lee Cataluna's newspaper column critiquing local ethnic humor and Frank De Lima in particular). Zach and Trina, who are student leaders in the University of Hawai'i at Mānoa Timpuyog Organization,[50] are having a spirited conversation before their club meeting. Trina is second-generation Filipino in Hawai'i while Zach is 1.5-generation, having immigrated to Honolulu when he was nine years old. Both grew up in a predominantly Filipino neighborhood, Trina in Waipahu and Zach in Kalihi. I ask them what they think about Local humor in general and Filipino jokes in particular. Trina says somewhat nonchalantly, "Personally, I don't see anything offensive with the jokes. It's something I grew up with. Frank De Lima came to my school when I was a kid. Manapua man. No one gets offended by his jokes. Everyone gets made fun of." Zach slightly countered, "But not everybody thinks they're funny." Trina responded quickly, "They're too sensitive, that's why. I'm fine with the jokes just as long as they're not mean-spirited." In slight exasperation, Zach asks, "But what's so punny?" Trina bursts out in laughter. Zach's native tongue has betrayed him.

Cataluna's initial column, and particularly her criticism of De Lima, generated public discussion and prompted a series of letters to the editor, much like the conversation I had with Zach and Trina. In a follow-up column a week later, Cataluna observed the split in opinion about Frank De Lima and ethnic jokes more generally: "Portagee jokes, a genre of local humor beloved by some as integral to our culture and, I found, loathed by as many as tiresome, asinine and hurtful" (Cataluna 2000b). Some claimed that Cataluna's critique was nothing more than "PC shibai" (political correctness gone awry or simple oversensitivity) with an undercurrent of bitterness, jealously, and resentment aimed at a popular local comedian. It was also argued that in Hawai'i's "racial paradise" where "we can laugh at ourselves," ethnic jokes have the effect of "bringing us closer together by highlighting and caricaturing our differences" (Coleman 2003), which in the end seemingly helps ease racial tensions. In this sense, ethnic jokes function as "an equalizer" that flattens cultural differences, although they do not directly challenge socially distributed wealth and power. Moreover, some reason that because each group is an equal target of racial stereotyping and ethnic jokes, these kinds of jokes are a type of equal-opportunity discrimination, so to speak. Those who support ethnic jokes claim that those who are critical, like Cataluna and Zach, simply need to "lighten up," that they have no sense of humor, they are too sensitive or are unable to laugh at themselves. In this regard, Local joking can be understood as race-conscious, but racism-aversive.

Cataluna's criticism of "Portagee jokes" also escalated into broader discussions of race and ethnicity-based humor in Hawai'i and their emotional, psychological, and social force. What began as a critique of ethnic jokes targeting one ethnic group, the Portuguese, expanded to include other racial/ethnic groups. As Cataluna wrote,

> People who identified themselves as Filipino or black or Hawaiian or haole wrote about the careless insults they've been subjected to under the guise of 'Local humor.' People wrote about being the target of racial jokes at work, at school, even church. The letters that were the most painful were from parents talking about how their children were made to feel ashamed of who they are (2000b: B1).

The debate no longer centered solely on "Portagee jokes" but Hawai'i ethnic humor in general. Some asked whether the race- and ethnicity-based "Local humor" still had a place in contemporary Hawai'i society. Given the changing political climate, shifting demographics, and the "political correctness" movement in the continental United States reaching the shores of Hawai'i, some wondered whether ethnic jokes were a tradition worth maintaining. In this regard, Okada (2007) uses a legal framework to explore Local ethnic humor in the public sphere (primarily in schools and comedy performances) as possible "fighting words" or racist hate speech, acknowledging the potential harm, even if unintended, of this type of joking. She issues a challenge to Hawai'i's multiculturalist ideology: "If Hawai'i is ever to truly move closer to the ideal of the 'racial paradise,' it is important to bring to light and look critically at practices—such as racial humor—that may be preventing genuine inter-racial harmony" (2007: 232). In a place fabled for its "harmonious race and ethnic relations" and heavily marketed as a "multicultural paradise," others argued that ethnic jokes "represent a powerful link to our past that we hate to lose" (Sodetani 2001: 6). But what is "our past" and who actually is included in "our past"? Are ethnic jokes still the glue that binds the "people of Hawai'i"? Is ethnic humor still relevant given the social, political, and economic changes in Hawai'i? Or are ethnic jokes merely nostalgic residues of a much-celebrated originary past that provided the conditions for the dispossession and displacement of Native Hawaiians and the exploitation of Asian labor as well as the basis for the islands' contemporary multicultural social formation? Are these jokes reflective of a multiculturalist ideology that supports Hawai'i's multicultural settler state?

Furukawa (2007) offers an alternative reading of Local comedy performances. Following Bhabha (1994), he suggests that Local comedy produces
a Third Space that challenges the status quo and, in that sense, can be better understood as carnivalistic practice. Focusing on Local comedian Andy
Bumatai's discursive practice in one of his comedy CDs, Furukawa argues
that through double-voicing via code switching, laughter, parody, and a joke-
within-a-joke structure, Bumatai is able to challenge Filipino marginalization
and disrupt official views of reality. Though perhaps an exception to the
rule in everyday and publicly staged Local racial/ethnic humor, Bumatai's
comedy and discursive practice maintains a type of "Local elitism" (Hiramoto 2011). Such comedy performances do indeed distort official views of
reality, particularly when they challenge white supremacist ideology and
the racial/ethnic ordering founded on the colonization of Native Hawaiians. However, such distortions also reinscribe their own official view of
reality, one dependent on a multiculturalist ideology and settler hegemony
established as part of the islands' plantation past. Rather than viewing Local
ethnic humor as carnivalistic acts, it is perhaps more instructive to consider
this kind of joking, particularly more so in everyday practice than in public
performance, as racially cannibalistic[51] or as a type of "racial minstrelsy"
(Lott 1992; Lott 1993) that uses devices like ventriloquized speech (via
"accents" and mock languages) and burlesque (via linguistic, cultural, and
costumed racial borrowing, masquerading, and cross-dressing) to mask
the uneven structures and relations of power in a settler-dominated society.
There is a particular racial/ethnic economy encoded in Local ethnic humor
performance, one dependent on a "racial unconscious" (Lott 1992) and
"unconscious racism" (Lawrence 1987; Lawrence 2008) that allows for its
continued legibility and intelligibility.

In December 1994, there was a similar debate on the role and place of
Local ethnic humor in Hawai'i society. This debate focused on Filipino jokes
and the release of a video by Frank De Lima that included a song parody
called "A Filipino Christmas," prompting a variety of public discussion,
particularly in the local Filipino community newspapers, about the negative
representations of Filipinos in Hawai'i.[52] In Mock Filipino style, the song
begins with "Macadangdang saluyot billy goat ganga bala bod bod . . ." It
has been noted that "only a few Filipino words are actually in the lyrics.
A lot of the words are just made up" (Seneca 1995).[53] In addition, a por-
tion of De Lima's song parody was sung to the traditional "The Christmas
Song" and included the lyrics "Black dog roasting on an open fire." Critics
claimed that the song was part of a decades-old stigmatizing discourse
that perpetuated lingering stereotypes of Filipinos. Supporters of De Lima

claimed that the song was nothing more than part of the Hawai'i tradition of ethnic jokes and Local humor; these images had been part of his comedy routine for years and thus, they were in no way racist or discriminatory; that they are just instances of harmless joking. According to the *Hawaii Filipino Chronicle,* De Lima "argues that immigrant Filipinos, not local Filipinos, are the ones who object to his jokes" (1995). Thus, it is buk buks as a specific type of Filipino identity category, not Locals, who are the object of cultural denigration and ridicule. De Lima's "A Filipino Christmas" continues to be a Local mainstay, enjoying repeated radio play during the holiday season.

Framed within the islands' cultural politics of representation, De Lima's "A Filipino Christmas the interactions between Joe and Tata Cayatmo and Da Braddahs's depiction of Filipinos foreground issues of power and representation, challenging who can represent whom and the effects of such representation. Explanations and justifications of the persistence of ethnic humor view language, culture, and identity as objective facts in the natural order of things rather than constructions embedded in a network of social relations and underscored by struggles of representational power. Pidgin and Local are understood as neutral phenomena that do not help to constitute social, political, and economic realities, facilitating a depoliticized and ahistorical understanding of the foreign invasion and external domination of the islands that has led to the formation of the contemporary racial and ethnic terrain. Recontextualizing language, culture, identity, and representation by emphasizing the structures of inequality and the systems of power that underscore lived experiences and discourses points to issues of contestation and hegemony between and within racial/ethnic groups. In Hawai'i, this is an issue of who rightfully belongs to the islands, meaning, who are legitimate members and what criteria are used to determine membership, that is to say, who can legitimately laugh at themselves? Thus, "we can laugh at ourselves" also points to struggles over representation, in terms of which images, signs, and jokes are produced, consumed, and distributed. Who makes the jokes, who is made fun of, and who laughs involves discourses of inclusion and exclusion. Jokes can effectively tell us who belongs, and in the process they construct an order and hierarchy invariably linked to struggles for power.

CHAPTER 3

"Anything but . . ."

Ramon Jacinto is a well-respected senior Filipino community leader. Although he has spent most of his life on Oʻahu, he also spent significant amounts of time on another island. Ramon describes himself as "a child of the plantations"—he was born and raised in a plantation community, and both parents were first-generation agricultural workers. He is a veteran of struggles for educational equity, and much of his community work focuses on youth empowerment. During one of our interviews, I asked him how he would best characterize the Filipino community in Hawaiʻi. He paused for a moment and then said, "Filipinos have no sense of nationhood." His response took me aback slightly because it was a bit different from others who typically talked about Filipino plantation history and the now collective low status and low prestige of Filipinos in Hawaiʻi society. Because I was unsure about what he meant, I asked him to elaborate. He explained, "Filipinos have no national identity. There's no unity. We're all so divided." At this point, I wondered if he was talking about the stunted nationalism of the Philippine revolution against Spain and the United States, but our conversation then turned to the more typical descriptions of the reasons for "Filipino disunity," namely the lack of a common language or a common culture: "We got all kinds of Filipinos over here: Ilokanos, Tagalogs, Cebuanos." The "kinds of Filipinos" represent the three most commonly spoken languages and three largest ethnolinguistic groups in the Philippines and Hawaiʻi. According to the National Statistics Office of the Philippines, in 2000 roughly 29 percent of the Philippine population spoke Tagalog as their first language, the majority of whom live in and around metropolitan Manila, in the southern part of the island of Luzon. Another 26 percent spoke Cebuano, the language associated with the Visayan Islands in the central part of the Philippines. Approximately 10 percent spoke Ilokano, usually associated with the Ilocos region in the northern part of Luzon. The notion of linguistic differentiation among Hawai'i's Filipinos was also expressed by many of my interviewees. Although Filipinos in Hawai'i are traditionally perceived to be mainly speakers of Ilokano (stemming from the long history of agricultural laborers from the Ilocos region), there are large numbers of Tagalog and Cebuano speakers. In fact, contrary to commonly accepted belief (and perhaps an effect of self-reporting error), the 2010 U.S. Census indicates that the majority of Filipinos in Hawai'i speak Tagalog, although other research suggests that Ilokano descendants comprise 80 percent of the local Filipino population (Aquino 2000). In addition, many second-, third-, and fourth-generation Filipinos in Hawai'i claim Pidgin, or Hawai'i Creole English, as their native language.

Regardless of the actual numbers associated with each language, the multilingual situation among Filipinos in Hawai'i is characterized by competing claims for representational authority and legitimacy that are often based on a "nationalist ideology of language and identity" (Woolard 1998) that equates one language with one nation. Ilokano speakers can claim a long historical connection to Hawai'i via the sakadas, or Filipino plantation workers. Cebuano speakers also point to their history as Hawai'i plantation workers, and their numbers equal those of native Tagalog speakers both in Hawai'i and the Philippines. Tagalog speakers draw attention to the fact that the language they are associated with serves as the basis for the national language of the Philippines, the lingua franca of the Filipino diaspora, and along with English, it is a medium of instruction in Philippine schools as well as the prestige language of business, government, and academia. Pidgin speakers claim they speak the lingua franca of "Local" Hawai'i residents, situating themselves as "real" members of the island community and not as outsider immigrants.

As stated by Ramon Jacinto, the linguistic differentiation among Filipinos is often understood as the basis for "Filipino disunity" (part of the Filipino "identity crisis" discussed earlier) and the lack of a collective identity and cooperative political action. The logic is that the internal linguistic differentiation of Filipinos (both among and within language groups) hinders political unity and collective action. In other words, for him, a shared language can effectively erase or ignore linguistic (as well as cultural and class) differences. The suppression of differences delimits and polices the boundaries of the "Filipino" ethnic identity, serving as a basis for defining or constructing a singular, monolithic Filipino-ness that, in turn, can lead to a united political front that can potentially pull the ethnic collectivity over the top and out of the political and economic margins of Hawai'i society. Put another way, what is perceived to be an undifferentiated or homogeneous language serves as an important resource for imagining a similarly perceived undifferentiated or homogeneous community (Anderson 1991).

Underpinning the claims for representational authority and legitimacy is the simplification of language as whole and undifferentiated and the existence of a one-to-one correlation between language and people. Despite glossing over the complexities and fluidities of language, the notion of a whole language helps to make concrete the boundaries of the "Tagalog," "Ilokano," and "Cebuano" and is also a crucial component in struggles over defining the "Filipino" identity category. In this sense, there are competing assertions that claim Tagalog, Ilokano, or Cebuano as emblematic of Filipinos as a national collectivity. Because it is assumed there can only be one common language for one people, there is a clamor for language dominance amid the cacophonous linguistic multiplicity resulting in contests over representational authority to define the collective interests of Filipinos. Thus, Filipino struggles over language dominance are also political contests for representational legitimacy and authority; the literal and figurative fight for who can speak for whom.

In my conversation with Ramon Jacinto, his foregrounding of the absence of a shared language was particularly revealing because he pointed to the centrality of language in the production of identity. He seemed to suggest that language was important in not only constructing a unitary Filipino identity but also as a unifying force in Filipino political and economic struggles in the islands. In this sense, language is connected to larger macrosocial processes and forces, serving as a key battleground through which social, cultural, ideological, political, and economic struggles are expressed and fought over, a locus around which a social group can politically organize. In short, language serves a critical role in shaping the Filipino cultural politics of representation in terms of how the boundaries of the ethnic group are defined and what political interests are deemed meaningful and important. And as part of the feedback loop and though often unrecognized, the cultural politics of representation also shape understandings and uses of language.

In this chapter, I examine the relationship between language, identity and politics. Where does language and identity fit in the Filipino cultural politics of representation? How do language and identity relationships play out among dispersed peoples, particularly immigrant communities, in the contemporary late capitalist, transnational world? Specifically, I focus on the ethnicity-based language and identity projects carried out by the Katipunan Club at the University of Hawai'i at Mānoa. The Katipunan Club is a Filipino/Tagalog language-based student organization that is a major component of the Filipino and Philippine Literature program. In the chapter, rather than analyzing forms of talk or speech events, I briefly examine two events sponsored by the Katipunan Club: a one-day student conference called "Rediscovering Filipino Identity" (which took place in 2002 to commemorate the ten-year anniversary of the student organization) and a song festival entitled Pag-ibig Sa Tinubuang Lupa (Love for the Native Land), which involved the musical performance of a series of Philippine nationalist songs and was part of the centennial celebrations of Philippine independence from Spain. Further, I argue that such events sponsored by the Katipunan Club are both pedagogical exercises and primary mechanisms for an identity-making project that produces, consumes, and distributes ideas and images about what it means to be "Filipino," effectively constructing the boundaries of the "Filipino" ethnic category. Through these events, the Katipunan Club and the larger Filipino Language and Philippine Literature program employ a nationalist ideology of language and identity that equates one language, "Filipino/Tagalog," with one nation-state, "the Philippines," to create one people, "Filipinos." In addition, the nationalist ideology of language and identity works in the "erasure" (Irvine and Gal 2000) of linguistic, class, and immigrant generational differences in an effort to produce, for its participating students, a sense of nationhood or a unitary "Filipino" ethnic identity. In the process, this would provide a node around which Filipinos can politically organize in an effort to secure a prominent place in the multicultural fabric of Hawai'i and the United States as a whole.

Although this chapter focuses on the Katipunan Club and the larger Filipino Language and Philippine Literature program, it is also important to note that the University of Hawai'i at Mānoa is the only institution in the world to offer a bachelor of arts degree with a specialization in Ilokano. Through the Ilokano Language, Culture, and Literature program and its student organization, Timpuyog, students are able to earn a minor and a certificate in Ilokano in addition to the bachelor's. The Ilokano program was established in 1972 and became a permanent, degree-granting track in 2013. Students and faculty in the program are intensely engaged in local and international community and academic organizations. For example, many are involved with Nakem Conferences Philippines (now International),[1] an advocacy group comprised of individual scholars, academic institutions, creative writers, local government agencies, and culture-based agencies, which has supported Mother Tongue-Based Multilingual Education programs and the development of Amianan Studies[2] in the Philippines. The Ilokano program also works closely with Nakem Youth, a community organization that promotes social justice and the use of mother-language in education. The

Ilokano Program and Nakem Youth helped to publish three recent books focusing on Ilokano youth in Hawai'i: *Kabambannuagan: Our Voices, Our Lives* (2010), *On the Edge of Hope and Healing: Flipping the Script on Filipinos in Hawaii* (2012), and *Panagtaripato: Parenting Our Stories, Our Stories As Parents* (2011), a collection of writing by Ilokano parents in the islands.

The Katipunan Club

In the early 1960s, the University of Hawai'i at Mānoa began to offer Tagalog language courses, primarily for military personnel and Peace Corps volunteers headed for duty or service to the Philippines. In the mid-1970s, Philippine literature, folklore, and culture courses were introduced. By 1980, the University of Hawai'i at Mānoa was the only university in the United States that had a fully developed program in Tagalog language and literature. In 1992 Katipunan ("association" or "organization" in Tagalog) was established, which is the shortened version of Kapatiran ng mga Estudyantednd Nag-aaral ng Pilipino sa Unibersidad ng Hawai'i, loosely translated as "Confraternity of Students studying Filipino at the University of Hawai'i." First-, 1.5-, and second-generation[3] Filipino immigrants constitute the majority of Katipunan's membership. Every semester, Katipunan sponsors a variety of events for its members, which include social gatherings, movie nights (in which feature films from the Philippines are shown), and song and drama festivals/competitions (in Tagalog, "Paligsahan sa Pagkanta" and "Paligsahan sa Dula," respectively), of which Pag-ibig sa Tinubuang Lupa in 1998 is an example. The "Rediscovering Filipino Identity" conference in 2002 was the first Katipunan event of its kind. It is also significant to note that the student organization takes its name from Andres Bonifacio's revolutionary organization, Kataastaasan Kagalanggalang na Katipunan nang manga Anak ng Bayan. In a sense, Bonifacio's organization serves as a model for behavior against oppressive circumstances and conditions. As a faculty member told me, the student organization has an explicitly political agenda grounded in contemporary racial/ethnic politics in Hawai'i: "I want them to persist in the university. I want then to fight their own apathy caused by oppressive experiences in the elementary and high school. I want them to fight for their rights to be heard—in other words, to be strong leaders in the campus as well as in the community . . . some of our Katipunan officers have become role models and leaders in the community, like the ones in the Filipino Junior Chamber of Commerce and in the FilCom center." In this way, participating in Katipunan not only fulfills the university's foreign language graduation requirement, it also serves as a venue for student leadership development and activism.

According to its club brochure, one of the main objectives of the organization is "to promote and preserve the Filipino Language and Philippine Culture in Hawai'i." In addition, by encouraging language use and supporting the "promotion of cultural programs that teach and introduce Filipino language, art, and culture," the organization functions as "the resource center for the creation, preservation, and promotion of Filipino materials."[4] In this way, Katipunan functions much like racial/ethnic clubs, ethnic studies centers, programs, and departments across the country, and other supportive university institutions that "provide a setting for students of color to establish social ties and to discuss their common problems and experiences; in so doing, they have an opportunity to develop a racial/ethnic consciousness out of their shared history of discrimination" (Espiritu 1994: 262–63). In highly racialized environments, like college and university campuses, race/ethnicity-based student organizations like Katipunan help to facilitate racial/ethnic "awakening" and cultural awareness. Student-produced cultural performances often sponsored by such student organizations serve as venues for self-expression and the articulation and enactment of meaningful histories and identities. In this respect, the stage provides an avenue for consciousness raising and community building, an arena for articulating Filipino-ness and making sense of one's past, present, and future.

In an interview with Gabrielle, one of Katipunan's student leaders and an organizer for the "Rediscovering Filipino Identity" conference, I asked her why she enrolled in language classes. Half-jokingly, she told me that she thought the classes would be easy. But after her laughter subsided, she paused and tentatively talked about her upbringing on one of the "neighbor islands": "Yes, I grew up hiding and denying my culture and wanting to be something else. Growing up, I wanted to be anything but Filipino. I didn't want people to think I was buk buk. Up until I came to college, I denied Filipino culture because I didn't want to be known as the girl whose family ate dog, or wore mismatched clothing, or had parents who spoke with an accent." For Gabrielle and many other Locals, "Filipino" and "buk buk" are one and the same. And her definition of buk buk, as dog eater, no fashion sense, and speaking an accented English, all fall in line with broader understandings of the identity category. Knowing that her parents were Ilokano speakers, I then asked her about why she enrolled in Filipino/Tagalog language classes. In her initial response, which was accompanied by soft laughter, she said she wanted to be able to understand the shows her family watched on The Filipino Channel and the songs they listened to. But then she also explained her perceptions of the differences between Philippine languages: "I didn't want to speak Ilokano because I didn't want to be seen as a FOB. I always thought the Filipinos from the Philippines were FOBs. They stood out as FOBs because they spoke in Ilokano." Gabrielle's characterization of Ilokanos-as-FOBs speaks to contemporary Filipino immigration dynamics in the islands but also points to her understandings of language, language use, and speakers. She then quickly added, "I took Tagalog because it's the national language of the Philippines." For Gabrielle, Tagalog is indeed a language of power and prestige.

Interestingly, at the University of Hawai'i at Mānoa, "Filipino" and "Tagalog" are often used interchangeably, although "Filipino," an emerging but primarily Tagalog-based language, is considered the official national language of the Republic of the Philippines and Tagalog is one of the various regional languages. In this way, rediscovering Filipino identity via discovering Filipino language can be understood as an attempt to extend linguistic nationalism from the Philippines to Filipinos in diaspora. The Philippine population speaks nearly eighty grammatically and lexically similar but mutually unintelligible languages (with their own sets of dialects and registers) that belong to the Austronesian family of languages (Ramos 1996). Moreover, through past mercantile commerce and colonization, these languages have come into contact with and have been influenced by a variety of languages, including Sanskrit, Arabic, Chinese, Spanish, and English. Of the nearly eighty languages, there are six "major" ones (listed in decreasing order of the number of native speakers): Tagalog, Cebuano, Ilokano, Hiligaynon, Bicolano, and Waray (Ramos 1996). Ramos has also observed that all these languages, in addition to Pampango and Pangasinan, are spoken by Filipinos in Hawai'i, although Ilokano has the highest number of native speakers in the islands.

According to the 1987 Philippine Constitution, "Filipino" is designated as the national language. "Filipino" is intended to function as the "common language" with which Filipinos are to communicate with each other and "express themselves as one nation." In this way, "Filipino" is imagined as the linguistic basis of a national unity and identity. "Filipino" is an emerging language that is a combination of Pilipino/Tagalog and Spanish and English in respelled forms using Pilipino orthography (for example, "teacher" becomes "titser" and "lengua" becomes "linggwa"). Preceding "Filipino" as the national language was "Pilipino," a Tagalog-based tongue that was identified as the national language in 1959. Prior to "Pilipino," the Commonwealth of the Philippines selected Tagalog in 1937 as the national language. Despite the various name changes, the national language of the Philippines for the past seven decades has remained some form of Tagalog.

What these name changes reflect is that in the multilingual Philippines, there is a continuing effort to establish a nationalist ideology of language and identity that supports the perceived fundamental unity of people, nation, and state. For proponents of "Filipino" as the national language and "mother tongue," a shared language is crucial for the production of national unity and identity. A shared language also serves a unifying function by providing speakers of various languages a means to communicate with each other and "express themselves as one nation." However, in the Philippine multilingual setting, the highly politicized designation of a Tagalog-based national language has drawn attention to a contested Philippine nationalism and a sense of "disunity," what community leader Ramon Jacinto called the "lack of a sense of nationhood." In a nation-state where regional and ethnolinguistic affiliations often serve as the primary sources of identification, the construction of national symbols and narratives of identity are conceived to be an immediate political need, but they are also highly politically contested.

Language Iideologies and the Rediscovery of Filipino Identities

In recent years, there has been a rapid increase in the number of works relating to language ideologies. Although there have been several proposed definitions, Kroskrity (2000) suggests that it is more instructive to think of language ideologies as a "cluster concept" composed of four interrelated features: (1) "language ideologies represent the perception of language and discourse that is constructed in the interest of a specific social or cultural group" (2000: 8); (2) "language ideologies are profitably conceived as multiple because of the multiplicity of meaningful social divisions (class, gender, clan, elites, generations, and so on) within sociocultural groups that have the potential to produce divergent perspectives expressed as indices of group membership" (ibid.: 12); (3) "members may display varying degrees of awareness of local language ideologies" (ibid.: 18); and (4) "members' language ideologies mediate between social structures and forms of talk" (ibid.: 21). The first attribute points to the ways language and discourse are perceived, and is invariably connected to a group's political and economic interests. There is no such thing as a disinterested or neutral language user; language use and knowledge is always positioned. The second feature illustrates that language ideologies are understood as multiple and socially distributed, with differential access to language varieties and registers. The third dimension points to variation in the awareness or consciousness level of members. The final characteristic shows that language ideologies serve a mediating role between sociocultural experiences and languages and discourses.

Similarly, Irvine and Gal (2000) observe three semiotic processes by which ideological representations of linguistic variability are produced: iconization, fractal recursivity, and erasure. According to Irvine and Gal, iconization "involves a transformation of a sign relationship between linguistic features (or varieties) and the social images with which they are linked. Linguistic features that index social groups or activities appear to be iconic representations of them, as if a linguistic feature somehow depicted or displayed a social group's inherent nature or essence" (2000: 37). Fractal recursivity "involves the projection of an opposition, salient at some level of relationship, onto some other level . . . the oppositions do not define fixed or stable social groups, and the mimesis they suggest cannot be more than partial. Rather, they provide actors with the discursive or cultural resources to claim and attempt to create shifting 'communities,' identities, selves, and roles, at different levels of contrast, within a cultural field" (2000: 38). Erasure involves "the process in which ideology, in simplifying the sociolinguistic field, renders some persons or activities (or sociolinguistic phenomena) invisible. Facts that are inconsistent with the ideological scheme either go unnoticed or get explained away" (2000: 38). For my purposes here, iconization, particularly the way in which Tagalog iconically represents the Philippine nation, and erasure, which renders invisible Philippine linguistic differentiation, are the most important processes in Filipino identity making and the creation of a Filipino sense of nationhood. Through iconization and erasure, Filipinos in Hawai'i can "Rediscover Filipino Identity" as well as express their "Love for the Native Land."

The "Rediscovering Filipino Identity" conference was attended by several hundred students, mostly Katipunan members but also other students from Mānoa and other UH campuses. The panelists included undergraduate and graduate students as well as staff and faculty who spoke on a wide range of topics, including language, culture, history, literature, religion and folklore, community involvement, and campus activism. Regardless of their own specific topics, each of the speakers linked their specific talks to the conference theme, Filipino identity. I was interested in the conference not so much for the individual papers and panels that were presented but rather why the conference was organized and what it had to say about the relationship between language and identity.

According to a conference organizer and student leader, Rebecca, who self-identified as Local, one of the main objectives of the conference was to provide a venue for students to "reclaim their heritage and discover or rediscover our identities as Filipinos." I asked her why and how the theme for the conference was chosen. She told me, "When I was in high school, I was ashamed of being Filipino. I didn't want to be associated with Filipinos. I didn't know anything about the language, the culture, the history. It wasn't till college when I started taking Tagalog classes that I began to identify with being Filipino. That's when I started the discovery and developed ethnic awareness and political consciousness. The club was an important place for me to find my Filipino identity." Another student organizer, Diego, who also self-identified as Local, echoed Rebecca's words: "Taking Filipino classes at UH helps me to think about my identity. . . . When I started taking Filipino classes at UH, I started to change my thinking. It was not until being enrolled in classes and being part of the organization that I realized that I was not the only one who felt ashamed to be Filipino." What "Rediscovering Filipino Identity" attempts to get at is the "real" language, Filipino/Tagalog, and seeks to counter linguistic and cultural assimilation. This follows from Woolard's (1998) suggestion that accompanying "the equation of one language/one people has come an insistence on the authenticity and moral significance of 'mother tongue' as the one first and therefore real language of a speaker, transparent to the true self" (1998: 18). In this regard, Teresita Ramos, a former chair of the Department of Hawaiian and Indo-Pacific Languages and Literatures and the founder of the Tagalog program at the University of Hawai'i, has written: "Since most of the immigrants have already learned some English in the Philippines, and since it is the language of superior prestige, linguistic assimilation is rapidly taking place, and the home language is fast being replaced by English or the Hawaiian Creole (pidgin). . . . The use of the native tongue, then, is confined largely to the home and is used solely by parents and grandparents" (1996: 165). For 1.5-, second-, third-, and fourth-generation Filipino Americans, the fear is that Filipino (or other native Philippine languages) is no longer an important linguistic resource. Immigration acts as a point of disruption and discontinuity, and language loss and cultural estrangement are part of the inevitable path to assimilation. In this regard, Ramos has further remarked: "The issue of language is of course highly volatile, and even in multicultural Hawai'i, there is a strong tendency to argue that the straightest road to assimilation into American society is through the abandonment—or at least, the non-encouragement—of the immigrants' native tongue" (ibid.; 168). But through events like "Rediscovering Filipino Identity," Katipunan seeks to develop a type of Filipino nationalism and promotes a search for unifying symbols of ethnic and national identity, namely language. In the process, Filipino/Tagalog, the language, becomes emblematic of the Philippine nation. In this way, Filipino/Tagalog attempts to unify and authenticate a disunited Filipino identity, serving as a possible source of group cohesiveness and strength in Hawai'i.

Though the primary concern of "Rediscovering Filipino Identity" centered on issues of immigrant assimilation and language loss, the performance of *Pag-ibig sa Tinubuang Lupa* is anchored in a nationalist ideology of language and identity focused on the relationship between place and identity. *Pag-ibig sa Tinubuang Lupa* participates in a racial/ethnic and cultural cartographic imagining involving boundary construction and maintenance. It is contingent on remembrances/narration of the past that naturalize a shared history of oppression and racial/ethnic subjugation as well the resistance to the same structures of oppression and subordination.

Pag-ibig sa Tinubuang Lupa

Pag-ibig sa Tinubuang Lupa, loosely translated as "Love for the Native Land," was a four-hour-long theatrical performance presented in November 1998 by members of Katipunan. The student organization also includes past members and other university students interested in the languages, literatures, arts, and cultures of the Philippines. The student performers have spent countless hours preparing for this public presentation. The title of the theatrical production takes its name from a famous nationalist poem written by Andres Bonifacio, the leader of the revolutionary organization whose primary objective was to free the Philippines from Spanish colonial bondage, Kataastaasan Kagalanggalang na Katipunan nang manga Anak ng Bayan (loosely translated as "Highest, Most Venerated Association of the Children of the Country" and Katipunan for short).

This theatrical cultural performance was one of numerous events and productions in Hawai'i and elsewhere in the United States in 1998 that celebrated the centennial anniversary of Philippine independence from Spain. The outbreak of the Philippine Revolution in 1896 marked the beginning of the armed struggle, but the nationalism that sparked the drive for emancipation was initiated decades earlier, if not centuries. During the three centuries of Spanish colonial rule, there were more than two hundred reported uprisings, revolts, and rebellions throughout the Philippines. The more well-known of these insurrections were the uprisings led by Malong, which was initiated in Pangasinan and spread to Pampanga, Zambales,

Ilocos, and Cagayan (in the 1660s), Diego and Gabriela Silang in the Ilocos region (in the 1760s), and Apolinario de la Cruz in Laguna and Tayabas. In 1872, three Filipino priests, Gomez, Burgos, and Zamora, were executed by the Spanish for their alleged participation in a mutiny involving Filipino soldiers in Cavite and their campaigns for native clergy rights. This event helped to arouse nationalist consciousness among Filipinos and overcome the regional character of previous uprisings. In 1892, Jose Rizal, the national hero of the Philippines, formed La Liga Filipina, which sought peaceful reforms and Filipino representation in positions of power. In the same year, Andres Bonifacio founded the Katipunan, a secret revolutionary organization that sought to end Spanish colonialism and win freedom for Filipinos. In 1896, the Philippine Revolution began, and that same year, Rizal was executed, which intensified nationalist consciousness. On June 12, 1898 Emilio Aguinaldo, who had assumed leadership of the Katipunan after Bonifacio's execution in 1897, raised the Philippine flag and declared the independence of the Philippine Republic.

Pag-ibig sa Tinubuang Lupa illustrates one of the ways in which recent immigrants, particularly young Filipinos, theatrically perform narratives that produce and distribute ideas and ideologies about language, culture, and identity. As Ochs and Capps (1996) observe, narrative serves as a primary means for making sense of self and experience as well as an instrument for negotiating social relationships. Further, *Pag-ibig sa Tinubuang Lupa* is a type of "narrative of discent" (Duara 1995) in its privileging of a heroic and revolutionary past as well as privileging Tagalog as the language with which the story is told. Narratives of discent help to secure and naturalize identity consolidations, showing the march of history as series of relational alterities and structural oppositions between self and other. Further, "The narrative of discent is used to define and mobilize a community, often by privileging a particular cultural practice (or a set of such practices) as the constitutive principle of the community—such as language, religion, or common historical experience—thereby heightening the self-consciousness of this community in relation to those around it" (1995: 66). Along these lines, a purpose of the theatrical performance is to invoke an action-oriented understanding of the past so that it can be practiced in the present and used as a resource in the future. Echoing a famous quote by Philippine national hero Jose Rizal, an instructor told me, "If they know where they came from, at least they will know where they are going."

Pag-ibig sa Tinubuang Lupa (and other similar theatrical cultural performances that are performed annually by the Katipunan Club) comments on where Filipinos position themselves (and how they are positioned by others) in the Filipino community in Hawai'i, in the broader Hawai'i society, in U.S. society, and in the global Filipino diaspora. As another instructor told me, such cultural performances are "opportunities for students to find their place." "Place" here has multiple meanings. It suggests student identity development, racial/ethnic identity development, and political consciousness development. Along these lines, by literally placing language, culture, and identity center stage, "Theater becomes a place where we can recognize ourselves, be ourselves, perform ourselves, seemingly apart from the oppressive gaze of the dominant" (Kondo 1997: xii). As such and borrowing from Myerhoff, I also understand cultural performances like *Pag-ibig sa Tinubuang Lupa* as types of "definitional ceremonies" that "deal with the problems of invisibility and marginality; they are strategies that provide opportunities for being seen and in one's own terms, garnering witnesses to one's worth, vitality, and being" (Myerhoff 1992: 263). In effect, these theatrical performances display cultural and ethnic identity claims, constructing and enacting what it means to be "Filipino" and at the same time, addressing issues of authenticity, power, voice, and visibility.

The claims to authenticity are principally fought over the nature of "home," that is to say, what and where is "home" and what is the relationship to the "homeland." At this point, it would perhaps be useful to differentiate between "home" and "homeland," terms already used above. Gupta and Ferguson (1997) provide an insightful distinction. For them, "home" refers to the "specific towns and particular dwellings" that create a strong sense of belonging to one's land of origin, while "homeland" is more abstract, "an intensely romanticized place sometimes likened to a lost lover" (10). Key to the formulation of "homeland" is the work of the imagination (Appadurai 1996). The importance of the imagination, however, does not deny the experiential reality of communities and places. As transnational subjects or dispersed peoples, "imagined communities (Anderson 1983) come to be attached to imagined places, as displaced peoples cluster around remembered or imagined homelands, places, or communities in a world that seems increasingly to deny such firm territorialized anchors in their actuality" (Gupta and Ferguson 1997: 39). Put another way, displaced peoples use social memory of places to create their new lived situations but also to construct affiliations with others in similar circumstances. Thus, "'homeland' in this way remains one of the most powerful unifying symbols for mobile and displaced peoples, though the relation to homeland may be very differently constructed in different settings" (ibid.: 39). From this definition, what differentiates "home" and "homeland" are feelings of attachment to places of origin and settlement.

Avtar Brah (1996) adds another dimension to this distinction. For Brah, "home" can be understood as "the site of everyday lived experience" (1996: 4); it is a place of everyday interaction and practice. Further, she notes that "home" is "a discourse of locality, the place where rootedness ensues from the mundane and the unexpected daily practice. Home here connotes our networks of family, kin, friends, colleagues, and various other 'significant others.' It signifies the social and psychic geography of space that is experienced in terms of a neighborhood or a home town" (ibid.: 4). An implicit assumption in Brah's definition is that the construction of "home" requires physical proximity and face-to-face interaction. However, Appadurai suggests that "home" can be, given the recent technological innovations in communication and transportation, a virtual community or neighborhood that involves the production of translocality. In constructing notions of "home" and "homeland," transnational or diasporic subjects create feelings of belonging that provide conditions for "dwelling-in-displacement," a type of "lived tension, the experiences of separation and entanglement, of living here and remembering/desiring another place" (Clifford 1997: 255).

So how are "home" and "homeland" constructed by Filipinos in Hawai'i? On one hand, there is a more geographically particular notion of "home" that symbolizes belonging to the "Local" Hawai'i community and the working-class plantation history. On the other hand, there is an invocation of a nationalistic and diasporic notion of ethnic identity, one that represents and indexes membership in the Philippine nation-state and a "Filipino" transnational community. In Hawai'i (as elsewhere), there is no unified "Filipino" identity. One reason for this is that there are multiple origins and discrepant histories among Filipinos in Hawai'i; they come from different parts of the Philippines and arrived in Hawai'i under different historical circumstances. Another reason is a sense of ambivalence toward the Philippine homeland. For some, the desire is not to return to the "homeland" but to belong to Hawai'i, the new "home." In this sense, the Philippines functions more as a spiritual homeland, a center from which "authentic Filipino culture" emanates. In this situation, Filipino constructions of homes away from home involve competing myths of origin and cultural purity (that is, "I'm from the Philippines" means "immigrant"; "I was born in Hawai'i" refers to being "Local"; and "I'm from the mainland—the continental U.S." is equated to a "haolefied" Filipino), which characterize discourses of identity. The adjective—immigrant, Local, or mainland—attached to "Filipino" indexes specific identities and triggers a chain of cultural associations, its social manifestations a type of identity-play in different cultural fields. What this identity-play and play of symbols draws attention to is that in different

Diff. places = Diff ways being "Filipino" (handwritten annotation)

places, there are different ways of being "Filipino" and that the construc-tions of "home" and "homeland" involve a politics of cultural authenticity and continuity. *Pag-ibig sa Tinubuang Lupa* intervenes on a representational tension between the local (Filipino Hawai'i) and global (the Filipino trans-nation), providing its own identity story that territorializes Filipino-ness and in the process, it constructs a collective sense of place and sense of self for its participants. In addition to finding a "common language," *Pag-ibig sa Tinubuang Lupa* is tethered to a nationalist ideology of language and identity, where the nationalist story is narrated in Filipino.

The performance of *Pag-ibig sa Tinubuang Lupa* followed the Music-Text-Dance (MTD) theatrical form. Generally speaking, in the MTD theatrical form human actors present scripted and semiscripted material using music, sung or spoken text, and dance (Beeman 1993: 381). When I asked a faculty member about the use of the theatrical form for the cultural performance, she commented on the interconnectedness of language, culture, and ideol-ogy: "Theater is the most effective way to put across any ideology and also most effective in teaching language. . . . The theater forms help us to teach culture most effectively. It is complete—linguistic, cultural, historical, so-cial, etc. Both audience and performers experience some form of catharsis, a cleansing of old, unpleasant knowledge or belief and a learning of new ones (history, words, phrases, folktales, melodies, etc.)." As for the specific theater form for *Pag-ibig sa Tinubuang Lupa*, she told me that, "I had in mind the theater forms used by writers in the early American occupation in the Philippines. The forms were also used to fight the dictatorship during the Marcos regime. The stage was used as a tool to inform people of the American takeover, to unite the audience in an ideology and to touch their feelings, incite if you may." Imitating the protest theater used to challenge American colonialism and the Marcos dictatorship also enables the students to comment on the sociopolitical conditions of Filipinos in Hawai'i and the rest of the United States.

In *Pag-ibig sa Tinubuang Lupa,* the students were the principal actors, although some faculty members served as narrators. The script was com-posed of popular nationalist Philippine songs and poems dating from the Spanish colonial era to the current period. The numbers in the production were either in song form (with solo and group singing to taped and live music) or dramatic readings of poems, with the exception of one interpre-tive dance that was accompanied by a group song. The spectators in this particular event at the University of Hawai'i were a mix of those who had prior familiarity with the content of the performance and others who had no previous exposure to the material presented. The primary role of the audience was to bear witness to the presentation, but at times the spectators were encouraged to participate in the presentation through vocal display, which made them not merely passive recipients of the identity story but active participants in co-constructing the narrative.

In terms of program and format, *Pag-ibig sa Tinubuang Lupa* (and the song and drama festivals/competitions in general) is similar, but also different in significant ways, to the Pilipino Cultural Night (PCN) productions performed by Filipino student groups on college campus in the continental United States.[5] According to American Studies scholar Theo Gonzalves (1995),[6] there are five constituent elements of the traditional PCN model: "the opening of the show with both the Philippine and U.S. American national anthems, the use of Tagalog in the programs, the marking of bodies through Philippine costumes, the standard (required) inventory of Philippine dance styles, and the emplotment of a narrative within the show as a vehicle for historicizing the Filipino American experience" (134). During *Pag-ibig sa Tinubuang Lupa*, only the Philippine national anthem, "Pambansang Awit," was performed, albeit as the closing song. Because the cultural production was put on by students taking Filipino/Tagalog courses, all of the song and poetry numbers were performed in Tagalog, although the narration was done in both Tagalog and English, recognizing the mixture in the audience's languages and cultural and historical knowledge. Like in the traditional PCN model, several performers used "indigenized costume" to mark the "Philippine-ness" of the actors, particularly in the representations of the indigenous peoples of northern Luzon and Mindanao.[7] Aside from the interpretive dance, there were no performances of Philippine dance styles like the Tinikling or Muslim Singkil (traditional Philippine "bamboo dances"). Perhaps the most significant similarity between the traditional PCN model and *Pag-ibig sa Tinubuang Lupa* is their use of narrative to historicize the experience of Filipinos. However, unlike the traditional PCN model, to promote a Philippine-oriented nationalism, *Pag-ibig sa Tinubuang Lupa* focuses on Philippine history and experience (rather than Filipino American) in its narrative. There was no specific mention of Filipino communities, histories, and cultures in Hawai'i or in the United States.

Following a type of developmental narrative, the show opens with a narrator reading a poem about the physical and human geography of the Philippines. The poem is read as a voiceover, with a series of photographic stills projected onto a large screen that displays the various Philippine landscapes and ethnoscapes. This is then followed by a performance of a "kulintang,"[8] which the narrator tells us is an indigenous cultural form that avoided foreign influence and represents the Filipino "natives" from Mindanao, in the southern Philippines, who resisted colonial intrusion. What follows these two introductory scenes is a historical narrative that can be divided into five parts: (1) the Spanish colonial period, represented by nationalist songs and poems, including a reading of a poem by Jose Rizal, the national hero of the Philippines, entitled "Ang Kagandahan Ng Ating Sariling Wika" ("The Beauty Of Our Own Language") and a song version of Andres Bonifacio's poem, "Pag-ibig sa Tinubuang Lupa"; (2) American colonial rule, symbolized by patriotic songs and poems expressing Philippine opposition to U.S. domination, including "Pilipinas Kong Mahal" (loosely translated as "My Beloved Philippines," which was based, as the narrator points out, on the Maryland state song, "Maryland, My Maryland"), and "Bayan Ko" ("My Country"), originally a poem written by Jose Corazon De Jesus; (3) the questioning of Philippine national identity during 1960s and early 1970s, exemplified by the reading of the poem "Pilipino, Isang Depinisyon" ("Filipino, A Definition"); (4) martial law under Marcos, portrayed by reenactments of protests and demonstrations by students, political opponents, indigenous peoples, and workers yelling "makibaka" ("struggle" or "fight"), reminiscent of that historical period, and songs of resistance and opposition to the human rights abuses during that time, including "Ako ay Pilipino" by George Canseco, "Halina" ("Come") by Jess Santiago, and "Pagbabalik" ("The Return"). This last song marks Benigno Aquino's return from political exile to the Philippines, where he would be assassinated, setting off the People Power movement that would eventually remove Ferdinand Marcos from political power; and (5) the post-Marcos period, presented in nationalist songs about community, identity, and pride, like "Dakilang Lahi" ("A Noble Race") and a live band performing a song called "Pilipino Ako" ("I am Filipino"). The chronological sequence of historical events presented in the narrative imposes an internal order and coherence, connecting the past to the present which, in turn, opens up possible futures. The story told in the theatrical presentation attempts to produce a dominant narrative that makes the past relevant, creating a historical precedent for contemporary social realities.

For its largely Filipino performers and audience, *Pag-ibig sa Tinubuang Lupa* outlines a selective background on Philippine history and culture, narrating a type of story of origin. The narrative emphasizes a history of resistance and persistent struggle against oppression, with the oppressors represented by the Spanish and American colonial powers, the martial law regime of Ferdinand Marcos, and the current operations and structures of global capitalism that underlie the movement (and exploitation) of Filipino workers throughout the world. In its narrative, *Pag-ibig sa Tinubuang Lupa*

sharply illustrates that the discourse on the formation of Filipino and Filipino American racial/ethnic and cultural identities has been and continues
to be conditioned by its engagement with white American colonial history
and hegemony that is maintained by the Philippine state. And more specifically, as Espiritu explains, "the making of a Filipino American culture and
identity is not done in isolation, but in dialogue with and in opposition to
the racist ideologies and practices with the United States" (1994: 268).[9] The
public performance is an identity act in which Philippine history is reframed
as a history of resistance, highlighting opposition to Spanish, American, and
Japanese colonialism. The net effect of this reframing or retelling of Philippine history is the reinscription of Filipino agency, where they are no longer simply victims or passive subordinates willingly consenting to external
imperial domination and being lulled into inaction by colonial mentality.
The story told in the cultural production is a project in identity and history
making, an "identity tale" that seeks to draw out the historical and cultural
continuities between the Philippines and Filipinos in Hawai'i (and in the
United States). Although it does not include Filipino history in Hawai'i or
in the United States, especially labor history, *Pag-ibig sa Tinubuang Lupa*
constructs a unifying narrative that attempts to produce a coherent Filipino
cultural imaginary and social unity. The identity narrative territorializes
the Filipino American social imaginary in an intimate relationship with the
Philippine nation-state and at the same time, Filipinos are positioned at the
ethnicized and minoritized margins of U.S. and Hawai'i society.

Although typical song and drama festivals are judged competitions that
enable individual and group contestants to showcase their music and acting
skills and talents as well as their language abilities, *Pag-ibig sa Tinubuang
Lupa* and the narrative it presents can be understood in four interconnected
ways: (1) a "definitional ceremony" that provides a means for collective self-
definition and self-construction through staged display; (2) the expression
of a diasporic Filipino consciousness; (3) an example of the "born-again
Filipino experience" (Strobel 1996); and (4) a type of "cultural activism"
(Ginsburg 1997).

Using Myerhoff's notion of "definitional ceremony," *Pag-ibig sa Tinubuang
Lupa* is a theatrical performance that dramatizes "collective self-definitions
specifically intended to proclaim an interpretation to an audience not otherwise available" (1992: 234–35) and provides "opportunities to appear
before others in the light of their own internally provided interpretation"
(ibid.: 235). Throughout the event, the students are both performers and
spectators, dramatizing and witnessing the stories they tell through the various songs and poems. The students are given the power and responsibility

to define themselves, to "exercise power over their images, in their own eyes and to some extent in the eyes of whoever may be observing them" (ibid., 232). The students are thus self-conscious performers, keenly aware of their participation in their own history making, constructing their own definitions of themselves and producing their understanding of the knowledge and truth of their past and present. In a sense, the students have power, control, and responsibility over the images and discourses.

What occurs in the theatrical performance is a type of "cultural mirroring" where a community reflects its understanding of itself. As Myerhoff explains, "Cultural performances are reflective in the sense of showing ourselves to ourselves. They are capable of being reflexive, arousing consciousness of ourselves as we see ourselves. As heroes in our own dramas, we are made self-aware, conscious of our consciousness" (ibid.: 234). The "mirroring" effected in the cultural production points to a process of creating and understanding a collective sense of self through self-representation and public performance. The students construct and perform their own definitions of themselves and in turn, they can become what and who they (re)present. *Pag-ibig sa Tinubuang Lupa* enables students to transport the past into the present, where they come to know and embody Andres Bonifacio and Jose Rizal, asserting the contemporary relevance of the courage and nobility represented by these national heroes in the students' current social, political, and economic circumstances.

The narrative in *Pag-ibig sa Tinubuang Lupa* also reveals the racial/ethnic and cultural cartographic imaginings of a dispersed people and their remembrances/narration of a common history of colonial oppression and shared experiences of racial subjugation, signaling the beginnings of an emergent diaspora consciousness. According to Okamura (1998), changes in the U.S.–Philippine relationship, new U.S. immigration policies, and technological advances in communication and transportation have created and supported the maintenance of transnational relations between diasporic Filipinos in the United States (and other parts of the world) and the Philippines. For Okamura, a crucial element of the Filipino diaspora is the circulation of "people, money, goods, and information to and from the Philippine homeland" (1998: 117). Through "visits to their home town or city by Filipinos residing or working abroad, remittances and consumer items sent to relatives in the Philippines, and international telephone communication that provides for information flows" (ibid: 117). Filipinos in diaspora maintain social, cultural, economic, and political ties to the Philippines. These types of ongoing transnational relations with the Philippine homeland, for Okamura, are the defining factors in the construction of Filipino communities in diaspora. However, as *Pag-ibig sa Tinubuang Lupa* demonstrates, the stories that people tell also prove to be important resources for the constitution of diasporic identities and the constructions of "home" and "homeland."[10] In this respect, the cultural production is a site of racial/ethnic and cultural identity production, consumption, and distribution, a place where the articulation of historical events and struggles (which represent the Philippine nation-state) enables the construction of affiliations and sentiments of national belonging for dispersed Filipinos.

Along the same lines, another effect of *Pag-ibig sa Tinubuang Lupa* is similar to Strobel's (1996) notion of the "'born-again' Filipino experience." According to Strobel, the "born-again Filipino experience" points to processes of self-(re)discovery and the return to Philippine racial/ethnic and cultural roots. In this regard, she remarks, "What I have come to label as the process of cultural identity formation among Filipino American college students and some community and cultural workers is the attempt to comprehend the interrelatedness of 1) the need for Philippine historical and cultural knowledge, 2) the function of personal memory, and 3) the consequences of language loss" (1996: 33). The experiences of "born-again Filipinos" is characterized by attempts to confront the legacies of the colonization of the Philippines, the disruption of immigration, and the racial subjugation of Filipinos in the United States. As a result, the racial/ethnic and cultural awakening is embedded in discourses of decolonization and indigenization.[11] The political awareness and consciousness characteristic of "born-again Filipinos" points to an understanding of the conditions of racial domination in which they live but also looks to the Philippines as the source of history and culture. The search for origins and purity inevitably leads to the Philippines. In engaging in the processes of social subjectivity formation, these young Filipinos in Hawai'i are involved in a spatialized politics of identity in which they create feelings of belonging to a sociopolitical imaginary amid ruptures and displacements brought on by experiences of immigration and sociopolitical marginalization.

"Born-again Filipinos" are members of the legions of nomads whose experiences have been constituted by the itinerary of immigration. *Pag-ibig sa Tinubuang Lupa* and other similar cultural productions and performances produced by "born-again Filipinos" question the relationship between "home" and "homeland." Where is "home" for those living in places where they were not born? Is "home" simply where one considers their place of origin, their natal/native land? Is "home" the place(s) of (temporary) arrival and settlement? And what is the relationship to the "homeland" (and to the other communities-in-displacement)? Is the Philippines the "homeland," the native, original, or authentic "home"? The historical narrative in *Pag-ibig sa Tinubuang Lupa* unambiguously marks the Philippines as the "homeland," extending the metaphor of kinship in which genealogical connections are based on a "temporal continuity of essence and territorial rootedness" (Malkki 1992: 27–28). In other words, Filipinos, in and outside the Philippines, belong to the same "place" and to the same "family" (with the same apical ancestors). According to *Pag-ibig sa Tinubuang Lupa*, the Philippines is the "homeland" because it is the place to which Filipino ancestry is traced and the place of the purported natural and rightful belonging of Filipinos everywhere. That is to say, for dispersed Filipinos the Philippines signifies the "roots" and the source of origin and heritage, where Filipinos are both "at-home" and "in-place." The Philippines symbolizes the spiritual center and origin of Filipino-ness. The itinerary of Filipino immigration to the United States is a disruptive process in which the "original" culture and language are lost and the cultural productions of "born-again Filipinos" function as sites and instruments for their recovery. The cultural production enables diasporic Filipinos to be (re)introduced to the homeland and to show their "Love for the Native Land." In the end, the mythologizing of the Philippines as "homeland" functions as a unifying narrative for those in diaspora, encouraging a type of "symbolic transnationalism" (Espiritu 2003).

Pag-ibig sa Tinubuang Lupa can also be understood as a type of "cultural activism" (Ginsburg 1997). As Mahon explains, activism-oriented cultural productions attempt "to shift the terms of debates circulating in the dominant public sphere, to attack stereotypes and perceived prejudices, and to construct, reconfigure, and communicate meanings associated with their racial, ethnic, gender, sexual, and national identities" (Mahon 2000: 475). Seen in this way, *Pag-ibig sa Tinubuang Lupa* serves as a site of critical intervention, mediating issues related to race/ethnicity, culture, representation, and power. According to Quemuel, Filipino student groups in Hawai'i, like Katipunan, take an activist stance and have a political function "in the sense that they are taking positive action to retain and promote Filipino cultural awareness and pride" (Quemuel 1996: 17). Like the racial/ethnic and cultural awakening of "born-again Filipinos," these student clubs promote awareness, pride, and "preservation of Filipino heritage through cultural activities" (ibid.: 17).

Further, Quemuel argues that the cultural productions and practices performed by such student organizations "constitute activism as they occur within a society that constantly degrades and devalues most things Filipino" (ibid.: 17). They are attempts to counter societal denigration and self-denial/self-hate: "These various cultural clubs are fighting the internalized self-hatred and racism and trying to rebuild a strong sense of pride and identity" (ibid.: 18). The loud, passionate, and repeated declarations of "Ako ay Pilipino" and "Pilipino Ako" ("I am Filipino") during the performance are fervent proclamations of self that reclaim and affirm racial/ethnic and cultural pride. They announce that being Filipino is something to be proud of and not a source of shame, that indeed, Filipinos constitute a "noble race." For these students, to take pride in being Filipino means to recognize their marginal and minority status and to take steps in the direction of subverting the existing systems and structures of power that position them at the margins. In this way, the cultural presentation can be seen as a project that strategically essentializes "Filipino" as part of efforts to develop solidarity and political mobilization to challenge the prevailing social order and hierarchy.

During the performance of *Pag-ibig sa Tinubuang Lupa*, the students, to a large extent, are also able to control the discourse and practice of representation. In deciding how the narrative is to be represented, the students "engage in a visible and frequently influential form of cultural politics" (Mahon 2000: 476). The construction and invocation of "Filipino" in the performance is a resistance against marginalization and minoritization, calling into question and destabilizing the current consensus existing in Hawai'i and U.S. racial/ethnic and cultural discourses and practices. As Mahon observes, "Indeed, people who historically have been marginalized from institutional power create self-representations of their groups—both idealized and accurate—to counter widely disseminated negative images, the absence of images, and images produced by others" (2000: 470). Through cultural productions and public performances, Filipinos are able to tell their own stories about who they are (their own self-perceptions and how others view them) and ultimately how they want to be seen and heard. They challenge external categorization and articulate counternarratives "that decenter notions of cultural inferiority based on master narratives that portray Filipinos as either having a 'damaged' culture or none at all" (Strobel 1996: 40). As such, they are consciousness-raising and pride-instilling vehicles that articulate shared experiences and histories that help to strengthen group solidarity and underwrite racial/ethnic and cultural coherence and unity. As Shapiro reminds us, "The production of identity coherence and exclusivity continues to be a matter of how a people's story is told" (1999: 54).

Like the traditional PCN model and the "born-again Filipino" experience, *Pag-ibig sa Tinubuang Lupa* is susceptible to charges of essentialism. It reflects the lure of (racial and) ethnic absolutism that persists as part of the "continuing aspiration to acquire a supposedly authentic, natural, and stable 'rooted' identity" (Gilroy 1993a: 30). However, perhaps it would be more instructive to view the cultural production not for its racial/ethnic and cultural reductionisms but instead as a project of constructing an essentialized story that seeks to stabilize an ambiguous and tenuous racial/ethnic and cultural coherence and unity. In its performance and overall narrative, the cultural production secures its own territorializations and representations of Filipino-ness. They are self-authenticating staged displays that repurpose "Filipino."

The struggles over configuring Filipino social identities can also be understood as part of the current phase of cultural politics that, according to Hall (1992), signals the "end of the innocence," the departure from the innocent notion of the essential racialized subject and the emergence of "new ethnicities." For Hall, the "end of the innocence" not only involves rethinking race and ethnicity but identity in general (he mentions class, gender, sexuality, and nation in particular). Speaking specifically about the category of "black" but applicable to "Filipino" (and other identity categories and forms of social differentiation), he explains the stakes underlying the "end of the innocence" in the following way: "What is at issue here is the recognition of the extraordinary diversity of subjective positions, social experiences and cultural identities which compose the category 'black'; that is, the recognition that 'black' is essentially a politically and culturally constructed category, which cannot be grounded in a set of fixed transcultural or transcendental racial categories and which therefore has no guarantee in Nature" (1992: 254). It is an attempt to rethink racial and ethnic categories and other social identities in nonabsolutist and sociopolitically strategic ways rather than talking about essences and nature.[12] Thus, identity categories and Hall's "new ethnicities" are understood as positionings, that is to say, they are contested, relational, and strategic (Hall 1996c). Identity and identity formation in the contemporary period points to a generative tension between Hall's "end of the innocence" (1992), which marks the departure of the unproblematic notion of the essential racialized subject, and the persistent lure of (racial and ethnic) absolutism, which according to Paul Gilroy reflects the "continuing aspiration to acquire a supposedly authentic, natural, and stable 'rooted' identity" (Gilroy 1992: 30). The search for an essential and authentic self often misrecognizes temporary closures of fundamentally porous boundaries for fixed internal coherence, unity, and uniformity. The search for essences is an attempt to naturalize unnatural boundaries and construct "misplaced concreteness" (Alonso 1994).

Following from this rethinking of identity, we can understand "Filipino" as a social imaginary that can never be fully attained, and instead is characterized as provisional and momentary. The coherence and unity of the "Filipino" category is under constant threat, its boundaries are fundamentally porous, and its points of intersection and divergence are nondeterminative. Thus, each historical specificity enables the reformulation and reformation of boundaries that potentially threatens/strengthens such sociopolitical consolidations. Each historical moment enables new (or emerging) constructs to be socially mediated. In this way, these identity consolidations can be understood as unstable sociopolitical positionings whose articulations about its content and boundaries must be consistently asserted and affirmed. Seen from this perspective, the "Filipino" category is a socially constructed and negotiated reality, characterized by the interplay between self-ascriptions (that coexist and compete) and externally imposed categories; the category is contested from within and without, among Filipinos themselves and in interaction with non-Filipinos. What this reveals is that identities are sites of emergence and becoming; they enable productive places and moments for active agency, creativity, and imagination.

As we see in the "Rediscovering Filipino Identity" conference and *Pag-ibig sa Tinubuang Lupa*, a nationalist ideology of language and identity underlie the narration of a sense of self and the creation of a sense of place and belonging. *Pag-ibig sa Tinubuang Lupa* shows us that place-based affiliations and linguistic attachments continue to provide anchors for perceptions and experiences of self in a time when the spatial supports of our identities supposedly no longer matter. In addition, stories in what they tell and how they are told provide an important means for people to demarcate boundaries, a type of "home"-making. Through processes of inclusion, exclusion, and othering in their narration, narratives, and commentary, stories territorialize a collective sense of self and attempt to reconcile experiences of dispersal/fragmentation and centeredness/integration. In the end, a story's setting continues to be meaningful. Where a story takes place and what language is used conditions how a story is told and ultimately, it tells us who matters.

CHAPTER 4

"THE CENTER IS NOT JUST FOR FILIPINOS, BUT FOR ALL OF HAWAI'I NEI"

Vignette #1: Waiting outside at the gates
June 11, 2002. 9:30 a.m. The grand opening and dedication
ceremony of the Filipino Community Center in Waipahu,
O'ahu, a former plantation town that is commonly viewed as
a Filipino residential enclave riddled with crime, drugs, youth
gang activity, and juvenile delinquency.

It is a typical hot, dry summer morning in Waipahu, a rural, working-class
neighborhood and historic plantation town located near Pearl Harbor on the
leeward (western) side of O'ahu. It is sunny and eighty-five degrees, and only
a few white clouds dot the skies. It is what people usually imagine and expect
Hawai'i weather to be. The old Waipahu sugar mill smokestack, the most
recognizable community landmark, sits only a few hundred yards away. Although the sugar mill closed in 1995, it continues to loom in the background.
The sugar plantation in Waipahu was established in the 1890s, turning the
community into a large sugarcane-processing area until the demise of the
sugar industry in the mid-1990s. Waipahu is steeped in plantation history (it
was the site of numerous significant strikes, specifically the 1906 and 1909
strikes by Japanese workers), and many of Waipahu's current residents are
somehow connected to the plantation history, but are mostly a mixture of
Local and immigrant Filipinos. A few months prior to the grand opening of
the Filipino Community Center, Nestor Garcia, a longtime Waipahu resident
and former state representative and Honolulu City Council member, wrote
in an article titled "The Waipahu OF My Youth" (1997):

Figure 7. A view of the smoke-stack from the FilCom Center parking lot, photo taken by author.

I look around now and I see a Waipahu that is more of a sprawling bedroom community, with pockets devoted to commercial and industrial use. Gone are Arakawa's, Gems, and the Sky Slide. The Oahu Sugar Mill, was the nucleus of the town, has also been shuttered. In its place, we have the Leeward YMCA, the light industrial park, and the soon-to-be opened Filipino Community Center. Neighborhoods such as Village Park, Royal Kunia, Waikele, and Gentry-Waipio, have sprouted where sugar cane and pineapple once grew. In my youth, I saw a town in transition. We have had our growing pains, and we continue to evolve. Now, the challenge is to dispense with the thinking that Waipahu is a place where gangs and graffiti rule.

The FilCom Center was expected to serve as a hub of economic activity and to help revitalize the neighboring community with much-needed economic investment. As former U.S. congressman and now governor, Neil Aber-crombie, wrote in a Filipino community newspaper, "the FilCom Center will serve as a 'beacon of light' for Filipino immigrant families, who have dreams of receiving the services necessary to build a better life for their

Figure 8. The old Waipahu sugar mill smokestack, photo taken by author.

families." As an economic "beacon of light," many hoped the FilCom Center would help transform the Waipahu community from "a place where gangs and graffiti rule" to a prosperous and thriving neighborhood alive with economic activity.

In addition to the sugar mill, just a few blocks away is the Hawai'i Plantation Village and Cultural Gardens, an outdoor history museum that exhibits, in a rather idyllic and romanticized fashion, the "lifestyles and experiences" of Hawai'i's plantation laborers. The Plantation Village contains restored structures and replicas of plantation buildings (like the general store), furnished homes of the different ethnic groups (including domestic tools, implements, and clothing), and other community structures as well as artifacts, photographs, a library collection, and other documents. The indoor exhibit and walking tour harkens back to the plantation era, circa 1900–1930, what is perceived as the foundational period of "Hawai'i's multiethnic heritage" and the basis of cultural diversity in contemporary society. The FilCom Center subscribes to the dominant plantation history narrative (similar to that told by the Plantation Village), which asserts that the development of a Filipino sense of solidarity stems from shared labor history, and that this plantation labor history serves as the backdrop for their "Filipino success story." In this chapter, I examine the building and the grand opening ceremonies of the Filipino Community Center (henceforth

PLANTATION ERA = 1900-1930

Figure 9. View of the Waipahu Street end of the Consuelo Zobel Alger Courtyard, photo courtesy of Took HNLA.

referred to as the FilCom Center) held on June 11, 2002, one day before the 104th anniversary of Philippine independence from Spain, and eleven years after the project was first initiated by the Filipino Chamber of Commerce of Hawai'i.

I attended the FilCom Center and other community organization meetings, performed participant observation of the two-week-long 2002 Mabuhay Festival, of which the opening of the Center was a central part, and conducted interviews with community leaders and other residents prior to the grand opening celebrations. This chapter relies heavily on my observations during that day, my interviews with FilCom Center board members and staff, and the stories written about the Center in the two Filipino newspapers, the *Hawaii Filipino Chronicle* and the *Fil-Am Courier*. In the chapter, I ask how the Center represents Filipinos in terms of which identity symbols and narratives are privileged and what political and economic claims are made. In short, I ask how the FilCom Center participates in the cultural politics of representation among Filipinos in Hawai'i, particularly as it pertains to the "ethnic myth of success" (Steinberg 1989), and I use the Center as a window for viewing broader discourses of race/ethnicity, class, immigration, and multiculturalism in Hawai'i. This is similar to Bonus's observations that suggest, "Filipino Americans have resorted to using the spaces of the community centers to organize themselves and build networks of mutual support outside the traditional or mainstream political venues that usually exclude or marginalize them" (Bonus 2000: 102). Specifically in this chapter, I look at how those in the middle class engage in a "class project" (Ortner 2003) to seize the symbolic in an attempt to overcome the demographic (similar to the ethnoracial assignment/identity dynamic discussed by Brodkin 1998) and address class anxieties of being down-classed or out-classed by other Local Asian immigrants. For Bonus, "community centers represent and constitute Filipino American politics to the degree that they serve as sites for articulating a kind of politics that may fall outside the state but adamantly part of the nation . . . such a politics is a response to the unwillingness and limited ability of the state to serve their interests. And it is a politics that nevertheless attempts to retain and sustain its ties with, not separate itself from, both Filipino and American realms." (2000: 103). As I show in this chapter, Hawai'i also functions as an important third realm that is connected with and separate from the Philippines and the continental United States.

The successful completion of the FilCom Center is commonly referred to as "a dream come true" or "a dream realized." This image is particularly compelling because the notion of a "dream" indexes the American Dream, American promises of opportunity and equality, and the fantasy of multiculturalism in Hawai'i. The FilCom Center version of the "ethnic myth of success" is also predicated on an assimilationist ideology and a view of Hawai'i as a "multicultural and racial paradise" and "a land of immigrants," something repeated throughout the speeches in the grand opening ceremony. In fact, one of the local Filipino politicians boldly remarked: "Filipinos built the Center for all immigrants. All the people of Hawai'i are immigrants." This view essentially configures Hawai'i as a settler society, a sociopolitical formation in which "Local" Asian claims to historical, social, economic, and political belonging prevail over and negate those of indigenous Hawaiians. In the end, the FilCom Center story of Filipinos finally "making it" in Hawai'i is about achieving social, political, and economic parity with other racial/ethnic groups. It is a demand for full participation in Hawai'i society, for moving out of the margins and into the mainstream. The story is about Filipinos becoming a "power player" in Hawai'i, having access to political and economic power, but without making fundamental changes to the structures of inequality and the patterns of racial and ethnic stratification that underpin Hawai'i society. In this regard, Stephen Steinberg suggests that when ethnicity is associated with class disadvantage—with poverty, hardship, low standard of living, and so on—then powerful inducements exist for the members of such groups to assimilate into the mainstream culture, since this will improve their chances for a better life. Especially when racial or ethnic stigma is attached to a group and the economic consequences that flow from it individuals are forced to shed the marks of ethnic difference. Indeed, most disadvantaged minorities have been willing to compromise their ethnicity for the sake of economic security, social acceptance, and a sense of participating fully in society instead of living precariously on the periphery (1989: 256).

In the case of Filipinos in Hawai'i, the desired assimilation into the mainstream is a process of becoming "Local" and shedding the stereotypical and negative image of Filipinos. No longer on the outside looking in, the FilCom Center seeks to interweave Filipinos into the multicultural fabric of Hawai'i. Ultimately the Localization of Filipinos is about social, political, and economic incorporation. Instead of radical social change and societal transformation, empowerment from the FilCom narrative keeps intact the political, economic, and racial/ethnic terrain of contemporary Hawai'i and reinscribes Asian immigrant hegemony and settler domination.

For many Filipinos and non-Filipinos alike, despite the reality that collectively, Filipinos continue to occupy the lower rungs of the socioeconomic ladder (along with Native Hawaiians, Samoans, and Micronesians), the Filipino Community Center has come to symbolize "Filipino success and achievement" and "the coming of age" of the community. The FilCom Center narrative of achievement and political and economic maturation supports an "ethnic myth of success" (Steinberg 1989) in which Filipinos supposedly have "made it," to be considered equals to mainstream "Local" Asians, particularly the Japanese, Okinawans, and Chinese who all have their own community or cultural centers and have undergone similar processes of fighting disadvantage and eventually gaining sociopolitical prominence and mainstream status. Furthermore, the FilCom Center story is a middle-class narrative with its own ethnic heroes. It depends on creating and displaying political stability and unity (countering notions of a Filipino "identity crisis" and "Filipino disunity") as part of its class interests, a way to mobilize Filipinos toward political and economic empowerment. In this way, the FilCom Center symbolizes the realization of immigrant dreams of middle-class prosperity, privilege, and status and constructs a "Filipino success story." This success story was produced in two specific ways: (1) the creation of "ethnic heroes" who serve as the prototype for individual success and socioeconomic mobility, and (2) the FilCom Center building itself as

Figure 10. Waiting outside the gates of Bahay Harry and Jeanette Weinberg during the grand opening ceremony, photo taken by author.

symbolic of the community's "coming of age" in terms of the attainment of political and economic clout—basically the story of how Filipinos are becoming "Local" and demanding inclusion into the mainstream and entry to power. This chapter examines these two mechanisms for producing and disseminating a "Filipino success story."

> Vignette #1A:
> Still waiting outside at the gates . . .

It is now ten in the morning and in the parking lot immediately outside the gates of Bahay Harry and Jeanette Weinberg,[1] and there are several hundred people huddled together, waiting in the midmorning sun. Despite some controversy over what the building should be called, the board reached a compromise, naming the structure after the individuals considered to be the Center's most important donors, Harry and Jeanette Weinberg. Their Foundation donated $3 million for construction, the largest amount given to the Center by an individual donor.

Outside the gates, there are young people, seniors, Filipino and Filipino American World War II veterans, Philippine government officials, families, community leaders, and university folks waiting to get in. Some are dressed casually, but the vast majority are in their formal wear—whether decked out in "Aloha attire" or in traditional Philippine dress (the women in their *terno* gowns and the men in their *barong tagalog*). And the local politicians, Filipino and non-Filipino, are en masse. It is an election year after all, and this year more than in years past it seems that the politicians all want (and need) Filipinos to vote for them. Like everyone else, they think that this year Filipinos will constitute the all-important swing vote, and perhaps the "sleeping giant" will finally awake from its political slumber. On numerous occasions, I have been told, "We have the numbers." But the numbers have not necessarily translated into collective political empowerment or political clout. For the most part, Filipinos in Hawai'i are still "the invisible community." As journalist and community leader Zachary Labez has observed: "The numbers tell the story. There are enough voting-age Filipinos capable of making a big difference in the results of any county or state election. Getting Filipinos to understand the importance to go out and vote is the challenge" (*Fil-Am Courier,* July 1–15, 2001).

Local politicians are quite conscious of the large pool of Filipino voters and Filipino activism. In the election for governor in 1998, the Filipino American Democratic candidate and incumbent governor barely won. Only five thousand votes separated the winner from the Republican loser. The slim margin of victory was particularly significant because since the mid-1950s Democrats have politically controlled Hawai'i. Although the narrow Democratic victory in the gubernatorial election did not set off panic alarms, it was a quiet but palpable wake-up call for the party. It is interesting that although the governor was Filipino American, it seemed that in his bid for reelection, Filipinos did not initially stand behind him as fervently as they did during his first run at the governor's seat. In fact, there was a much-needed massive voter registration campaign to get Filipinos to go out and vote and reelect one of their own. Zachary Labez describes the impetus for the voter registration drive and the impact of the project in the following way:

> Seeing the tight race between Governor Ben Cayetano and Republican-ticket challenger Linda Lingle going into the general election, community leaders [from the Filipino Coalition for Solidarity, Inc. and the O'ahu Filipino Community Council] quickly put together a voter registration and get-out-the-vote project [called Tanikala '98] to increase the number of Filipino voters. Every day, an average of 100 new voter applications were turned in at the Honolulu City Clerk's office. Going into the general election, over 5,000 new voters were registered. . . . When the results of the gubernatorial race showed Governor Ben Cayetano leading by some 5,000 votes, even the project organizers were dumb-founded. They realized that pollsters estimated over 80 percent of Filipino voters reported voting for Cayetano (*Fil-Am Courier,* July 1–15, 2001).

The 1998 election highlighted the importance of Filipino voters, and four years later at perhaps one the most important events for Filipinos in Hawai'i in the new millennium, numerous local politicians, including the Republican candidate who nearly defeated Cayetano, were on hand to shore up support for their bids for public office.

As we continue to wait outside, it starts to get hotter and hushed complaints begin to emerge: "They're running on Filipino time." In this occasion,

Figure 11. The unveiling of the José Rizal statue at the grand opening ceremony, photo taken by author.

"Filipino time" is actually only a few minutes late, but this moment has been a long time coming. The guests of honor start to gather outside the gates, indicating that the ceremony is about to begin. The island "cultural protocol" in these types of occasions usually includes some type of recognition or acknowledgment of the host culture (that is Native Hawaiians) via a co-opted, misappropriated, or invented tradition involving a *lei* or chant. Though it is often understood as a sign of respect, this protocol also symbolizes that the land in which we have settled is home to an indigenous people who have been displaced, dispossessed, and often rendered marginal and anachronistic in contemporary Hawai'i society.

As anticipated, the opening ceremony festivities formally begin with religious blessings, a Hawaiian chant (representing the Native Hawaiian hosts, though they did not seem to be in attendance), and a Catholic prayer (representing the Philippine guests). The blessings are followed by a *maile lei* ceremony (similar to a ribbon cutting), in which the honored guests and dignitaries, Honolulu Mayor Jeremy Harris, Lieutenant Governor Mazie Hirono, Philippine Consul General Rolando Gregorio, Philippine Undersecretary of Foreign Affairs Merlin Magallona, Philippine Secretary for Local Government Joey Lina, Patti Lyons from the Consuelo Alger Foundation, Gailene Wong from the Weinberg Foundation, and FilCom Center board of directors Eddie Flores Jr., Roland Casamina, and Lito Alcantara, untie the

Figure 12. Igorot youth perform in front of the *bahay kubo* at its permanent place during the grand opening ceremonies, stage right next to the José Rizal exhibit, photo taken by author.

lei. The white mayor and Japanese American lieutenant governor symbolize the racial/ethnic and class hierarchy and order in contemporary Hawai'i society, pointing to where power, privilege, and status are located. The two older Filipino men, the consul general and undersecretary, are surrogates for the Philippine homeland and the *sakadas.* With the untying of the *maile lei,* the past and present collide and the Filipino masses are finally allowed entry.

But before we can completely enter the courtyard, there is another highly symbolic activity. A small replica of a *bahay kubo,* or nipa hut, is to be wheeled across the gates and into the courtyard of the three-story, Spanish-style structure. The *bahay kubo* is a "native" Filipino house that is typically constructed from bamboo for the structure, and leaves of nipa, a type of palm tree, are woven together and used for roofing. I was told by one of the event organizers that the *bahay kubo* is a symbol of "the Filipino," representing their simplicity, resiliency, and their rural and agricultural roots. I also learned that wheeling the *bahay kubo* across the gates and into the courtyard represented the *bayanihan* spirit, the Philippine tradition of villagers helping one another move their houses to new locations. In its more contemporary usage, *bayanihan* is commonly regarded as "a core Filipino cultural value" (often detached from material conditions) that refers to a "communal spirit" in which unity, harmony, and cooperation can overcome overwhelming or impossible obstacles. So as the *bahay kubo* is wheeled across the gates, we are encouraged to reexperience the communal spirit and "the coming together of Filipinos and the putting aside of their differences" that resulted in the FilCom Center, despite the tremendous odds. The *bahay kubo* and *bayanihan* spirit finally carry us through the gates and into the courtyard, and it is the white Honolulu mayor dressed in a *barong tagalog* and draped with *lei* who leads the procession. He is the frontrunner for the Democratic nomination for governor (although he dropped out of the governor's race a few months later amid highly publicized political and financial scandals). The other candidates, both Democrats and Republicans, are also there to show their support, shake some hands, and secure some votes. But it is the mayor, a favorite politician among Filipinos, who leads the Filipino masses across the threshold. I follow them in.

As I wait to enter the gates of the Center, I keep thinking about all the Filipinos around me. There were all types: locals, immigrants, mainlanders, rich, poor, young, old, men, women, and children. I also thought about their collective social, political, and economic position in contemporary Hawai'i society. Ever since the racial and class oppression experienced during the plantation days and the struggles for better working and living conditions during union organizing, it seems that Filipinos in Hawai'i have been at the gates, waiting to enter not as second-class citizens, an "invisible community," or "a sleeping giant," but as equals, the ideal promised by multicultural

Figure 13. View of the Consuelo Zobel Alger Courtyard from the Waipahu Street end of the Center, photo courtesy of Took HNLA.

Hawai'i. And there we all were, still knocking at the gates, on the outside looking in. With the successful construction of the FilCom Center and its grand opening, had Filipinos finally "arrived"? Had Filipinos in Hawai'i finally "made it" like I was hearing and seeing everywhere and reading in the mainstream and Filipino newspapers? Is Filipino identity really no longer about the working class but now about business, entrepreneurship, and middle-class status?

"A Dream": The Making of the Filipino Community Center

According to Rose Cruz Churma, then the former interim executive director of the FilCom Center, Inc., the desire for a Filipino community center has been a longstanding but failed series of dreams: "For years, the Filipino community in Hawaii has dreamed of creating a gathering place it could call its own" (*Fil-Am Courier,* June 1–15, 2002). Since 1954, when the Filipino Chamber of Commerce in Hawai'i was established, there have been numerous attempts at building a Filipino community center. For the most part, the Filipino Chamber of Commerce in Hawai'i has carried the torch for such a project, having discussions about building a center back in the 1950s. Depending on whom you ask, there have been anywhere from three to eight previous attempts to construct a Filipino community or cultural center. The most concrete effort was in the late 1960s when Soledad Alconcel, the founder of the Philippine Cultural Foundation, sought to construct a Philippine Cultural Center. The Cultural Center never materialized and the idea lost steam when Alconcel passed away. In the early 1980s there was talk about building a Filipino Garden on the grounds of the East-West Center at the University of Hawai'i at Mānoa. There was a fund-raising drive with a good amount of community support for the garden and even a ground-breaking ceremony, but the monies raised disappeared and there is no Filipino Garden to date. Thus in 1991, when talks about building a Filipino community center resurfaced, there was a tremendous amount of community skepticism and suspicion.

The FilCom Center traces its immediate roots to 1991. That year, the Filipino Chamber of Commerce of Hawai'i (FCCH) under the leadership of Lito Alcantara, an engineer and president of the construction company Group Builders, began talks about a project to build a Filipino community center. Although in the early stages of planning there existed a lot of doubt and cynicism among Filipinos and non-Filipinos, there was an unwavering and unrelenting enthusiasm for the proposal. To solidify the project, in

September 1992 The Filipino Community Center, Inc., was founded and incorporated as a Hawai'i nonprofit corporation, with members of the FCCH serving as the leadership and planning committee. Roland Casamina was elected president, Mario Ramil vice president, Lito Alcantara secretary, and Stanley Suyat director. A few months later in March 1993, the organization adopted a mission statement. According to the statement, the purpose of The Filipino Community Center, Inc., was "To establish a community center which will preserve and perpetuate the Filipino culture for all of Hawaii." (Was "Filipino culture" vanishing?)

As part of its mission, The Filipino Community Center, Inc., under the leadership of Eddie Flores Jr., sponsored its inaugural Filipino Fiesta and Parade in Waikiki in May 1993 where Filipinos—local leaders and celebrities involved in politics, business, education, sports, entertainment, and beauty pageants (the young, old, and adolescents)—could be put on display to "help unify the community by having something fun and culturally meaningful." Since then the Filipino Fiesta and Parade has become an annual event and every year, there are more floats, more participants, more businesses and food booths, more spectators, and more politicians (Filipino and non-Filipino). In this regard Zachary Labez has observed: "A decade ago, when I chaired the first Filipino Parade of Filipino Community Center, Inc., we had 35 floats and marching units; except for a handful of elected government officials, there were no political groups in the event. The following year, there were approximately 90 participating units with more politicians and a voter registration booth at the end of the parade route. Earlier this month, we counted 25 floats and marching units, smaller than in the past, but this time the parade included floats or marching units of the Republican Party and the Young Democrats of Hawaii, five Honolulu council members, four state legislators, Honolulu Mayor Jeremy Harris, and Lieutenant Governor Mazie Hirono" (*Fil-Am Courier,* July 1–15, 2001). In addition to providing a venue for local politicking, the Filipino Fiesta and Parade was an important site for promoting the FilCom Center project and garnering community awareness and political support.

From the beginning of the project, it was clear that the making of the FilCom Center would require a tremendous political and economic undertaking. For the FilCom Center to actually materialize, support from state legislators and fund raising were crucial. In a speech at the Federation of the Philippine American Chambers of Commerce (FPACC) convention in 1998 Eddie Flores Jr. is quoted as saying, "To build the Filipino Community Center, my decision was to be active in the political arena because this is the only way we could get the funding. This is the only way we could get

Figure 14. View of the Consuelo Zobel Alger Courtyard from the third floor, photo courtesy of Took HNLA.

the land" (*Fil-Am Courier,* June 1–15, 2002). In August 1993, the initial effort to raise monies for the Center began with the first "Tee off a Dream" golf tournament. Later in the year, fund-raising possibilities were bolstered by the establishment of The Filipino Community Center, Inc., as a 501(c) (3) nonprofit corporation, receiving tax-exempt status from the IRS, which allowed the organization to apply for federal and state government grants and monies from local and national foundations.

In August 1994, the Center began discussions with AmFac/JMB Hawai'i to acquire a two-acre parcel of land in Waipahu that was previously owned by the O'ahu Sugar Company. This was particularly interesting and rather ironic because AmFac started out in 1849 as Hackfeld and Company, a German-owned firm. Hackfeld and Company first began as a small general store on the Honolulu waterfront, which eventually swelled into financing and supplying sugar planters (that is, developing into a factor in an investment sense), leading the company to become owners of large sugar and pineapple plantations throughout the islands, which included land around the town of Waipahu in leeward O'ahu. As the sugar factors (that is, the financial intermediaries and funding sources for the plantations) evolved, providing larger amounts of capital to the plantations, they were able to take over the plantations they were financing and servicing (eventually consolidating into five main corporations, the "Big Five"). After World War I, because the assets of German-owned businesses were seized by the federal government, Hackfeld and Company went through a name and ownership change. The company was sold to a group of Hawai'i businessmen who took on the rather patriotic name, American Factors. In 1966, American Factors became AmFac and in 1988, JMB Realty Corp. bought Amfac. The FilCom Center had begun talks with the company because with the demise of the sugar industry and the closing of the Waipahu plantation in 1995, AmFac/JMB sought to rezone forty acres of land near the old Waipahu sugar mill. Seeing this as an opportunity, "The Center's supporters proceeded to organize the Filipino community, particularly those living in Waipahu, to support the rezoning [which included a Filipino Community Center as part of the community's long-range plan], which the City Council approved in 1998" (*Fil-Am Courier*, June 1–15, 2002). In 1998, during a deed-signing ceremony at the AT&T Filipino Fiesta, AmFac/JMB Hawai'i transferred the property to the FilCom Center. By this time, with a site having been determined, the early skepticism had waned and instead, talk turned to when construction of the Center would begin, when it would be completed, and where the money would come from.

Inclusion into the Waipahu Special Area Plan as a "center of influence" and identified as a "beacon of light" that could promote the economic revitalization of the community paved the way for raising funds to plan, design, and build the Center. As part of the fund-raising drive, the FilCom Center turned to the City and County of Honolulu and in particular the Community Development Block Grant (CDBG) program. The FilCom Center was represented as a potential neighborhood savior and as a vehicle for economic development that could create jobs and open up small business opportunities in the community: "The areas around and near the old sugar mill in Waipahu need a catalyst for economic revitalization. The FilCom Center intends to do just that. The FilCom Center will benefit not only Filipinos but other ethnic groups that comprise the rich tapestry of Hawaii's multi-cultural population. Its name is a source of pride for us all who dared to dream, but its ultimate mission is to serve the community at large, because it is only through our collaborative efforts that we can revitalize our blighted neighborhoods and eliminate slums and blight, create meaningful employment and provide services to those less fortunate than us" (*Fil-Am Courier*, July 1–15, 2001). In May 1998, the City and County of Honolulu, under the leadership of Mayor Jeremy Harris, approved the first $500,000 grant that enabled the FilCom Center to begin the planning and design for the project. The City and County of Honolulu, using federal Housing and Urban Development's (HUD) Community Development Block Grant (CDBG) funds, ultimately would contribute $2 million by 2001 and another $500,000 in 2002. The FilCom Center would also receive funds from the state government and federal agencies. In May 2000, Governor Benjamin Cayetano approved the release of $1.5 million appropriated by the state legislature for the construction of the FilCom Center. In October 2000, the U.S. Department of Commerce's Economic Development Administration approved a $1.125 million grant, and a VA/HUD grant of $800,000 was awarded to the FilCom Center. In addition, the U.S. Department of Agriculture committed to a $5 million loan guarantee to the Center. The Center would also receive a $3 million donation from the Harry and Jeanette Weinberg Foundation and $500,000 from the Consuelo Zobel Alger Foundation. By the time of the grand opening, more than $14 million had been raised, including more than $1.3 million in pledges from thousands of individuals and families, and the Center's goal of opening the facility debt-free was achieved and "an impossible dream had come true."

Vignette #2—Inside the Courtyard: "A Dream Come True"

Inside the uncovered courtyard, the midday sun blazes, even hotter than when we were outside the gates. Paper lanterns drape across the width of the courtyard. This scene propels me back to my early childhood in the Philippines, to the town plaza during festival time. There are rows of chairs in the sun, but few can tolerate the direct rays. Several individuals with camcorders brave the heat, using programs and handkerchiefs to fan themselves. It seems like some of the dignitaries are starting to wilt in the heat, losing a bit of their luster as they watch the festivities. There are hundreds of people jammed into the courtyard's perimeter, seeking shade and relief from the heat. Only a few chairs are arranged in this area, the majority of which are occupied by older women and some of the World War II veterans. The cramped crowd standing in the breezeways has actually generated more heat, and it is difficult to view the on-going program in the courtyard.

The *bahay kubo* has been set down at the front right corner of the courtyard, next to an educational exhibit on the life and significance of José Rizal,[2] the national hero of the Philippines. A podium is centered in the courtyard. This is where the speeches and cultural performances take place. In the background lies a clear view of the town of Waipahu and Pearl Harbor.

The opening festivities had four main parts: (1) the *maile lei* untying ceremony; (2) the singing of the Philippine and United States national anthems; (3) the opening remarks, acknowledgments, and speeches by Casamina,

Figure 15. A view from inside the courtyard during the grand opening ceremony, photo taken by author.

Flores, and members of the Filipino Caucus in the Hawai'i State Legislature; and (4) the cultural show/ethnic spectacle and extravaganza. Before all the opening remarks, acknowledgments, and speeches, young Filipino American children (who appear to range in age from six to thirteen) dressed in traditional Filipino attire perform a traditional Philippine dance called *putong*. Traditionally, the *putong* is a crowning ceremony that is performed to mark festival queens or princesses. It is a Christianity-based ceremony, modeled after the crowning of Jesus, and usually involves flowers. In this case, the

Figure 16. The beginning of the *putong* ceremony, photo taken by author.

putong has been adapted. Instead of flowers, red, white, and blue origami paper star *lei* are used. At the end of the performance, the children present the paper *lei* to the FilCom Center Board of Governors and Directors and to other dignitaries.

The *putong* ceremony is rife with symbolism. The obvious symbols are of American patriotism, a nod to Native Hawaiian host culture (via the *lei*) and the children as the future of Americans of Filipino ancestry. The children and their costumes are an embodiment and a reminder of U.S. colonialism in the Philippines and U.S. colonialism in Hawai'i, which provided the conditions of Filipino immigration to the islands. The red, white, and blue star *lei* simultaneously elides and showcases the contemporary reality of Hawai'i as American military colony and tourist playground. The young performers also wear the red, white, and blue on top of their traditional Philippine costumes. It is the melding of Hawai'i as the United States and the Philippines in uniform. In Hawai'i tourist culture, a *lei* is presented to welcome visitors. In this case, the presentation of *lei* is a sign of gratitude, an acknowledgment of benevolence, and an assurance of assimilation. And foremost, the *putong* triumphantly proclaims that "we, as Filipino, like the Japanese, have arrived." In this way, the *putong* is a performance of normativity, upholding the existing racial and class hierarchy and order. At the end of the performance, everyone cheers and applauds loudly.

Figure 17. The end of the *putong* ceremony, photo taken by author.

Filipino "Success" and the Making of "Ethnic Heroes"

At the time of the FilCom's grand opening ceremonies, Filipinos were perceived to be a largely "uneducated" group of low-wage, low-status workers who cleaned hotel rooms and yards. Eisen's recent study (2011) suggests that these images remain in wide circulation among Filipinos and non-Filipinos, resulting in lack of access to social and economic capital for many local Filipinos. When the FilCom Center opened, the U.S. Census revealed that the majority of Filipinos in Hawai'i (race alone or in combination, twenty-five years and over) had a high school diploma or equivalency or less at 58.4 percent, compared to 37.9 percent for Japanese (alone or in combination, twenty-five years and over) and 14.0 percent for whites (alone or in combination, twenty-five years and over). In addition, 26.4 percent of the local Filipino population had some college or an associate's degree, compared to 27.4 percent for Japanese and 32.6 percent for whites. Lastly, 12.5 percent of the local Filipinos held a bachelor's degree, compared to 25.6 percent for Japanese and 21.1 percent for whites, while only 2.8 percent of Filipinos had graduate or professional degrees, compared to 9.3 percent for Japanese and 14.0 percent for whites. In terms of employment, Filipinos were overrepresented in service and sales and office occupations, 28.9 percent and 27.9 percent respectively, compared to 14.1 percent and 34.1 percent for Japanese and 20.4 percent and 25.0 percent for whites. Filipinos, however, were underrepresented in managerial, professional, and related occupations at 19.3 percent while Japanese were 38.4 percent and whites 39.0 percent. With respect to income, although Filipinos compared favorably to Japanese and whites in median household income and mean household earners (perhaps owing in large part to bigger Filipino households with multiple income earners, often with more than one occupation) they lagged behind in median family income ($59,754 compared to $76,381 for Japanese and $62,657 for whites) and per-capita income ($16,132 compared to $27,112 for Japanese and $26,762 for whites). These educational, occupational, and income statistics firmly position Filipinos at the bottom of Hawai'i's socioeconomic ladder, and those who helped to construct the FilCom Center sought to seize the symbolic as part of efforts to overcome these demographics. Integral to seizing the symbolic was to represent Filipinos in the media who had "made it" (despite the contrary demographic evidence for the vast majority of Filipinos), an identity claim in which they can now be considered equals to mainstream Local Asians, particularly the "model minority" Japanese, Okinawans, and Chinese who all have their own community or cultural centers and have undergone similar processes of fighting disadvantage, and have eventually realized immigrant dreams of middle-class prosperity, privilege, and status.

The media coverage of the FilCom Center, in the mainstream and Filipino newspapers as well as television and radio, overwhelmingly focused on the Center's two primary figureheads, Roland Casamina and Eddie Flores Jr., the president and executive vice president of the FilCom Center, respectively. It seemed like every news story, whether in the newspapers or on television, involved Casamina and Flores. In addition, my interviewees told me that the amount of media coverage they received was more than justified and that the Center would not have been built without these two men. As a whole, the stories about Casamina and Flores, in what was reported by the media and told to me from my interviews, depict a rags-to-riches "morality tale." They are the prototype of Filipino enterprise and entrepreneurship. The two men are portrayed as the Hawai'i Filipino equivalents to Horatio Alger. Like other Filipinos in Hawai'i, they started at the bottom but through their hard work, determination, industry, and perseverance, they were able pull themselves up by their own bootstraps.

Roland Casamina immigrated to Hawai'i more than thirty years ago. In 1968, his parents arrived first in Honolulu from Ilocos Sur, a rural province in the northern part of the Philippines, a region from which many earlier Filipino agricultural workers emigrated. Casamina and his three siblings arrived in Honolulu soon thereafter. According to *Midweek,* a local weekly publication, as a teenager while still in high school he cleaned yards on the weekends. In 1972, Casamina graduated from Farrington High School, a local institution located in a predominantly low-income, immigrant Filipino, and working-poor Filipino neighborhood known more for its poverty, high crime, and juvenile delinquency than academic achievement. And to save enough money to attend the University of Hawai'i, he worked as a janitor at the Honolulu airport and bussed tables in Waikiki. Casamina later obtained a bachelor's degree in business administration from the University of Hawai'i. In his early twenties, through his thrift, hard work, and determination, he became the youngest branch manager at International Savings & Loan. In addition, he was able to purchase his first house and start and own his own business, House of Finance, where he is president and CEO. He also serves on the Board of Directors for the Hawaii Financial Services Association. For the next ten years, Casamina would serve as the president of The Filipino Community Center, Inc.

Eddie Flores Jr. immigrated to Hawai'i in the 1960s with his parents and his six siblings when he was sixteen. He initially lived in Liliha, near the same neighborhood as Casamina's. Flores attended the University of Hawai'i and received a bachelor's degree in business administration. He later attended the University of Oklahoma, where he received his master's degree in liberal studies. He has taught courses on real estate, investments, management, travel, and business appraisal throughout the University of Hawai'i system. For more than ten years, Flores served as the executive vice president of The Filipino Community Center, Inc. He is also the president of the ubiquitous and popular L & L Drive-Inn and L & L Hawaiian Barbecue (as it is known outside Hawai'i). In Hawai'i, L & L Drive-Inn is the franchise equivalent to McDonalds, a fast-food restaurant chain that specializes in affordable plate lunches, the epitome of "Local" food. Since the opening of the first restaurant in 1976, the business rapidly expanded, with approximately two hundred locations in Hawai'i, the continental United States (in California, Oregon, Washington, Arizona, Colorado, Nevada, Utah, Texas, and New York), the Pacific (American Samoa and New Zealand), and Asia (Japan).

Although the paths of Casamina and Flores were slightly different, together they constitute the following form of and model for the Filipino success myth: third-world conditions in the Philippines have made life difficult, and there was a tremendous lack of economic opportunities. American colonialism via the educational system instills in the Filipino a colonial mentality in which he or she regards all things Filipino inferior to all things American. Thus, his "miseducation" (Constantino 1987) leads him to courageously cross the Pacific in pursuit of the American Dream and the American promise of freedom, opportunity, and equality. Upon arrival, our Filipino hero encounters prejudice, discrimination, and racism. However, his unfaltering belief in the American Dream pushes him to work hard, resist, and explain the oppression he faces as merely an inevitable part of the path to progress. Eventually, despite the uphill struggle and the unchanging structures of inequality, his children but mostly likely his grandchildren will fulfill the dream and succeed in American society. The overall moral of the story is that hard work, industriousness, thrift, and sacrifice will be eventually rewarded and redeemed.

In effect, the success stories of Casamina and Flores make them into the quintessential Filipino "ethnic heroes" and "model minorities" (see Okamura 2008). Although the individual achievements of Casamina and Flores should be applauded, these stories are set up as the prototype for achievement, success, and upward socioeconomic mobility; they narrate the path of class mobility and the possibility of achieving mainstream, middle-class status. These success stories are founded on immigrant dreams of prosperity and demands for full social, political, and economic participation in Hawai'i (and by extension, American society). Interestingly enough, the initial leadership of the FilCom Center is almost entirely composed of first-generation Filipino professionals affiliated with the Filipino Chamber of Commerce of Hawai'i and not directly connected to the earlier waves of immigrant Filipino agricultural workers. These success stories reflect the personal achievement and a collective wish to emerge out of the margins and climb into the mainstream. In a moralistic way, these success stories also serve as the model that the supposedly underachieving, hardly working, and socially immobile young Filipinos are to follow. Like in other myths of immigrant and ethnic success, the story constructs mobility as an individual process detached from material conditions and societal structures. In other words, success is achieved through individual effort, motivation, and aspirations and is disconnected from sociopolitical circumstances (that is, no racism or institutional discrimination).

In addition, the story of Casamina and Flores is an attempt to redefine and reclaim what it means to be Filipino. The stories suggest a potential shift in the image of Filipinos from working-class or working poor (that is, laborers formerly in agribusiness and currently in the tourism, service, and retail industries) to Filipinos as middle class (that is, the Filipino as professional, specifically as entrepreneur). As the *Honolulu Advertiser* stated in an editorial: "Indeed the three-story center is a tribute to Filipino resilience and entrepreneurship" (June 12, 2002). This shift in definition and image is

Figure 18. One of the long arcades that flank the interior and exterior walls. This corridor includes the entrance to the Casamina-Flores Ballroom, photo courtesy of Took HNLA.

a move that can possibly secure for Filipinos a rightful and a central place in Hawai'i's multicultural order.

The ideologies of self-help (Kelley 1997), self-sufficiency, and self-reliance are integral components of these Filipino success stories as well as to the underlying mission of the FilCom Center. Through the examples of Casamina and Flores, Filipino progress and mobility is achieved through enterprise and the promotion of Filipino business. In addition, a key part and fundamental rationale for the Center was its expected lead role in the economic revitalization efforts not only in the Waipahu community (a key economic player to the neighborhood's Special Area Plan) but also throughout the state. As then-U.S. Congressman and now Governor Neil Abercrombie stated in a letter of congratulations to the FilCom Center, the economic potential of the Center ranges from "helping individuals realize their dreams to stimulating the economy of the community and the states with its many activities and programs." One such activity supported by the FilCom Center is the Hanapbuhay-Hawai'i program, a training workshop cosponsored with Hawai'i's Small Business Development Center Network. *Hanapbuhay*, in Tagalog, generally means "livelihood" or "means of living" but can also refer to "occupation" or "employment." The Hanapbuhay-Hawai'i program specifically targets "aspiring entrepreneurs" and so in this case, *hanapbuhay* also refers to "business." The program includes a micro-enterprise workshop called "How to Start a Really Small Business" that has a specific goal "to encourage immigrants to be more entrepreneurial." The program follows the success stories of Casamina and Flores by focusing on Filipino entrepreneurship and encouraging Filipinos, particularly immigrant Filipinos, to start their own small businesses.

Along the same lines, the first-ever Philippines-Hawai'i Import/Export Trade Expo was held as part of the grand opening ceremonies at the FilCom Center. The Bank of Hawai'i and the City and County of Honolulu sponsored the three-day event, in collaboration with the Philippine Consulate of Hawai'i, Filipino Chamber of Commerce of Hawai'i, and the FilCom Center, Inc. The primary goal of the Import/Export Trade Expo was to strengthen trade relations between Hawai'i (and the United States) and the Philippines as well as to showcase products and services from the Philippines (many of the exhibitors were businesses from the Philippines whose primary products were foodstuffs, textiles, and arts and crafts). The expo provided opportunities for local and Philippine-based entrepreneurs and businesses to network. A central component of the Import/Export Trade Expo was a two-part, one-day seminar called "Doing Business in Hawai'i" and "Doing Business in the Philippines." Essentially, the seminar provided logistical and legislative information (for example, relevant laws and business trends) for

Figure 19. View of the wooden ceiling and metal chandelier at the Waipahu Street end of the Consuelo Zobel Alger Courtyard, photo courtesy of Took HNLA.

enabling and encouraging capitalist ventures in Hawai'i and the Philippines. Like the Hanapbuhay-Hawai'i program, the Philippines-Hawai'i Import/ Export Trade Expo focused on self-help and the creation of Filipino business as the most effective means for community social, political, and economic empowerment. It is hoped that the benefits of FilCom Center–sponsored business will gradually spread to the rest of the Filipino community and the broader Hawai'i population, fulfilling what Rose Churma, the former interim executive director of the Center, states is part of the Center's mission to "revitalize our blighted neighborhoods and eliminate slums and blight, create meaningful employment and provide services to those less fortunate than us" (*Fil-Am Courier,* June 1–15, 2002). Thus continuing with the epidemiological metaphor used by Churma, self-help through entrepreneurship is understood as a fundamental basis for community self-medication.

A Filipino "Coming of Age" in Hawai'i and the "New Filipino"

For many in the local community, the successful completion of the FilCom Center is often told as a story of the "arrival" and the "coming of age" of the Filipino community as a political and economic force in the islands; it is a settler Filipino narrative of development. Ideologies and narratives of development often characterize peoples, cultures, or political movements using the un/developed and im/mature binaries. Fujikane notes that developmental narratives are especially troubling for minority groups: "Accounts of development have proved to be particularly dangerous for minority or colonized peoples, who are often assigned to the infantilized, 'immature' end of a developmental narrative that privileges the 'maturity' of the dominant or colonizing group. Such narratives of development have often been utilized in 'civilizing' missions serving colonial purposes, and colonized peoples are expected to forsake their own cultures and histories in order to conform to the colonizer's definition of 'maturity'" (Fujikane 1997: 43). The successful completion of the FilCom Center represents a Filipino "coming of age," and "political maturation" exemplifies a developmental narrative. In this regard, using the trope of redemption and underscored by the ideals of ethnic success, Caroline Ahn in an article in the *Hawaii Filipino Chronicle* wrote: "The Filipino community in Hawaii can now celebrate a coming of age in Hawaii with the completion of the long awaited Filipino Community Center, often referred to as the FilCom Center. The FilCom Center is much more than a gathering place for the community, it's the building of a dream with hard work and dedication that finally become a reality. After nearly fifty years, a long cherished goal has finally reached fruition and can now be looked upon as a symbol of what the Filipino peoples' dedication and perseverance can accomplish." Similarly, before the grand opening of the Center, the editor of the *Hawaii Filipino Chronicle* proudly proclaimed, "Although the Center may represent different meanings to different people, to us it symbolizes the crowning glory of Filipinos' achievements in Hawaii's rich history. It represents the 'coming of age' of Filipinos" (June 1, 2002). According to the accounts, the history of Filipinos in Hawai'i follows a linear, developmental path from a lower to a higher stage of social, political, and economic progress and "maturity." Echoing this view and perhaps stating it even more pointedly, Casamina told the *Honolulu Star-Bulletin*: "We have been at the bottom of the economic social ladder for many years. This is a symbol of our success" (June 6, 2002). Thus, the FilCom Center itself symbolizes a collective success story and serves as an assertion of economic and political advancement. The Center's success story declares that Filipinos have ascended from the lower rungs of Hawai'i society and can now lay claim to economic and political power and active participation in island politics. As Belinda Aquino, a professor at the University of Hawai'i and then-director of the Center for Philippine Studies has written, the FilCom Center "should be seen in the context of a maturing political community able to participate more fully in the life of the state" (*Fil-Am Courier,* June 1–15, 2002).

The Filipino political and economic "coming of age" is also reflected in the ways in which individual, community, state, and federal resources were mobilized in the making of the FilCom Center. In this regard, the *Hawaii Filipino Chronicle* wrote, "The many years of planning and fundraising finally paid off for the Filipino Community that first settled in Hawaii close to a hundred years ago. The achievement of the FilCom Center signaled the arrival of the Filipino people as a group with clout. The magnitude of such a project required political and economic influence to raise millions of dollars, as well as possess a high level of technical 'know-how' to get much of the work in *gratis*" (January 1, 2003).

According to popular perception, key to the "achievement of the FilCom Center" were the types of Filipinos involved in its making. Casamina explained to *Midweek* that the earlier failed attempts to build a community center were caused by past organizational problems within the Filipino community and "the members' lack of maturity in the community." He further stated: "The Filipinos then, compared to now, were much more different," noting that the Filipinos of the past were laborers and the Filipinos of the present "are better educated and have better jobs with more freedom and resources" (April 19, 2000). Again, we see it is a "new breed" of Filipinos, "more mature" and more self-reliant than their working-class predecessors, who are responsible for Filipinos finally "making it." From the bottom of Hawai'i society and through the FilCom Center, a different sort of Filipino has emerged.

The new breed of Filipino is politically sophisticated, a "power player" and leader in Hawai'i society. Prior to the grand opening of the Center, Rose Churma asked, "How could the Filipino community of Hawaii pull off something like this? Some say it is due to a 'new' type of leadership, that we've grown more politically savvy, more sophisticated to the ways of this country. Maybe it is due to all that, and more" (*Fil-Am Courier,* June 1–15, 2002). In this way, we see that Filipinos have assimilated "to the ways of this country" and the leadership has become more politically involved. According to Raymund Liongson, a professor at Leeward Community College (located in Waipahu): "The FilCom Center is itself a political assertion: that the Filipinos in Hawaii are a people who have the capacity to muster a socio-political base. . . . [Unlike previous generations] [t]his generation of Filipinos is more politically aware and involved. They constantly talk about political empowerment. We have Filipinos occupying significant government positions in the executive, legislative, and judicial branches. More and more

Filipinos are getting involved in political races" (*Hawaii Filipino Chronicle Mabuhay Festival Supplement*, June 1, 2002).

In addition to individual political participation, Belinda Aquino also highlights the "sophistication" and positive personal characteristics of the "new Filipino leadership" in the following way: "a definitive element is the increasing sophistication of leadership in Filipino communities in America today, i.e. one propelled by ideas rather personalities, long-term vision rather than short-run goals, deeds, rather than words. In short, a leadership that cuts through the barriers posed by traditional hesitation or defeatism. The observation was then made that the present generation of Filipinos in America, both immigrant and local, is probably much more enterprising, much less conservative, less risk-averse, and much more astute in its understanding of social and political reality than its predecessors" (*Fil-Am Courier,* June 1–15, 2002).

The explanations and descriptions offered by Churma, Liongson, and Aquino are founded on perceived binary oppositions and underscored by moralizing overtones. In a rather Manichean fashion, strict distinctions are drawn between what are understood to be conflicting and divergent views of the old and new Filipinos. In addition, Churma, Liongson, and Aquino provide a linear and evolutionary historicizing of the Filipino community in which the old, uneducated, unrefined, politically immature, and socioeconomically marginal Filipinos are now being substituted with the new, educated, sophisticated, politically shrewd, and socioeconomically mainstream Filipinos. This historicization often has a polarizing effect and potentially sets up the "old" as deficient and deprived, the alterity against which the new and improved are measured, and glosses over the long history of Filipino worker resistance and union participation. Furthermore, in the temporal unfolding of this history, the sacrifices and struggles faced by the "old" are redeemed by the "new," an important part of the procession to an inevitable closure that fulfills the desire for an equal position for Filipinos in multicultural Hawai'i.

In his opening speech at the FilCom Center grand opening ceremony, Eddie Flores Jr. fully captured this narrative of redemption and the Filipino "coming of age" story. In the speech, he compared the history of the FilCom Center with the history of the *sakadas*, remarking that the trials and tribulations the sakadas encountered paralleled the difficulties the Center faced in getting off the ground and eventually becoming a reality. Flores proclaimed, "The center is a symbol of Filipino achievement. We are no longer second-class citizens." He went on to say, "Who would have thought that Filipinos would have the business sense and know-how? No one believed in us. The

Center is not just for Filipinos, but for all of Hawai'i nei." Flores's brief opening remarks are particularly instructive. They touch on several themes that are central to the FilCom Center narrative. First, there is the tribute to the *sakada* generation, highlighting their hard work and sacrifice. Second, his remarks speak to the history of Filipino subordination in Hawai'i and their collective marginalization as second-class citizens. The story that Flores tells in his opening remarks and the overall FilCom Center narrative is one of success and redemption. Narratives of immigrant success become problematic when positioned within the context of Native displacement and dispossession: "antiracist projects that celebrate an American nationality must be rethought, for the grim reality of that U.S. citizenship and 'success' as a good citizen is contingent upon the success of U.S. settler colonization of indigenous people" (Saranillio 2008: 265). In Hawai'i, the narrative of immigrant success points to the transformation of the island society from a white racial plantation oligarchy to a multicultural state where power is shared among the various settler groups. In this regard, Fujikane notes, "Asian political and economic 'successes' in Hawai'i have been represented as evidence of Hawai'i's exceptionalism as a multicultural state, proof that Asians have been able to overcome the racist treatment and policies of the American sugar planters to form what several scholars have described as 'harmonious multiculturalism' " (Fujikane 2008: 3). To a large extent, the immigrant success story celebrated by the FilCom Center validates and justifies contemporary Asian settler colonial power that rests on and was built on top of U.S. settler colonialism.

The FilCom Center narrative of success is coupled with a narrative of redemption. The hard work and subjugation the *sakadas* faced are now redeemed by a new generation of Filipinos, entrepreneurs with the proper "business sense and know-how"; it is deferred gratification par excellence. This narrative structure is part of the need to create a historical continuity between the multiplicity of Filipino histories and identities. This orientation to history is not so much a nostalgic remembering of an idealized *sakada* past but a re-valuation and re-presentation of "the *sakada* story" used to construct a metaphorical genealogy. The connection to the past enables the desired present where Filipinos are no longer marginalized and "no longer second-class citizens." Filipinos can now claim incorporation into the mainstream and a place in Hawai'i nei (the land of Hawai'i). Flores's use of the Hawaiian *nei* indicates a symbolic and settler appropriation of Hawai'i as "home" which marks a "Local" (that is to say, no longer from the perspective of an immigrant/sojourner but that of a settler) claim to place and belonging. For Flores, Filipinos can now take their place in the multicultural fabric of the islands as one of the colors of Hawai'i's racial and ethnic rainbow. As a FilCom Center board member told me, "The Center is the most public and tangible proof of Filipino success and achievement. The FilCom Center is the clearest and most visible way to say to the non-Filipino community to take us seriously." Thus, the FilCom Center can be understood as a call for social, political, and economic recognition and incorporation as well as a challenge to Hawai'i society to uphold its ideal of racial equality and maintain the settler, multicultural order. The narrative attempts to disrupt the image of Filipinos for the purpose of crossing the social boundaries that have historically excluded them from the mainstream and from full participation in island social, political, and economic life; it is a claim for inclusion via incorporation. The FilCom Center's logic of incorporation illustrates an intertwined doubleness: assimilation styled after Robert Park race-relations cycle and class mobility through business and entrepreneurship. The FilCom Center plotline effectively recasts Filipinos as main characters in the broader Hawai'i settler story.

In this chapter, I have suggested that the FilCom Center, in its promotion of ethnic heroes, success stories, and "coming of age" story, participates in a Filipino cultural politics of representation that retells a settler colonial narrative. The FilCom Center story is simultaneously an attempt to privilege

Figure 20. View of the Consuelo Zobel Alger Courtyard, exhibit room, classroom, and belfry, photo courtesy of Took HNLA.

specific symbols and narratives of Filipino identity and to make political and economic claims on behalf of Filipinos in Hawai'i. The construction of the FilCom Center can be understood as a middle-class project that campaigns for the assimilation of Filipinos into mainstream Hawai'i society. The FilCom Center supports a claim for Filipinos as "Local." Okamura (1983) has suggested that a nested hierarchy of relational alterities and structural oppositions underscore the assertion of "Local" identity. Fujikane (1997) further suggests that "Local" is a problematic relationship and commitment to Hawai'i: "locals who claim Hawai'i as *home* often do not understand Native Hawaiian nationalists who claim Hawai'i as *homeland,* and as non-Hawaiian locals, we need to ask ourselves what our commitment to Hawai'i and its peoples really means (Fujikane 1997: 43, emphasis in original). As such, competing claims to Hawai'i as home/land by settlers and natives are fraught with issues of power and representation.

The FilCom Center narrative expresses a desire for social, political, and economic integration into mainstream Hawai'i society. By affirming a "Local" identity or becoming "Local" in the mainstream sense, the FilCom Center claims a place for Filipinos as equals among the other racial and ethnic groups in multicultural Hawai'i. Okamura explains the lure and danger of a multiculturalist ideology in the following way: "Despite its liberal rhetoric of tolerance, acceptance, and equality of opportunity, multiculturalism in Hawai'i represents an argument for the stability and continuation of the status quo rather than for substantial change in the current structure of race and ethnic relations" (Okamura 1994: 21). In the end, the making of the FilCom Center is part of the never-ending pursuit of the American Dream, what Zachary Labez calls the "quest for a fair share of the proverbial pie in [the] 'Land of Immigrants'" (*Fil-Am Courier,* June 1–15, 2001).[3] In this "quest for a fair share," the racial hierarchies in the settler colonial state are reinforced, while the colonization of Native Hawaiians continues. Along these lines, Saranillio notes that the politics of community empowerment resists racialized labor exploitation but is blind to indigenous struggles for sovereignty: "our quest for our 'share of the proverbial American pie,' becomes oppressive because the American political and economic system relies on denying Native Hawaiians their right to self-determination" (Saranillio 2008: 267). How then can Filipinos organize for community empowerment without being complicit with the continued colonization and dispossession of Native Hawaiians?

Unsettling Hawai'i

In the November 2002 gubernatorial election, Republican candidate Linda Lingle, a former mayor of Maui County, soundly defeated Lieutenant Governor Mazie Hirono. Lingle's victory was particularly significant because not only was she the first woman governor of the state of Hawai'i, she was also the first Republican governor elected since statehood in 1959. Since the "Democratic Revolution" in 1954, the Democratic Party has dominated state politics and continues to hold the majority in the state senate and House of Representatives. Although the election of Linda Lingle signaled a potential shift in the islands' political environment, the governor's race itself demonstrated the workings of traditional racial and ethnic politics and highlighted the growing importance of Filipinos in the political and economic lives of the islands.

Like in the past two governor's races, throughout the campaign the Filipino community was projected to play a crucial role in determining the election results. In fact, local newspaper and television polls indicated that undecided Filipino voters were key to the outcome. As in the past two gubernatorial elections, Filipinos were viewed as the all-important swing vote. However, unlike the two previous elections in which Filipinos supported the Filipino American candidate, Benjamin Cayetano, Filipinos were largely undecided in 2002. It seemed as if even up until Election Day, both candidates were courting Filipino voters.

Because of their working-class history and their close relationship to the labor unions, Filipinos traditionally have been strong supporters of the Democratic Party. In addition, the two predominantly Filipino neighborhoods on O'ahu, Kalihi and Waipahu, are traditional Democratic strongholds. Conventional wisdom would suggest that because of the race's closeness, Filipinos would rally behind the Democratic candidate. However, just weeks prior to Election Day, there was major concern that Filipinos were going to break tradition and vote Republican. This concern developed even earlier when Eddie Flores Jr., then the executive vice president and chair of the Filipino Community Center, Inc., decided to endorse the Republican candidate. Prior to his endorsement of Linda Lingle, Flores historically supported Democratic candidates, particularly former Governor Benjamin Cayetano and former Honolulu Mayor Jeremy Harris (who was the 2002 Democratic front-runner for the governor's race before bowing out amid political and financial scandals). Because Flores was closely associated with the Filipino Community Center and had served as the primary Filipino public figure, his individual support for Lingle was seen as representative of the Filipino vote. In addition, Flores was an active supporter of the Lingle campaign, helping to organize huge rallies in Kalihi and Waipahu that involved extravagant door prizes (like free trips to the Philippines and Las Vegas). These rallies further demonstrated a strong base of support for the Republican ticket but also created a stir in the Filipino community and among the Filipino Caucus of Hawai'i's Democrats, many of whom were members of the Filipino Chamber of Commerce of Hawai'i and strong supporters of the Filipino Community Center, Inc.

In response to the rallies and to Flores's support for the Republican candidate, members of the Filipino Caucus of Hawai'i's Democrats organized a press conference in which they denounced the rallies as a ploy to buy Filipino votes and stressed the need to vote Democrat. Besides saying that Filipinos could not be bought, there were subtle reminders that it was the Democratic Party that helped to secure resources to build the Filipino Community Center in Waipahu, and it was because of Democratic leadership and support that Hawai'i was able elect the first Filipino American governor in the United States (and even earlier, have the first Filipino American as a justice in the State of Hawai'i Supreme Court). Further, the press conference reiterated the Democratic Party's commitment to immigrant issues, social equality, and social justice. In contrast, Flores told the *Honolulu Advertiser,* "Filipinos in Hawai'i are going to vote for the candidate that can offer us a future." Essentially, Flores was making a break with the past, symbolized by the loyalty to the Democratic Party and its commitment to the working class, the labor unions, and the plantation era, which suggested a reformulation of how Filipino identity is understood and practiced.

One of the net effects of the gubernatorial campaign was the reinscription of the image of Filipinos as a divided community. There was a reemergence of "Filipino disunity," a community with leaders who cannot agree politically. It seemed as if this was a substantiation of the incessant fears of community fragmentation, disabling hard-fought and hard-earned alliances and coalitions by revealing a lack of unity, a divided political front. But instead of the traditional divisions of culture and language, it was politics and class that surfaced as points of contention.

Like many Filipinos on O'ahu, Andy Tabangcura was especially excited about the possibility of having a community center for Filipinos. As someone born in the 1940s, he remembers the various attempts at building a center since the 1950s. He tells me that although there was already a smaller Filipino center built by Visayans, "people have been talking and dreaming about building a bigger community center for decades." Tabangcura was very hopeful that the "business guys could get it done" (he was referring to Roland Casamina, Eddie Flores Jr., and rest of the members of the Filipino Chamber of Commerce). He rejoiced in the completion of the Filipino Community Center. During the grand opening ceremony in 2002, he whispered to me, "They did it. The dream came true." During the gubernatorial campaign later that year, his joy had turned to disappointment. He lamented, "It took the FilCom Center years and a lot of hard work to unite the community. And it took a matter of days to divide us back up again." Tabangcura asked somewhat rhetorically, "How are we supposed to build community?" He paused, and as if to answer his own question he shrugged and bemoaned, "I guess the building wasn't enough. We're back to where we started. Divided."

Beyond the idea of a divided community, the governor's race also called attention to what it means to be Filipino in Hawai'i. Does "Filipino" mean working class, as the Democrats suggested, or probusiness and entrepreneurial, as indicated in Flores's support for the Republicans? Was Flores a legitimate and representative voice of the local Filipino community? Whose and what interests did Republicans represent and would Flores's break with traditional political loyalties encourage a rethinking of what it means to be Filipino in Hawai'i? Would Flores's support for the Republicans translate into increased access to political and economic power for the broader Filipino community and facilitate the mainstreaming of Filipinos? These questions point to a Filipino cultural politics of representation in terms of which symbols of Filipino identity are privileged and how they are used in struggles for power. These questions also suggest the need to recognize the constructedness and heterogeneity of the "Filipino" identity category, as opposed to a commonly misrecognized homogeneity that excludes and eradicates differences on behalf of a common collective political struggle.

I began this book with a relatively simple and general question: "What does it mean to be Filipino in Hawai'i?" Asking the question has required examining the history of Hawai'i, from precapitalist society to the confrontation with Westerners and other settlers, to colonization and incorporation into the capitalist world economy (via the sugar industry), to the contemporary period dominated by a tourism-driven economy and Native Hawaiian struggles for sovereignty amid the political symbol and ideal of multiculturalism. This study has also drawn attention to how we understand identity in the current late capitalist, transnational world. When we ask, "Who is Filipino?" and "What is Filipino?" the discussion often begins with an examination of the articulations about the content and borders of the identity category that is founded on invented, imagined, and imposed linguistic and cultural commonalities. Although a singular, monolithic "Filipino" or "Filipino American" identity is often presupposed and sought after, it is also observed that Filipinos are internally differentiated along lines of class, language, religion, nationality, period of immigration, region, and so forth. In Hawai'i, there are "Local" Filipinos, "immigrant" Filipinos, and "mainland" Filipinos.

When we ask, "Who is Filipino?" and "What is Filipino?" the discussion must also turn toward discourses relating to political cartographic imagination and practices, that is to say, how identities are mapped out in terrains of struggle. In a political climate of racial and ethnic stratification and inequality, and where the state and its various agencies and institutions function as the principal arbiters of the distribution system, like that of Hawai'i and in the rest of the United States, politics have become racialized and ethnicized, which has fed the politicization of identity. In other words, political and economic antagonisms are being articulated in racial and ethnic ways and at the same time, race and ethnicity are encoded in the political economy. In this context, race and/or ethnicity serve as a rallying point in struggles over communal entitlements and privileges amid asymmetrical relations of power. It is a political game in which the state provides the conditions that enable the politicization and legitimization of race and ethnicity. Racial and ethnic groups (and the boundaries associated with them) often begin as arbitrary state constructs, but nevertheless subscription to these state-assigned categories usually opens up points of entry into the political and economic system and lead to their naturalization.

As this book illustrates, "Filipino" has served and continues to function as a primary organizing principle for collective identification and political participation for persons of Filipino ancestry in Hawai'i. In this sense, ethnicity is not merely a cultural attachment but also acts as a basis of political identity and loyalty, serving as a political resource for collective action in a political system where strength is drawn from size, numbers, and money. The "Filipino" identity formation is thus understood as a situationally activated ethnic formation, a political resource for uniting diverse groups and mobilizing solidarity. The invocation of ethnicity, then, is often an appropriate and effective political strategy that involves processes of internal assertion (or self-identification) and external ethnoracial assignment (or categorization) (Brodkin 1998). Thus, we see that race and ethnicity serve as organizational strategies that respond to a community's needs in a racialized and ethnicized political system.

My investigation of Filipino identities has involved interrogating the processes of boundary construction and maintenance as well as how these identity formations are practiced politically. In short, I suggest that "Filipino" is a culture- and politics-based collective identity category that reveals a tension between its sociohistorical constructedness (and hence, its fundamental contestability) and the political need (as part of the efforts to disrupt existing systems and structures of domination) to stabilize its tenuous coherence and unity. Because identity categories are socially and politically constructed, each historical moment enables new (or emerging) constructs to be mediated. In this way, these identity consolidations can be understood as political positionings which can reinforce or displace the existing hierarchy and order.

The fundamental contestedness of "Filipino" underscores the situations, positions, and negotiations in the identity formation process, revealing not only the mobility of identities but also their motility.[1] Here, borrowing from biology, I understand motility as active and seemingly spontaneous movement. Focusing on motility highlights the actors' agency as a type of self-propulsion where actors produce and are produced by the context, which include power dynamics. The focus on motility also directs our attention on the gradients around which identity movements pivot. Traditional examples of identity gradients include race, ethnicity, gender, class, culture, and sexuality. My fieldwork demonstrates other types of gradients including language, speech community, place-based ideologies, and immigration generation. Further, movement along these identity gradients is not necessarily a conversation between two (or more) equal agents who are in opposition. Instead it is a multivocal conversation between agents who may or may not be diametrically opposed to one another. In other words, Filipino identity is an internally and externally contested reality, in which multiple definitions coexist and often challenge one another. There is often a privileged and dominant definition that enforces a particular understanding of Filipino-ness. The privileged understanding does not deny the existence of alternate interpretations of Filipino identity, but it demonstrates how an interpretation can dominate under specific conditions, in a particular time, place, and relations of power. Motility avoids predetermination or situational essentialism by suggesting that identities are negotiated along gradients of nonprescriptive oppositions. Motility embodies the shifting, relational, relative, situational, and negotiated reality of identities, suggesting that "Filipino" is not unitary and monolithic but instead involves a contested terrain of coexisting and often competing definitions, interpretations, and boundaries.

It has been ten years since the Filipino Community Center opened. Thus far, it has not become the "economic beacon of light" that now-Governor (and then-Congressman) Neil Abercrombie predicted. For many in the community, the Filipino Community Center is a place where graduation parties, wedding receptions, birthday parties, and similar events are held. The three-and-a-half-million-dollar construction loan needed to complete the center remains outstanding. This outstanding loan reflects the changing dynamics of the American Dream; home ownership is not what it used to be. The paths to upward socioeconomic mobility and immigrant success are not assured. Andy Tabangcura's question hangs in the air. The Filipino building has been built, but how do we now build community? Can the "Filipino home" capitalize on its assets, cash in on its equity, or will it undergo foreclosure?

The changes in demographics in the 2010 Census offered hope and optimism for many in the community. With Filipinos now Hawai'i's second-largest population group, would the "sleeping giant" finally awake and move up? At a recent political fundraiser, I asked an aspiring state legislator whether or not he thought Filipinos would finally become "equals in multicultural Hawai'i," especially in light of the numbers increase the census highlighted. He was cautiously optimistic: "Numbers don't mean anything unless we vote and elect people. Even then, that doesn't mean we have power." I asked him to explain further. He remarked that there were "plenty Filipinos in office" but "we don't move the political needle. No one asks us how high to jump." Later in the conversation, he talked about the need to create more alliances and to find connections with others. In other words, he was telling me that Filipinos still need to build community.

Andy Tabangcura's lamentation, "How do we build community?" points to the problematics of a politics of empowerment among Filipinos in Hawai'i. Saranillio has argued that the current Filipino "strategy of empowerment does not disrupt the colonial power structures oppressing Native Hawaiians and instead reinforces colonialism by making use of American patriotic narratives" (Saranillio quoted in Fujikane 2008: 9). Saranillio's argument raises several important questions about the politics of community and community empowerment. Are Filipinos in Hawai'i Asian settlers participating in the double colonialism of Hawai'i (Saranillio 2008)?[22] Trask explain the dynamics of Asian settler colonialism in the following way:

> Our Native people and territories have been overrun by non-Natives, including Asians. Calling themselves "local," the children of Asian settlers greatly outnum-

ber us. They claim Hawai'i as their own, denying indigenous history, their long collaboration in our continued dispossession, and the benefits therefrom. Part of this denial is the substitution of the term "local" for "immigrant," which is, itself, a particularly celebrated American gloss for "settler." As on the continent, so in our island home. Settlers and their children recast the American tale of nationhood: Hawai'i, like the continent, is naturalized as but another telling illustration of the uniqueness of America's "nation of immigrants" (Trask 2000: 2).

In Hawai'i, the settler colonial framework is dependent on a particular type of erasure and a recasting of the indigenous population: "the use of the term ['land of immigrants'] exposes a U.S. narrative that constructs a phantasmatic land with no indigenous people, vacant land where immigrants have settled to construct a 'modern' democratic society. Often implicit in such a narrative is the argument that indigenous peoples also are immigrants, that Native Hawaiians immigrated to Hawai'i some fifteen hundred years ago" (Saranillio 2008: 267). How then do migrant Filipino identity territorializations politically engage the Native Hawaiian sovereignty movement and struggles for indigenous rights? As I have discussed in this book, the Filipino history of labor exploitation and struggles for upward mobility are often framed within a problematic multiculturalist ideology. In other words, Filipino identity making in Hawai'i is constructed within the context of an illusion of a racial or multicultural paradise (Okamura 1998). Yet, multiculturalism in Hawai'i is rooted in U.S. colonialism and the exploitation of immigrant labor, with the conquest of Native Hawaiians (their displacement, dislocation, and population collapse) providing the conditions for the development of U.S. capitalism and the importation of Filipinos and other Asian immigrants as sources of cheap labor for Hawai'i agribusiness (and later, the tourism industry). The subjugation of Native Hawaiians and the oppression of Asian laborers is the foundation for the highly praised and oft-celebrated racial and ethnic diversity in Hawai'i. But as Saranillio warns, the false equivalences drawn in a multiculturalist ideology can effectively erase indigeneity; the exploitation of Asian labor is not the same as Native Hawaiian dispossession and the continuing U.S. occupation of Hawai'i. He notes, "While Filipino communities must continue to resist oppressive systems that perpetuate various inequalities, we must also be aware of the colonial structures ingrained in U.S. nationalism that render invisible the U.S. violation of Native Hawaiians' human rights to self-determination" (ibid., 257).

Is it then possible to relieve colonial amnesia and imagine cartographies of colonial violence against both natives and migrants that link Filipino struggles against marginalization in Hawai'i and the United States, Filipino decolonization and anti-imperialism in the Philippines to Native Hawaiian self-determination? San Juan suggests the possibility of a revolutionary internationalism that is attentive to indigenous struggles for sovereignty:

> With the tide of globalised capitalism sweeping over national boundaries, partisans of revolutionary hope need to lend support to the indigenous peoples of Hawaii and elsewhere in their struggle for sovereignty. Reason dictates the priority of self-determined locations for unique aboriginal cultures to flourish. Their singular forms of life remain the touchstones for realizing visions of popular, egalitarian democracy sustainable for constructing a global ecumene (San Juan 2002: 78).

As San Juan suggests, there must be a migrant engagement with indigeneity. To engage indigeneity is to confront the operations of U.S. empire and race as well as our sense of self and place, while working toward social justice and paving paths to our collective liberation. Engaging indigeneity seeks connectedness without drawing false equivalences in search of commonalities. Engaging indigeneity points to the processes and dynamics of larger-scale identity consolidations, and the way their constructedness and contestedness are embedded in historical, social, political, and economic specificities. In the islands, engaging indigeneity challenges images of Hawai'i as "tropical paradise" (a global tourist destination) and as "racial paradise" ("the melting pot in the Pacific"), and instead shifts the view of the islands as a U.S. militarized zone (an occupied Hawaiian nation), a settler colony (including settlers of Asian ancestry) founded on ideologies of white supremacy and fantasies of multiculturalism, and as a site of active indigenous resistance and opposition against U.S. empire. Engaging indigeneity requires centralizing the experiences of Native Hawaiians, the histories of Hawai'i (the *'āina*) and its people, and the history of U.S. empire.

In the end, Filipino struggles for empowerment and resistance against marginalization must challenge the logic of incorporation, an "assimilative politics" (San Juan 2009) that seeks entry into the islands "multicultural paradise." Filipino struggles must also be a diasporic politics that attend to struggles not only in the islands but also in the continental United States, the dozens of countries Filipino labor is being exploited as well as the national popular democracy movement in the Philippines. In this way, Filipino migrant "home"-making need not be a "home"-invasion. It is possible to seek migrant empowerment outside the dominant confines of a Hawai'i multicultural utopia that transforms the current settler colonial relations, not simply in the service of the status quo but to achieve a liberatory politics that can reconcile the problematic polarities of human rights/civil rights, the international/national, and settler/indigenous. This is the struggle that continues and where we need to build.

NOTES

Introduction. "Why do you want to go Hawai'i?"

1. This corresponds to Catherine Ceniza Choy's work that examines the interrelatedness of U.S. colonialism, nursing, migration, and the racialization of Filipinos. See her *Empire of Care: Nursing and Migration in Filipino American History*.

2. I have chosen the states with the highest number of people of Filipino descent according to the 2010 Census.

3. Following standard practice, I use the *'okina* (or glottal stop) whenever appropriate, as in "Hawai'i," unless the word appears in a quote or name where it is absent. Also in some cases, I do not use the *'okina* in English-language–derived words, like "Hawaiian."

4. For early work on "the racial melting-pot of the Pacific," see Adams (1937), Lind (1938), and Park (1926, 1937). For more recent discussions of Hawai'i as "multicultural, multiethnic society," see Okamura (1998) and Rosa (2001).

5. Following convention applied to other racial/ethnic categories such as "Asian American" or "Pacific Islander," here I use the term "Local" with a capital "L." My use of "local" with a lowercase "l" refers to the more general use of the term, which, in this case, points to the relatedness, situatedness, and/or typicality of an object and/or phenomenon to Hawai'i.

6. Hereafter, I use "Local" (with a capital "L") to refer to the racialized panethnic identity category and "local" to characterize a particular place or spatial location. Furthermore, as I discuss later in chapter 2, I understand "Local" as a racialized identity category, a panethnic formation composed primarily of the various non-white groups that usually trace their settlement in the islands to the plantation era. Thus, Local is also the label for those who are usually classified as "Asian American," "Asian Pacific Islander," or "Asian Pacific American" in the continental United States. For many Hawai'i residents, particularly those of Asian and/or Pacific Islander ancestry, Local is often the most salient category for sociocultural and political identification.

7. As I discuss in chapter 2, Filipinos in Hawai'i do not suffer from the types of misrecognition, misunderstanding, and invisibility their counterparts in the continental

United States endure (see Isaac 2006 and Pisares 2006). Instead, Filipinos in Hawai'i are highly visible even if their publicity tends to be negative. Okamura (2009) has argued that the media representation of Filipinos during the 2006 centennial celebrations positioned them as both immigrant menace and immigrant success. However, he further argues that the social, political, and economic force of dominant stereotypes (and Hawai'i's political economy) severely curtail Filipino attempts to challenge the dominant imagery and redefine Filipino-ness. In other words, given the existing relations and power structures in Hawai'i, Filipinos in the islands are limited in their abilities to (re)define themselves; to a large degree they are overpowered by a largely negative, externally assigned hypervisibility.

8. Beginning in the late 1980s through the Center for Philippine Studies at the University of Hawai'i at Mānoa, Virgilio Enriquez, the father of "Filipino psychology," published two reports that offered culture-based explanations for the Filipino youth gang issue.

9. Here I borrow from Yen Espiritu's (2003) immigrant menace/success binary. In recent years, however, "Micronesians" unfortunately have increasingly been perceived as the new "immigrant menace" who experience similar types of societal denigration and institutional violence described in this book.

10. Since 1988, the University of Hawai'i Pamantasan Council, a task force designed to address issues and concerns relating to Filipino Americans in higher education, has sponsored an annual conference for students, faculty, staff, and the broader community that usually has a panel focusing on "Filipino/Filipino American identity." The identity panel is typically the highest attended session.

11. Frank DeLima is usually regarded as one of the pillars of Hawai'i ethnic humor.

12. In 1998, the confrontation between Filipinos in Hawai'i (and in the continental United States) and Lois-Ann Yamanaka reached its peak during the annual meeting of the Association for Asian American Studies (AAAS) in Honolulu. For a comprehensive treatment on the AAAS controversy and a reading of Yamanaka's work, *Blu's Hanging*, see Fujikane (2000).

13. A similar commission was established by Governor Cayetano to celebrate in 2006 the one-hundredth anniversary of the first Filipino laborers' arrival in Hawai'i. See Jonathan Okamura's book, *Ethnicity and Inequality in Hawai'i* (2008) for an analysis of the representation of Filipinos during the 2006 centennial celebrations.

14. It is also important to note that the seventy-fifth anniversary activities did not solely focus on pointing out structural inequalities, but they also emphasized the celebration of achievements often associated with community events. For example, the publication *Filipinos in Hawaii...The First 75 Years* celebrates Filipina/o progress and "success stories" in government and politics, labor, education, medicine, arts and entertainment, religion, military, sports, and communications.

15. This self-identification dynamic played out in many of my interviews where interviewees often stated, "I'm Spanish-Chinese, but my parents are Filipino" or "I'm Local, but my parents are Filipino."

16. This book focuses primarily on the constructions of "Local" and "immigrant" Filipinos but it is important to note the significance of the "mainland" category and its connections to "performative haoleness" (Rohrer 2010). For example, when I first moved to Honolulu, many of my friends characterized me as an "haolefied Filipino." When I asked them what they meant, they often remarked that I "acted haole" and I "talked like a haole," which marked language and culture (expressed in attitudes and behaviors) as points of distinction rather than solely based on racial difference. As Rohrer suggests, haole is not simply translated as the "white" racial category but must also be understood as a relationally and structurally constructed identity marker. My friends who described me as "acting haole" pointed to a performative haoleness that "manifests in behavioral excesses: being too loud, taking up too much space, demanding too much attention, and acting with disregard to local custom" (Rohrer 2010: 80). And because I spoke "standard English" or "proper English" (as opposed to Hawai'i Creole English or a Philippine language) they marked me as non-Local and nonimmigrant and instead placed me as "mainland."

17. Here I borrow from Kroskrity's (1993) notion of "repertoire of identity."

18. This is usually related to the image of Visayans as being fond of social gatherings and being good musicians. "Visayan" usually refers to those populations who trace their ancestry to the central region of the Philippines that includes Cebu, Samar, Leyte, Negros, Siquijor, Panay, Guimaras, Biliran, and Romblon. Visayans are important players in Filipino Hawai'i's plantation and post-plantation history, comprising a majority of the early plantation recruits who were eventually replaced by Ilokanos as the largest group of *sakadas* by the 1920s.

19. I am intentionally not using the term "native anthropology," because of the problematic native/settler dynamics in Hawai'i (for a longer treatment, see Fujikane and Okamura's edited book, *Asian Settler Colonialism: From Local Governance to the Habits of Everyday Life in Hawai'i*).

20. As I have described elsewhere and discuss further in chapter 2, the term *buk* is often used in local ethnic humor and everyday speech to index "immigrant Filipinos and is the primary marker of linguistic and cultural otherness" (Labrador 2004: 301).

21. According to the 2010 U.S. Census, Filipinos constitute 33.2 percent of the Daly City population, and as Benito Vergara (2009) notes, the community as a whole exhibits middle-class characteristics.

22. Although the book attends to "Filipinos in Hawai'i" I fully acknowledge the centrality of O'ahu in my analysis. In addition, my data collection and analysis is also reliant on and shaped by my own linguistic competence in the standard variety of English, Hawai'i Creole English, Ilokano, and Tagalog.

CHAPTER I. OVERLAPPING ARCHITECTURES

1. *Marunggay* is the Ilokano name for the tree; it is also known as *kalamunggay* in Tagalog. These are the small horseradish tree that belongs to Moringa family,

with fernlike pinnate leaves, small white fragrant flowers, roots, and young green pods that are common in Filipino cooking.

2. *Bahay na bato* is usually translated as "stone house" and the style incorporates indigenous Filipino, Spanish, and Chinese architectural features. Historically, the nipa hut or *bahay kubo* gave way to the *bahay na bato* and became the typical house of the colonial Philippine elite. The *bahay na bato* followed the nipa hut's architectural arrangements, such as open ventilation and elevated living areas. The most obvious difference between the *bahay kubo* and *bahay na bato* are the building materials; the *bahay na bato* was constructed out of brick and stone rather than traditional bamboo and nipa palm materials. Interestingly, in Waipahu, *bahay na bato* could also evoke a different set of imagery, one related to crime and drug use. *Batu* is used as local street slang for the crystalline and smokable form of methamphetamine, or crystal meth or "ice." *Bahay na bato*, as "rock house," can also be understood as a haven for drug users, a meth lab used to process the drug from its powder to crystal form, and a place were "ice" is distributed or purchased. Waipahu is often perceived as a community where *batu* is processed, sold, and/or used.

3. Here, following Eric Wolf, I understand mode of production as "a specific, historically occurring set of social relations through which labor is deployed to wrest energy from nature by means of tools, skills, organization, and knowledge" (Wolf 1984: 75). For Wolf, there are three dominant modes of production: kin-ordered, tributary, and capitalist. By the early 1800s, Hawai'i utilized a combination of kin-ordered and tributary modes of production.

4. See the Filipino Community Center website for the vision behind the design of the building: www.filcom.org. Intramuros was originally located along Manila Bay near the Pasig River and was guarded by the Fuerte de Santiago, a citadel located at the mouth of the river. It was destroyed during World War II, and attempts to restore and rebuild it began in the 1950s.

5. The Spanish mission style is different from Hawai'i's plantation architecture and the precolonial Philippine architecture, of which the *bahay kubo* or nipa hut is exemplary. Traditionally the *bahay kubo* is a single-room structure raised slightly above the ground on stilts and is constructed by tying together bamboo for the walls, which are covered by a steep, thatched roof made from the leaves of the nipa palm.

6. The tympanum of the pediment above the front entrance is decorated with seventeen rays of half a sun and has a blue background, reminiscent of the sun in the Philippine flag.

7. There is a statue of a sakada cutting stalks of sugarcane in the Filipino Community Center that is accompanied by a plaque entitled, "The Arrival of Filipino Plantation Workers in Hawaii." The plaque lists the names of the fifteen pioneering sakadas who arrived in Honolulu from the Ilocos region in December 1906. The statue and plaque were unveiled in September 2006 by then-Philippine president Gloria Macapagal-Arroyo as part of the Filipino centennial celebrations. There is also a large mural inside the Casamina-Flores Ballroom in which the figure of a sakada is in the center. He holds a machete in his left hand and three stalks of sugarcane in his right.

8. To use another somewhat clichéd metaphor of the "hotspot origin" of the Hawaiian archipelago, a geologically important feature of the islands, we can imagine these historical layers (or migrations and modes of production) corresponding to the oceanic lithosphere, the oceanic crust, and the earth's crustal layer, with the magma representing Native Hawaiian sovereignty, which is simultaneously productive and destructive. When the magma rises to the earth's surface, the lava flow can be unpredictable, changing locations and activity levels leading to different types of formations.

9. In Hawaiian, *ahupuaʻa* literally means "pig altar," but it also refers to the political and economic land division that runs from the mountains to the sea.

10. See Pukui, Elbert, and Mookini's *Place Names of Hawaii (1976)*.

11. Kelly explains that the "*ahupuaʻa* is a land division, usually extending from the sea to the mountains and is allocated to senior chiefs. An *ʻili* is generally a subdivision of the *ahupuaʻa* given to lesser or junior chiefs" (1980: 71).

12. (Personal communication, July 4, 2007). For more than fifteen years, Moniz has provided education and training opportunities for public and private school teachers who work with K–16 students from the leeward coast. See also Kalākaua's *Legends and Myths of Hawaiʻi* (1990) and Beckwith's *Hawaiian Mythology* (1977). Munro (1983) recounts a similar story in her dissertation.

13. Kapa is similar to the tapa found in other part of Polynesia. It is a fabric made from the skin fibers of trees, like *wauke* or paper mulberry. The kapa is made by cutting and soaking the skin fibers, which are then placed on a tablet or board and beaten, which usually involved two phases.

14. *Aloha* is perhaps most commonly defined as the touristy "hello and goodbye." It was this cultural value of *aloha* that was betrayed by foreigners who sought political and economic control of the islands, leading to U.S. colonization, dispossession, and native resistance. This is a nod to Noenoe Silva's work, *Aloha Betrayed: Native Hawaiian Resistance to American Colonialism, 2004.*

15. San Buenaventura (1995) understands Filipino immigration to Hawaiʻi and the United States as part of "the second phase of their colonial history" (the first phase was Spanish colonialism). In this phase, labor and education (via the pensionado program) are the primary catalysts for immigration. In 1903, the U.S. colonial administration passed the Pensionado Act. The act enabled "the best and brightest" Filipino students to study in prestigious American colleges. In effect, pensionados were government-sponsored students and the program highlighted the idea that education is the primary avenue for socioeconomic mobility. Also, as San Buenaventura notes, "the *pensionado* program became the mechanism for the advanced training of the personnel needed to run the government bureaucracy. It was consistent with the policy of preparing the Filipinos for 'self-government' and satisfied the American desire for educational reforms."

16. While the makaʻainana were being transformed into wage earners, similar processes were already underway in the Philippines, where the Manila Galleon Trade (involving Spain, Mexico, the Philippines, and China) was at its peak.

17. In Hawaiian, *ʻohana* means "family."

18. Formed in 1895, the HSPA centralized the management of information, conducted agricultural research, established policies for the importation and management of laborers, served as the primary mechanism for controlling wages, and was the key decision-making body of the sugar planters. From its inception, the HSPA was central in shaping Hawai'i's racial/ethnic terrain and the political economy of the islands.

19. See Baldoz's *The Third Asiatic Invasion* and Poblete's forthcoming book, *Islands in the Empire: Filipino and Puerto Rican Migrants to Hawai'i* for further discussion about the effect of the "U.S. Nationals" status on Filipino migration and settlement in Hawai'i and the United States.

20. See Sharma (1984).

21. It is perhaps important to note here that the gender imbalances were not as severe among the Filipino "bachelor societies" forming on the West Coast of the continental United States during this same time period.

22. For a closer reading of Pablo Manlapit, see Melinda Tria Kerkvliet's *Unbending Cane: Pablo Manlapit, a Filipino Labor Leader in Hawai'i.*

23. Other Hawai'i labor historians, particularly Anderson et al. (1984), argue that instead of a truly unified and singular interethnic strike, the 1920 event was actually two separate but simultaneous strikes. Regardless of the degree or level of cooperation between the Japanese and Filipino unions, the 1920 strike is popularly regarded as the first time in which two ethnicity-based unions cooperated for a common purpose.

24. For example, the first Filipino ILWU president was Tony Rania, preceding Carl Damaso. Other high-ranking Filipino labor leaders included Eddie Lapa, Emilio Yadao, Ric Labez, and Richard Dumancas (of the Sheet Metal Workers Union).

25. See Saranillio (2010b).

CHAPTER 2. "WHAT'S SO P/FUNNY?"

1. See Sarita See (2009) for a fuller treatment of Rex Navarrete's comedy performances.

2. Outside Local comedy, examples of Mock Filipino can also be found in local greeting cards (Da Kine Cards) and heard in various morning radio shows in which deejays tell jokes using a "Filipino accent."

3. De Lima began doing "Local comedy" in the late 1970s and since then, his Filipino song parodies (particularly those that include depictions of Filipinos as dog-eaters) have prompted lively public discussion in the Filipino community newspapers. De Lima's critics claim that his song parodies are part of a decades-old stigmatizing discourse that perpetuates lingering negative stereotypes of Filipinos. For example, in an editorial in the *Fil-Am Courier* Mila Medallon asked if ethnic jokes were "camouflaged racism" (1993b). Supporters of De Lima claim that his representations are nothing more than part of the Hawai'i tradition of ethnic humor that has a defined target audience and a specific target of ridicule. To this end, the *Hawaii Filipino Chronicle* noted that De Lima "argues that immigrant Filipinos, not local Filipinos, are the ones who object to his jokes" (1995, 5).

4. The founding trio of Booga Booga included Ed Kaʻahea, James Grant Benton, and Rap Reiplinger. Booga Booga began performing as a group in 1974 at the University of Hawaiʻi at Mānoa. Rap Reiplinger, as a solo artist and as part of Booga Booga, is arguably the most revered among Local comedians.

5. "Foreigner" in Hawaiian, but refers to "white" in its more racialized contemporary usage.

6. In Hawaiian, *kumu* means "foundation," "source," "tree," or "teacher." In this sense, *kumu hula* means "hula teacher."

7. In Hawaiian, *alakaʻi* means "leader" or "to lead."

8. It is also interesting to note that in their videos and on the television show, Da Braddahs also have a character named "The Governor," a caricature of the former governor of Hawaiʻi, Benjamin Cayetano. Cayetano is a Filipino American who by most standards speaks a standard variety of American English and Pidgin but has a "Filipino accent" in the sketches.

9. *Kanaka* means "person" or "human" in Hawaiian, but in contemporary usage it has come to connote "Native Hawaiian."

10. "Portuguese" in Pidgin.

11. See Pizon 1999.

12. For other examples, see Paul Ogata's (1998) comedy CD, *Mental Oriental,* especially "Dr. Ay Seuss, parts 1 & 2," which employs Mock Filipino and caricatures the "Filipino" preference for eating black dog.

13. A kin term that means 'older brother' but in Local usage refers to 'older Filipino man.' The Localized pronunciation of the term places the accent on the second syllable rather than the first, as it is pronounced in Ilokano.

14. This is often the evidence used in "positive" stereotypes of Filipinos which characterize them as hardworking and industrious.

15. The song originally appears in *Frank De Lima's Joke Book* (1991) as "The Purple Danube." The song lyrics that I transcribe here are taken from a more recent version that appears in De Lima's *Silva Anniversary* (2001).

16. This is equivalent to the Ilokano term, *bugguong,* which is "salted fermented fish or shrimps used to season food" (Rubino 2000, 124) and is known for its pungent odor.

17. In Hawaiian, *opae* are "small shrimp" (see Simonson et al. 1981).

18. P.I. refers to the Philippine Islands, but is often used alongside terms like *buk buk, manong,* and Flip to refer to Filipinos.

19. *Salamat* means "thank you" in Tagalog.

20. Lanaʻi is one of the Hawaiian Islands that is heavily dependent on the tourism industry and has a large Filipino population.

21. A Hawaiian term that means "to carry," but refers to being pregnant.

22. Some of my interviewees told me stories about how they or their immigrant Filipino relatives would intentionally avoid wearing these colors for fear of being ridiculed.

23. The term *"buk buk"* is derived from a Tagalog term, *"bukbok,"* which means "to rot" and refers to something rotten (Alcantara 1981, 165). In Ilokano, *"bukbok"*

is a type of woodworm and also means "cavity (of teeth)" (Rubino 2000, 125; see also De Lima 1991, 67). The common onomatopoeic explanation for the term "*buk buk*" is that it mimics the clucking sound of chickens, pointing to how Filipinos are closely associated with fighting chickens. Take, for example, the following joke taken from De Lima (1991, 71): "Official Filipino bird: Fighting chicken."

24. Representations of Filipino subordination have their historical origins in the plantation era (Okamura 1996, 3). Despite the large numbers of pre–World War II Filipino immigrants, the community was mostly composed of single men; it was a "bachelor society." At the height of Filipino immigration to Hawaiʻi, the male to female ratio was 3 to 1 in 1923 and 9 to 1 in 1927 (San Buenaventura 1995).

25. The /k/ is usually preferred in contemporary standard Ilokano orthography.

26. Cayatmo could also be a play on "Cayetano," referring to the former Filipino American governor of Hawaiʻi.

27. Contemporary depictions of Filipino male sexual violence also appear in Local literature, particularly in the works of Lois-Ann Yamanaka, like her *Saturday Night at the Pahala Theatre*. For a textual analysis of Yamanaka's most controversial work, *Blu's Hanging*, see Fujikane (2000).

28. For nearly a decade, *Hawaiʻi Stars* aired weekly on local television. The half-hour show was a judged karaoke-style singing competition that showcased the singing talents of people from the islands.

29. *Kadugo* is an Ilokano term that can be translated as "family member" or "relative."

30. *Barok* is an Ilokano term that can be translated as "young man."

31. *Kalamunggay* is the Tagalog term for a vegetable, from the horseradish tree family, often used in Filipino dishes. *Marunggay* is the Ilokano equivalent.

32. The Ilokano phrase "*naimas kayatmo*" can be translated as "It's delicious, do you want some?"

33. In Ilokano, "*suksok*" is loosely translated as "insertion" or "penetration."

34. In Ilokano, this phrase can be loosely translated as "that girl is not respectable."

35. A multiethnic, urban, working-class neighborhood on the island of Oʻahu that has a high concentration of immigrant Filipino residents.

36. A reference to the Philippines, "PI" = "Philippine Islands."

37. This is a local clothing store.

38. I discuss this idea of "retarded/retired" further below.

39. This is a reference to TFC (The Filipino Channel), a twenty-four-hour Philippine-language channel available on cable television. TFC broadcasts a wide range of programs from the Philippines, including news, entertainment, music, feature films, soap operas, and so on.

40. See Okamura's (2010) discussion of the stereotype of Filipinos as "poke-knife".

41. In her analysis of Rex Navarette, Asian American studies scholar Sarita See (2009) illustrates the oppositional functions "accent puns" and "punning" can play in Filipino American identity territorializations. In contrast, in this chapter I point to the ways these accent puns, what I call Mock Filipino, create other hegemonies, primarily generational and linguistic ones, within Filipino Hawaiʻi.

Anticipating this possibility, See writes: "Perhaps the jokes' reliance on the Filipino accent in English reinscribes the racialized inferiority of both Filipinos and Filipino languages" (2009: 80).

42. "UH" refers to the University of Hawai'i.

43. De Lima (1991: 72).

44. Here, I use the Odo orthography to represent pidgin and Mock Filipino, in italics (see Odo 1975, 1977; Sakoda and Siegel 2003; Talmy 2009). Other transcription conventions used in the example:

-	sudden cut-off
:	Lengthening
.	Falling contour
?	Rising contour
((comments))	Transcriber comments
(h)	Breathiness, laughter
[word	Onset of overlapping talk

45. The /b/ → /v/ labiodentalization does not occur in this particular example, but it is an important feature of Mock Filipino and appears in other parts of the CD.

46. See Hiramoto (2011) for more detailed characterizations of Mock Filipino.

47. Augie Tulba is a popular Local comedian who is Portuguese, Irish, and Filipino. This quote is taken from an article by Naomi Sodetani (2001: 5) titled, "Local Humor and the New World Order," which appeared in the *Honolulu Weekly*.

48. These are race/ethnic labels commonly used in pidgin: "Portagee" = Portuguese, "Pake" = Chinese, "Buddha Head" = Japanese, "Sole" = Samoan, "Yobo" = Korean, "Kanaka" = Native Hawaiian, and "Haole" = white.

49. This was not the first time the issue of Local comedy and ethnic jokes was brought up in the local newspapers. Larger-scale discussions were included in the *Honolulu Weekly* in 1992, in the *Honolulu Star-Bulletin* in 1994 and in the *Honolulu Advertiser* in 1998.

50. Timpuyog is the Ilokano language student organization on the Mānoa campus.

51. I use the idea of "racial cannibalism" as both a type of homophonic (Mock Filipino) play on carnival but also to extend the food metaphor often associated with Hawai'i's multiculturalism, whether it be the "melting pot," "mixed plate," or "chop suey nation." In this sense, racial cannibalism involves the literal and figurative eating of the other, where food functions as a proxy for race/ethnicity and culture.

52. The song, "A Filipino Christmas," was actually released three years earlier. Since then, the song has become a Hawai'i "holiday tradition, treat." As Harada (2003) has observed, "As sure as there is a Christmas, there is Frank De Lima singing 'A Filipino Christmas,' all decked out with boughs of the jollies . . . making like a singing Christmas tree."

53. The only decipherable word in the song introduction is the Ilokano word, *saluyot*, which is a type of herb "with edible spinachlike leaves famous in Ilocano cuisine" (Rubino 2000: 528).

CHAPTER 3. "ANYTHING BUT . . ."

1. In 2013, Nakem Conferences held its eighth annual conference in Honolulu.

2. "Amianan" is the Ilokano term for "north." Amianan Studies refers to scholarship by, about, and for the peoples of the northern Philippines, where Ilokano is the primary language in the region.

3. At a basic level, I suggest that 1.5-generation immigrants constitute an in-between space at the interstices of the first and second generations—the former refers to the adult immigrant population, while the latter designates those born in the host country or those who immigrated at a very young age, the children of the first generation. Put simply, 1.5ers are located in-between first- and second-generation immigrants. However, unlike the first and second generations, linguistic and cultural socialization and formal education for 1.5-generation immigrants occur both in their home and host countries.

4. The Timpuyog Organization, Katipunan's Ilokano counterpart, has very similarly stated goals (as they appear in their brochure: "To serve the needs of students of the Ilokano language and theater program and others interested in the Ilokano the Ilokano language and Philippine culture; to promote the Ilokano language and Philippine culture in the community; to instill pride in our Ilokano heritage; to develop leadership skills among the students; to help students develop proficiency in Ilokano and awareness of Filipino traditions and values through meaningful language and cultural activities; to serve the community through cultural presentations; to encourage Ilokano students to speak Ilokano; and to serve as role models for our Filipino youth.").

5. See Gonzalves (1995) for a more in-depth analysis of the PCN as well as his most recent book, *The Day the Dancers Stayed: Performing in the Filipino/American Diaspora*).

6. For his more recent treatment on the Pilipino Cultural Nights, see *The Day the Dancers Stayed: Performing in the Filipino/American Diaspora* .

7. In the performance, the indigenous populations are represented by the peoples of the Cordillera and the Filipino Muslims, who are also commonly known by their historically pejorative names, the "Igorots" and "Moros" respectively.

8. The kulintang is a type of musical ensemble featuring gongs and drums usually associated with the indigenous peoples of the southern Philippines. The ensemble is similar to the better-known Indonesian gamelan.

9. For a further analysis on U.S. production of the "Filipino," see E. San Juan Jr.'s "One Hundred Years of Producing and Reproducing the 'Filipino,' " *Amerasia Journal*, 1–33.

10. See also S. L. Mendoza, *Between the Homeland and the Diaspora: The Politics of Theorizing Filipino and Filipino American Identities, A Second Look at the Poststructuralism-Indigenization Debates.*

11. For Strobel, the "indigenous" refers to the "worldviews, values, beliefs, and practices which define Filipino-ness . . . [that] come mainly from cultural or tribal

communities which resisted colonization and were therefore to maintain their indigenous cultures" (1996: 38).

12. For similar arguments, see Spivak (1988), Lowe (1996), and Gonzalves (1995).

CHAPTER FOUR. "THE CENTER IS NOT JUST FOR FILIPINOS, BUT FOR ALL OF HAWAI'I NEI"

1. There was some controversy over the naming of the building. I was told of a stipulation in the Weinberg Foundation award (of which FilCom Center Board members were unaware) that required the center to be named after the donors. Some board members felt that the building should be called "The FilCom Center" and the Weinberg money returned. After much discussion, the board agreed on the name Bahay Harry & Jeanette Weinberg, even though it continues to be popularly known as "The FilCom Center." *Bahay* means "house" or "dwelling" in Tagalog, and the word was chosen by the FilCom Center Board "as a symbol of the nurturing spirit that the FilCom Center hopes to perpetuate through the center."

2. The exhibit was created by the Filipino Historical Society of Hawai'i and members of the Knights of Rizal. The Knights of Rizal is an organization that studies the life and teachings of José Rizal. In addition to the grand opening, the exhibit has been displayed in different venues throughout the islands. The grand opening ceremonies also included the unveiling of the Dr. José Rizal statue on the FilCom Center grounds. The bronze statue was donated to the Center by the Philippine National Centennial Commission–Committee on International Relations (NCC-CIR).

3. In the same community newspaper, Mila Medallon (1993a) expressed a similar sentiment nearly ten years earlier in her editorial entitled, "Filipinos are now going for a piece of the pie."

CONCLUSION. UNSETTLING HAWAI'I

1. The focus on mobility usually recognizes that identities move and are never static. My focus on motility acknowledges that identities are neither completely free-floating self-ascriptions nor entirely context-dependent entities.

2. The first colonialism is associated with white racial dominance during the plantation years, and the second colonialism is the current multicultural order where power is shared by whites and Local Asians.

BIBLIOGRAPHY

Acido, Jeffrey T., and Gordon Lee, eds. 2012. *On the Edge of Hope and Healing: Flipping the Script on Filipinos in Hawaii*. Honolulu: Timpuyog Dagiti Mannurat nga Ilokano (TMI) Press.

Adams, Romanzo. 1937. *Intermarriage in Hawaii: A Study of mutually Conditioned Processes of Acculturation and Amalgamation*. New York: Macmillan.

Agbayani, Amefil R. 1991. "Community Impacts of Migration: Recent Ilokano Migration to Hawaii." *Social Process in Hawaii* 33: 73–90.

———. 1996. "The Education of Filipinos in Hawaii." *Social Process in Hawaii* 37: 147–60.

Agcaoili, Aurelio S., and Jeffrey T. Acido, eds. 2010. *Kabambannuagan: Our Voices, Our Lives*. Honolulu: Timpuyog Dagiti Mannurat nga Ilokano (TMI) Press.

Agcaoili, Aurelio S., ed. 2011. *Panagtaripato: Parenting Our Stories, Our Stories As Parents*. Honolulu: Timpuyog Dagiti Mannurat nga Ilokano (TMI) Press.

Alcantara, Ruben. 1981. *Sakada: Filipino Adaptation in Hawaii*. Washington, D.C.: University Press of America.

Alegado, Dean T. 1991. "The Filipino Community in Hawai'i: Development and Change." *Social Process in Hawaii* 33: 12–38.

———. 1996. "Carl Damaso: A Champion of Hawaii's Working People." *Social Process in Hawaii* 37: 26–35.

Alonso, Ana M. 1988. "The Effects of Truth: Representations of the Past and the Imagining of Community." *Journal of Historical Sociology* 1(1): 33–57.

———. (1994) "The Politics of Space, Time and Substance: State Formation, Nationalism, and Ethnicity." *Annual Review of Anthropology* 23: 379–405. Andaya, Leonard Y. 1996. "From American-Filipino to Filipino-American." *Social Process in Hawaii* 37: 99–111.

Anderson, Benedict. 1991. *Imagined Communities: Reflections on the Origin and Spread of Nationalism*. 2nd ed. London: Verso.

Anderson, Robert N., Richard Coller, and Rebecca F. Pestano. 1984. *Filipinos in Rural Hawaii*. Honolulu: University of Hawaii Press.

Anzaldúa, Gloria. 1987. *Borderlands/La Frontera: The New Mestiza*. San Francisco: Spinsters/Aunt Lute.

Aquino, Belinda A. 2000. "The Politics of Ethnicity among Ilokanos in Hawaii." In Charles J-H Macdonald and Guillermo M. Pesigan, eds., *Old Ties and New Solidarities: Studies on Philippine Communities, 100–16*. Quezon City: Ateneo de Manila University Press.

Appadurai, Arjun. 1990. "Disjuncture and Difference in the Global Cultural Economy." *Public Culture* 2(2): 1–24.

———. 1991. "Global Ethnoscapes: Notes and Queries for a Transnational Anthropology," in Richard G. Fox, ed., *Recapturing Anthropology: Working in the Present*. Santa Fe, N.M.: School of American Research Press.

———. 1996. *Modernity at Large: Cultural Dimensions of Globalization*. Minneapolis: University of Minnesota Press.

Baldoz, Rick. 2011. *The Third Asiatic Invasion: Migration and Empire in Filipino America, 1898–1946*. New York: New York University Press.

Basch, Linda, N. Glick Schiller, and C. Szanton Blanc. 1994. *Nations Unbound: Transnational Projects, Postcolonial Predicaments, and Deterritorialized Nation-States*. Langhorne, Pa.: Gordon and Breach Science Publishers.

Beechert, Edward D. 1985. *Working in Hawaii: A Labor History*. Honolulu: University of Hawaii Press.

Beeman, William O. 1993. "The Anthropology of Theater and Spectacle." *Annual Review of Anthropology* 22: 369–93.

Berger, John. 1998. "Buckaloose: Da Braddahs." *Honolulu Star-Bulletin*, July 31.

———. 2002. "Two wild and crazy guys! Tony Silva and James Roché [*sic*] may look lolo and act lolo, but they know what they're doing." *Honolulu Star-Bulletin*, June 27.

Bhabha, Homi. 1994. *The Location of Culture*. New York: Routledge.

Bonus, Rick. 2000. *Locating Filipino Americans: Ethnicity and the Cultural Politics of Space*. Philadelphia: Temple University Press.

Brah, Avtar. 1996. *Cartographies of Diaspora: Contesting Identities*. London and New York: Routledge.

Brodkin, Karen. 1998. *How Jews Became White Folks and What That Says About Race in America*. New Brunswick, N.J.: Rutgers University Press.

Cariaga, Roman R. "The Filipinos in Hawaii: A Survey of Their Economic and Social Conditions." Master's thesis, University of Hawaii, 1936. Also published by the Filipino Public Relations Bureau, 1937.

Carter, Erica, J. Donald, and J. Squires, J., eds. 1993. *Space and Place: Theories of Identity and Location*. London: Lawrence & Wishart Limited.

Cataluna, Lee. 2000a. "'Portagee' Jokes Born of Cruelty." *Honolulu Advertiser*, November 21.

———. 2000b. "Readers, Too, Hate 'Portagee' Jokes." *Honolulu Advertiser*, November 28.

Chang, Jeff. 1996. "Local Knowledge(s): Notes on Race Relations, Panethnicity and History in Hawai'i." *Amerasia* 22: 1–29.

Cheng, Lucie and Edna Bonacich, eds. 1984. *Labor Immigration Under Capitalism: Asian Workers in the United States Before World War II*. Berkeley: University of California Press.

Choy, Catherine Ceniza. 2003. *Empire of Care: Nursing and Migration in Filipino American History*. Durham, N.C.: Duke University Press.

Chun, Elaine W. 2009. "Ideologies of Legitimate Mockery: Margaret Cho's Revoicings of Mock Asian." In Angela Reyes and Adrienne Lo, eds., *Beyond Yellow English: Toward a Linguistic Anthropology of Asian Pacific America*, 261–87. New York: Oxford University Press.

City and County of Honolulu, Planning Department. 1995. "Waipahu Town Plan: A Special Area Plan of the Central Oahu Development Plan."

Clifford, James. 1988. *The Predicament of Culture: Twentieth-Century Ethnography, Literature, and Art*. Cambridge, Mass.: Harvard University Press.

———. 1997. *Routes: Travel and the Translation in the Late Twentieth Century*. Cambridge, Mass.: Harvard University Press.

Coleman, Mark. 2003. "Frank DeLima." *Honolulu Star-Bulletin*, March 2.

Coleon, Shayna. 2001. "Da Braddahs: Comic Pair Are Gaining Fame After a Somewhat Rough Start." *Honolulu Advertiser*, August 15.

Constantino, Renato. 1987. "The Miseducation of the Filipino." In Daniel B. Schirmer and Stephen Rosskamm Shalom, eds., *The Philippines Reader: A History of Colonialism, Neocolonialism, Dictatorship, and Resistance*, 45–48. Boston: South End Press.

Cordova, Fred. 1973. "The Filipino-American: There's Always an Identity Crisis." In S. Sue and N. W. Wagner, eds., *Asian-Americans: Psychological Perspectives*, 136–39. Palo Alto, Calif.: Science and Behavior Books.

———. 1983. *Filipinos: Forgotten Asian Americans. A Pictorial Essay, 1763–circa 1963*. Dubuque, Iowa: Kendall/Hunt

Da Braddahs. 1998. *Buckaloose*. CD. Hobo House on the Hill.

Da Pidgin Coup. 1999. "Pidgin and Education: A Position Paper." http://www.hawaii.edu/sls/pidgin.html and eric.ed.gov/id=EJ877775.

David, E. J. R. 2011. *Filipino-/American Postcolonial Psychology: Oppression, Colonial Mentality, and Decolonization*. Bloomington, Ind.: Author House Publishing.

Deleuze, Gilles, and F. Guattari, 1987. *A Thousand Plateaus: Capitalism and Schizophrenia*, translated by Brian Massumi. London: Athlone Press.

De Lima, Frank. 1991. *Frank De Lima's Joke Book: Having Fun with Portagees, Pakes, Buddha Heads, Buk Buks, Blallahs, Soles, Yobos, Haoles, Tidahs, Pit Bulls, and Other Hawaiian Minorities*. Honolulu: Bess Press.

———. 2001. *Silva Anniversary*. CD. Pocholinga Productions.

Dionisio, Juan C., ed. 1981. *The Filipinos in Hawaii: The First 75 Years*. Honolulu: Hawaii Filipino News Specialty Publications.

Duara, Prasenjit. 1995. *Rescuing History from the Nation: Questioning Narratives of Modern China*. Chicago: University of Chicago Press.

Eisen, Daniel. 2011. "Becoming Filipino in Hawaii: Rejection, Reframing, and Acceptance of a Stigmatized Identity." PhD diss., Department of Sociology. University of Hawai'i at Mānoa.

Enriquez, Virgilio G. 1989. "The Hawaii Youth Gang Issue: A Preliminary Research Report." Honolulu: Center for Philippine Studies, University of Hawai'i at Mānoa.

———. 1990. "Hellside in Paradise: The Honolulu Youth Gang." Honolulu: Community Affairs Committee, Center for Philippine Studies, University of Hawai'i at Mānoa.

Espiritu, Augusto. 2005. *Five Faces of Exile: The Nation and Filipino American Intellectuals*. Stanford, Calif.: Stanford University Press.

Espiritu, Yen L. 1994. "The Intersection of Race, Ethnicity, and Class: The Multiple Identities of Second-generation Filipinos." *Identities* 1(2–3): 249–73.

———. 1995. *Filipino American Lives*. Philadelphia: Temple University Press.

———. 2003. *Home Bound: Filipino Lives Across Cultures, Communities, and Countries*. Berkeley: University of California Press.

Fajardo, Kale. 2011. *Filipino Crosscurrents: Oceanographies of Seafaring, Masculinities and Globalization*. Minneapolis: University of Minnesota Press.

Fuchs, Lawrence. 1961. *Hawaii Pono: A Social History*. New York: Harcourt, Brace & World.

Fujikane, Candace. 1994. "Between Nationalisms: Hawai'i's Local Nation and Its Troubled Paradise." *Critical Mass: A Journal of Asian American Cultural Criticism* 2:23–57.

———. 1997. "Reimagining Development and the Local in Lois-Ann Yamanaka's *Saturday Night at the Pahala Theatre*." *Women in Hawai'i: Sites, Identities, and Voices*, eds. Joyce N. Chinen, Kathleen O. Kane, and Ida M. Yoshinaga. Special issue of *Social Process in Hawai'i* 38: 1–17.

———. 2000. "Sweeping Racism Under the Rug of 'Censorship': The Controversy of Lois-Ann Yamanaka's *Blu's Hanging*." *Amerasia* 26: 158–94.

———. 2008. "Introduction: Asian Settler Colonialism in the U.S. Colony of Hawai'i." In Candace Fujikane and Jonathan Okamura, eds., *Asian Settler Colonialism: From Local Governance to the Habits of Everyday Life in Hawai'i*, 1–42. Honolulu: University of Hawai'i Press.

Fujikane, Candace, and Jonathan Okamura, eds. 2000. "Whose Vision? Asian Settler Colonialism in Hawai'i." *Amerasia Journal* 26(2).

———. 2008. *Asian Settler Colonialism: From Local Governance to the Habits of Everyday Life in Hawai'i*. Honolulu: University of Hawai'i Press.

Furukawa, Toshiaki. 2007. "No Flips in the Pool: Discursive Practice in Hawai'i Creole." *Pragmatics* 17(3): 371–85.

Garcia, Nestor. 1997. "The Waipahu of My Youth." *Hawaii Filipino Chronicle Magazine*, summer.

Geertz, Clifford. 1973. *The Interpretation of Cultures*. New York: Basic Books.

———. 1983. *Local Knowledge: Further Essays in Interpretive Anthropology.* New York: Basic Books.

Gilroy, Paul. 1987. *There Ain't No Black in the Union Jack: The Cultural Politics of Race and Nation.* London: Hutchinson.

———. 1993a. *The Black Atlantic: Double Consciousness and Modernity.* Cambridge, Mass.: Harvard University Press.

———. 1993b. *Small Acts: Thoughts on the Politics of Black Cultures.* London: Serpent's Tail.

———. 1994. "Sounds Authentic: Black Music, Ethnicity, and the Challenge of a *Changing* Same." In S. J. Lemelle and R. D. G. Kelley, eds., *Imagining Home: Class, Culture and Nationalism in the African Diaspora,* 93–117. London and New York: Verso.

Ginsburg, Faye. 1997. "'From Little Things, Big Things Grow': Indigenous Media and Cultural Activism." In Richard G. Fox and Orin Starn, eds., *Between Resistance and Revolution: Cultural Politics and Social Protest,* 118–44. New Brunswick, N.J.: Rutgers University Press.

Goffman, Erving. 1959. *The Presentation of Self in Everyday Life.* New York: Doubleday.

Gonzalez, Joaquin J. 2009. *Filipino American Faith in Action: Immigration, Religion, and Civic Engagement.* New York: New York University Press.

Gonzalez III, Joaquin L., and R. D. Holmes. 1996. "The Philippine Labour Diaspora: Trends, Issues and Policies." *Southeast Asian Affairs* 1: 300–17.

Gonzalves, Theodore S. 1995. "The Show Must Go On: Production Notes on the Pilipino Cultural Night." *Critical Mass: A Journal of Asian American Cultural Criticism* 2(2): 129–44.

———. 2009. *The Day the Dancers Stayed: Performing in the Filipino/American Diaspora.* Philadelphia: Temple University Press.

Goodyear-Ka'ōpua, J. Noelani. 2009. "Rebuilding the 'Auwai': Connecting Ecology, Economy and Education in Hawaiian Schools." *AlterNative* 5(2): 46–77.

Grant, Glen, and Dennis Ogawa. 1993. "Living Proof: Is Hawai'i the Answer?" *The ANNALS of the American Academy of Political and Social Science* 530: 137–54.

Gupta, Akhil, and J. Ferguson. 1992. "Beyond 'Culture' : Space, Identity, and the Politics of Difference." *Cultural Anthropology* 7(1): 6–23.

Gupta, Akhil, and Ferguson, J., eds. 1997. *Culture, Power, Place: Explorations in Critical Anthropology.* Durham, N.C.: Duke University Press.

Hall, Stuart. 1989. "Ethnicity: Identity and Difference." *Radical America* 23(4): 9–20.

———. 1990. "Cultural Identity and Diaspora." In J. Rutherford, ed., *Identity: Community, Culture, Difference,* 222–37. London: Lawrence and Wishart.

———. 1992. "The New Ethnicities." In J. Donald and A. Rattansi, eds., *"Race," Culture, and Difference.* London: Sage Publications.

———. 1996a. "Gramsci's Relevance for the Study of Race and Ethnicity." In D. Morley and K-H. Chen, eds., *Stuart Hall: Critical Dialogues in Cultural Studies,* 411–40. London and New York: Routledge.

———. 1996b. "What Is This 'Black' in Black Popular Culture?" In D. Morley and K-H. Chen, eds., *Stuart Hall: Critical Dialogues in Cultural Studies*, 1–22. London and New York: Routledge.

———. 1996c. "Introduction: Who Needs 'Identity'?" In S. Hall and P. du Gay, eds., *Questions of Cultural Identity*, 1–17. London, Thousand Oaks, Calif., and New Delhi: Sage Publications.

———. 1997. "The Local and the Global: Globalization and Ethnicity." In A. Mc-Clintock, A. Mufti, and E. Shohat, eds., *Dangerous Liaisons: Gender, Nation, and Postcolonial Perspectives*, 173–87. Minneapolis: University of Minnesota Press.

Harada, Wayne. 2000. "For 25 Years, Always So Frankly DeLima." *Honolulu Advertiser*, July 11.

———. 2003. "DeLima's Zany Antics a Holiday Tradition, Treat." *Honolulu Advertiser*, December 19.

Harvey, David. 1989. *The Condition of Postmodernity: An Inquiry into the Origins of Culture Change*. Oxford: Basil Blackwell.

Hawaii Filipino Chronicle. 1995. "Filipinos Speak Out on DeLima Jokes," January 1.

Hill, Jane H. 1993. "Hasta la vista, baby: Anglo Spanish in the American Southwest." *Critique of Anthropology* 13: 145–76.

———. 1995. "Junk Spanish, Covert Racism, and the (Leaky) Boundary between Public and Private Spheres." *Pragmatics* 5: 197–212.

———. 1998. "Language, Race, and White Public Space." *American Anthropologist* 100: 680–89.

Hiramoto, Mie. 2011. "Is Dat Dog You're Eating? Mock Filipino, Hawai'i Creole, and Local Elitism." *Pragmatics* 21(3): 341–71.

Honolulu Advertiser. 1939. "Gushing Water Is Waipahu Meaning." October 22, p. 11.

Ignacio, Emily N. 2005. *Building Diaspora: Filipino Community Formation on the Internet*. New Brunswick, N.J.: Rutgers University Press.

Irvine, Judith T., and Susan Gal. 2000. "Language Ideology and Linguistic Differentiation." In Paul V. Kroskrity, ed., *Regimes of Language: Ideologies, Polities, and Identities*, 35–84. Santa Fe, N.M.: School of American Research Press.

Isaac, Allan P. 2006. *American Tropics: Articulating Filipino America*. Minneapolis: University of Minnesota Press, 2006.

Jameson, Frederic. 1984. "Postmodernism, or the Cultural Logic of Late Capitalism." *New Left Review* 146: 53–92.

———. 1991. *Postmodernism, or the Cultural Logic of Late Capitalism*. London: Verso.

Kame'eleihiwa, Lilikalā. 1992. *Native Land and Foreign Desires: Pehea lā e Pono ai?* Honolulu: Bishop Museum Press.

Kearney, Michael. 1991. "Borders and Boundaries of State and Self at the End of Empire." *Journal of Historical Sociology* 4(1): 52–74.

———. 1995. "The Local and the Global: The Anthropology of Globalization and Transnationalism." *Annual Review of Anthropology* 24: 547–65.

Keith, Michael, and S. Pile, eds. 1993. *Place and the Politics of Identity*. London and New York: Routledge.

Kelley, Robin D. G. 1997. *Yo Mama's Disfunktional! Fighting the Culture Wars in Urban America*. Boston: Beacon Press.

Kelly, Marion. 1980. "Land Tenure in Hawaii." *Amerasia* 7(2): 57–73.

Kent, Noel J. 1993. *Hawai'i: Islands under the Influence*. Honolulu: University of Hawaii Press.

Kerkvliet, Melinda Tria. 1996. "Interpreting Pablo Manlapit." *Social Process in Hawaii* 37: 1–25.

———. 2002. *Unbending Cane: Pablo Manlapit, a Filipino Labor Leader in Hawai'i*. Honolulu: University of Hawai'i at Mānoa Office of Multicultural Student Services.

Kondo, Dorinne. 1997. *About Face: Performing Race in Fashion and Theater*. New York: Routledge.

Kroskrity, Paul V. 1993. *Language, History, and Identity: Ethnolinguistic Studies of the Arizona Tewa*. Tucson: University of Arizona Press.

———. 2000. "Regimenting Languages: Language Ideological Perspectives." In Paul V. Kroskrity, ed., *Regimes of Language: Ideologies, Polities, and Identities*, 1–34. Santa Fe, N.M.: School of American Research Press.

Labrador, Roderick N. 2002 "Performing Identity: The Public Presentation of Culture and Ethnicity among Filipinos in Hawai'i." *Cultural Values* 6(3): 287–307.

———. 2004. "We Can Laugh at Ourselves": Hawai'i Ethnic Humor, Local Identity, and the Myth of Multiculturalism." *Pragmatics* 14(2/3): 291–316.

———and Erin K. Wright. 2011. "Engaging Indigeneity in Pacific Islander and Asian American Studies." *Amerasia Journal* 37(3): 135–47.

Lavie, Smadar, and T. Swedenburg. 1996. *Displacement, Diaspora, and Geographies of Identity*. Durham, N.C. and London: Duke University Press.

Lawrence, Charles R., III. 1987. "The Id, the Ego, and Equal Protection: Reckoning with Unconscious Racism." *Stanford Law Review* 39(2): 317–88.

———. 2008. "Unconscious Racism Revisited: Reflections on the Impact and Origins of 'The Id, the Ego, and Equal Protection.' " *Connecticut Law Review* 40(4): 931–78.

Lemelle, Sidney J., and R. D. G. Kelley, eds. 1994. *Imagining Home: Class, Culture and Nationalism in the African Diaspora*. London and New York: Verso.

Libarios, Ernest "Niki" D., Jr. 2013. "Social Stratification and Higher Education Outcomes: The Case of Filipinos in Hawai'i." PhD diss., Department of Educational Administration, University of Hawai'i at Mānoa.

Lind, Andrew. 1938. *An Island Community: Ecological Succession in Hawaii*. Chicago: University of Chicago Press.

Liu, John. 1984. "Race, Ethnicity, and the Sugar Plantation System: Asian Labor in Hawaii, 1850–1900." In Lucie Cheng and Edna Bonacich, eds., *Labor Immigration Under Capitalism: Asian Workers in the United States Before World War II*, 186–210. Berkeley: University of California Press.

Lott, Eric. 1992. "Love and Theft: The Racial Unconscious of Blackface Minstrelsy." *Representations* 39: 23–50.

———. 1993. *Love and Theft: Blackface Minstrelsy and the American Working Class*. New York: Oxford University Press.

Lowe, Lisa. 1996. *Immigrants Acts: On Asian American Cultural Politics*. Durham, N.C.: Duke University Press.

Lum, Darrell H. Y. 1998. "Local Genealogy. What School You Went?" In E. Chock, J. Harstad, D. Lum, and B. Teter, eds., *Growing Up Local: An Anthology of Poetry and Prose from Hawai'i*, 11–15. Honolulu: Bamboo Ridge Press.

Mabalon, Dawn Bohulano. 2013. *Little Manila Is in the Heart: The Making of the Filipina/o American Community in Stockton, California*. Durham, N.C.: Duke University Press.

Mahon, Maureen. 2000. "The Visible Evidence of Cultural Producers." *Annual Review of Anthropology* 29: 467–92.

Mallki, Lisa. 1992. "National Geographic: The Rooting of Peoples and the Territorialization of National Identity Among Scholars and Refugees." *Cultural Anthropology* 7(1): 24–44.

Manalansan, Martin, IV, ed. 2000. *Cultural Compass: Ethnographic Explorations of Asian America*. Philadelphia: Temple University Press.

Manalansan, Martin, IV. 2003. *Global Divas: Filipino Gay Men in the Diaspora*. Durham, N.C.: Duke University Press.

Mauricio, Michael. 1997. *Waipahu: Its People and Heritage*. Honolulu: P.O.S.E. Custom Publishers.

Medallon, Mila. 1993a. "Filipinos Are Now Going for a Piece of the Pie." *Fil-Am Courier*, March.

———. 1993b. "Camouflaged Racism in Aloha Land?" *Fil-Am Courier*, April.

Melendy, Brett H. 1972. "California's Discrimination Against Filipinos, 1927–1935." In Roger Daniels and Spencer Olin Jr., *Racism in California: A Reader in the History of Oppression*, 141–51. New York: Macmillan.

Mendoza, Susanah Lily L. 2002. *Between the Homeland and the Diaspora: The Politics of Theorizing Filipino and Filipino American Identities: A Second Look at the Poststructuralism-Indigenization Debates*. New York: Routledge.

Michaelsen, Scott, and D. E. Johnson, eds. 1997. *Border Theory: The Limits of Cultural Politics*. Minneapolis: University of Minnesota Press.

Munro, Leslie Ann. 1983. "Waipahu: An Historical Profile of Education and Community." EdD diss., Department of Educational Foundations, University of Hawai'i at Mānoa.

Myerhoff, Barbara. 1992. *Remembered Lives: The Work of Ritual, Storytelling, and Growing Older*. Ann Arbor: University of Michigan Press.

Nadal, Kevin. 2009. *Filipino American Psychology: A Handbook of Theory, Research, and Clinical Practice*. Bloomington, Ind.: Author House Publishing.

Nedbalek, Lani. 1984 (1997, second printing). *Waipahu: A Brief History*. Wahiawa, Hi.: Wonder View Press.

Ochs, Elinor, and L. Capps. 1996. "Narrating the Self." *Annual Review of Anthropology* 25: 19–43.

Odo, Carol. 1975. "Phonological Processes in the English Dialect of Hawaii." PhD diss., Department of Second Language Studies, University of Hawai'i at Mānoa.

———. 1977. "Phonological Representations in Hawaiian English." *University of Hawaii Working Papers in Linguistics* 9:7 7–85.

Ogata, Paul. 1998. *Mental Oriental*. CD. Tropical Jam Productions.

Ogawa, Dennis. 1978. *Jan ken po: The World of Hawaii's Japanese Americans*. 2nd ed. Honolulu: University of Hawai'i Press.

———. 1981. "Dialogue: What Is Local?" *Hawai'i Committee for the Humanities News* 2: 7.

Okada, Karyn R. 2007. "An Analysis of Hawai'i's Tradition of 'Local' Ethnic Humor." *University of Hawai'i Law Review* 30(1): 219–42.

Okamura, Jonathan. 1980. "Aloha kanaka me ke aloha aina: Local Culture and Society in Hawai'i." *Amerasia Journal* 7: 119–37.

———. 1990. "Ethnicity and Stratification in Hawai'i." *Operation Manong Resource Papers* 1: 1–11.

———. 1991. "Beyond Adaptationism: Immigrant Filipino Ethnicity in Hawaii." *Social Process in Hawaii* 33: 56–72.

———. 1994. "Why There Are No Asian Americans in Hawai'i: The Continuing Significance of Local Identity." *Social Process in Hawai'i* 35: 161–78.

———. 1996. "Historical Legacies, Contemporary Challenges, and Future Visions: The Filipino American Community in Late Twentieth Century Hawai'i." In *Pagdiriwang 1996: Legacy and vision of Hawaii's Filipino Americans*, ed. Jonathan Okamura and Roderick Labrador, 1–4. Honolulu: Student Equity, Excellence & Diversity and Center for Southeast Asian Studies, University of Hawai'i at Manoa.

———. 1998a. *Imagining the Filipino American Diaspora: Transnational Relations, Identities, and Communities*. New York and London: Garland Publishing.

———. 1998b. "The Illusion of Paradise: Privileging Multiculturalism in Hawai'i." In *Making Majorities: Composing the Nation in Japan, China, Korea, Fiji, Malaysia, Turkey and the United States*, ed. Dru Gladney, 264–84. Palo Alto, Calif.: Stanford University Press.

———. 2008. *Ethnicity and Inequality in Hawai'i*. Philadelphia: Temple University Press.

———. 2010. "From Running Amok to Eating Dogs: A Century of Misrepresenting Filipino Americans in Hawai'i." *Ethnic and Racial Studies* 33(3): 496–514.

Okamura, Jonathan Y., and R. Labrador, eds. 1996. *Pagdiriwang 1996: Legacy and Vision of Hawai'i's Filipino Americans*. Honolulu: University of Hawai'i, Student Equity, Excellence, and Diversity, and Center for Southeast Asian Studies.

Oliveira, Katrina-Ann K. (2009). "Wahi a Kahiko: Place Names as Vehicles of Ancestral Memory." *AlterNative* 5(2): 1–24.

Ong, Aihwa. 1993. "On the Edge of Empires: Flexible Citizenship Among Chinese in Diaspora." *Positions* 1(3): 745–78.

———. 1999. *Flexible Citizenship: The Cultural Logics of Transnationality*. Durham, N.C. and London: Duke University Press.

Ong, Aihwa, and D. M. Nonini, eds. 1997. *Ungrounded Empires: The Cultural Politics of Modern Chinese Nationalism*. London and New York: Routledge.

Ortner, Sherry B. 2003. *New Jersey Dreaming: Capital, Culture, and the Class of '58*. Durham, N.C.: Duke University Press.

Park, Robert. 1926. "Our Racial Frontier in the Pacific." *Survey Graphic* 9: 192–96.

———. 1937. Introduction. In *Intermarriage in Hawaii: A Study of Mutually Conditioned Processes of Acculturation and Amalgamation*, ed. Romanzo Adams, vii–xiv. New York: Macmillan.

———. 1938. Introduction. In *An Island Community: Ecological Succession in Hawaii*, ed. Andrew Lind, vii–xiv. Chicago: University of Chicago Press.

Parrenas, Rhacel S. 2001. *Servants of Globalization: Women, Migration and Domestic Work*. Stanford, Calif.: Stanford University Press.

———. 2005. *Children of Global Migration: Transnational Families and Gendered Woes*. Stanford, Calif.: Stanford University Press.

———. 2008. *The Force of Domesticity: Filipina Migrants and Globalization*. New York: New York University Press.

———. 2011. *Illicit Flirtations: Labor, Migration and Sex Trafficking in Tokyo*. Stanford, Calif.: Stanford University Press.

Pisares, Elizabeth H. 2006. "Do You Mis(recognize) Me: Filipina Americans in Popular Music and the Problem of Invisibility." In *Positively No Filipinos Allowed: Building Communities and Discourse*, ed. Antonio Tiongson, Ricardo Gutierrez, and Edgardo Gutierrez, 172–98. Philadelphia: Temple University Press.

Pizon, Elmer Omar. 1999. "Black Dog [pinoy style]." *Bamboo Ridge* 75:169.

Pukui, Mary, Samuel Elbert, and Esther Mookini. 1976. *Place Names of Hawaii*. Revised and expanded edition. Honolulu: University of Hawai'i Press.

Quemuel, Christine. 1996. "Filipino student apathy or activism? Examining the activism and activities of Filipino student organizations throughout the University of Hawai'i system." In *Pagdiriwang 1996: Legacy and Vision of Hawaii's Filipino Americans*, ed. Jonathan Okamura and Roderick Labrador, 17–19. Honolulu: Student Equity, Excellence & Diversity and Center for Southeast Asian Studies, University of Hawai'i at Mānoa.

Radhakrishnan, Rajagopalan. 1991. "Ethnicity in an Age of Diaspora." *Transition* 54: 104–15.

———. 1996. *Diasporic Mediations: Between Home and Location*. Minneapolis: University of Minnesota Press.

Ramos, Teresita. n.d. "Some Communication Problems of Filipino Students."

———. 1996. "Philippine Languages in Hawaii: Vehicles of Cultural Survival." *Social Process in Hawaii* 37: 161–70.

Rattansi, Ali. 1995. "Just Framing: Ethnicities and Racisms in a 'Postmodern' Framework." In *Social Postmodernism: Beyond Identity Politics*, ed. L. Nicholson and S. Seidman, 250–86. Cambridge, U.K.: Cambridge University Press.

Revilla, Linda. 1996. "Filipino Americans: Issues of identity in Hawai'i." In *Pagdiriwang 1996: Legacy and vision of Hawaii's Filipino Americans*, ed. Jonathan Okamura and Roderick Labrador, 9–12. Honolulu: Student Equity, Excellence & Diversity and Center for Southeast Asian Studies, University of Hawai'i at Mānoa.

———. 1997. "Filipino American Identity: Transcending the Crisis." In *Filipino Americans: Transformation and identity*, ed. Maria Root, 95–111. Thousand Oaks, Calif.: Sage Publications.

Robinson, Cedric. 1982. *Black Marxism*. London: Zed Press.

Rodriguez, Dylan. 2009. *Suspended Apocalypse: White Supremacy, Genocide, and the Filipino Condition*. Minneapolis: University of Minnesota Press.

Rodriguez, Robyn M. 2010. *Migrants for Export: How the Philippine State Brokers Labor to the World*. Minneapolis: University of Minnesota Press.

Rohrer, Judy. 2010. *Haoles in Hawai'i*. Honolulu: University of Hawai'i Press.

Rosa, John. 2000. "Local Story: The Massie Narrative and the Cultural Production of Local Identity in Hawai'i." *Amerasia Journal* 37(3): 93–115.

———. 2001. "'The Coming of the Neo-Hawaiian Race': Nationalism and Metaphors of the Melting Pot in Popular Accounts of Mixed-Race Individuals." In *The Sum of Our Parts: Mixed Heritage Asian Americans*, ed. Teresa Williams-Leon and Cynthia Nakashima, 49–56. Philadelphia: Temple University Press.

Rosaldo, Renato. 1989. *Culture and Truth: The Remaking of Social Analysis*. Boston: Beacon.

Rouse, Roger. 1991. "Mexican Migration and the Social Space of Postmodernism." *Diaspora* 1(1): 8–23.

Rubino, Carl. 2000. *Ilocano Dictionary and Grammar*. Honolulu: University of Hawai'i Press.

Safran, William. 1991. "Diasporas in Modern Societies: Myths of Homeland and Return." *Diaspora* 1(1): 83–99.

Sakoda, Kent, and Jeff Siegel. 2003. *Pidgin Grammar: An Introduction to the Creole Language of Hawai'i*. Honolulu: Bess Press.

San Buenaventura, Steffi. 1995. "Filipino Immigration to the United States History and Legacy." In *The Asian American Encyclopedia*, ed. Franklin Ng, 439–53. New York: Marshall Cavendish.

———. 1996a. "Hawaii's Filipinos: History and Legacy." In *Pagdiriwang 1996: Legacy and Vision of Hawaii's Filipino Americans*, ed. Jonathan Okamura and Roderick Labrador, 35–38. Honolulu: Student Equity, Excellence & Diversity and Center for Southeast Asian Studies, University of Hawai'i at Mānoa.

———. 1996b. "Hawaii's '1946 Sakada.'" *Social Process in Hawaii* 37: 74–90.

San Juan, Epifanio, Jr. 1994. "Configuring the Filipino Diaspora in the United States." *Diaspora* 3(2): 117–33.

———. 1998a. "One Hundred Years of Producing and Reproducing the 'Filipino,'" *Amerasia Journal* 24(2): 1–33.

———. 1998b. *From Exile to Diaspora: Versions of the Filipino Experience in the United States*. Boulder, Colo.: Westview Press.

———. 2002. *Racism and cultural studies: Critiques of multiculturalist ideology and the politics of difference*. Durham, N.C.: Duke University Press.

———. 2009. *Toward Filipino Self-Determination: Beyond Transnational Self-Determination*. Albany: State University of New York Press.

Saranillio, Dean I. 2008. "Colonial Amnesia: Rethinking Filipino 'American' Settler Empowerment in the U.S. Colony of Hawai'i." In Candace Fujikane and Jonathan Okamura, eds., *Asian Settler Colonialism: From Local Governance to the Habits of Everyday Life in Hawai'i*, 256–78. Honolulu: University of Hawai'i Press.

———. 2010a. "Kēwaikaliko's *Benocide*: Reversing the Imperial Gaze of *Rice v. Cayetano* and Its Legal Progeny." *American Quarterly* 62(3): 457–76.

———. 2010b. "Colliding Histories: Hawai'i Statehood at the Intersection of Asians 'Ineligible to Citizenship' and Hawaiians 'Unfit for Self-Government.' " *Journal of Asian American Studies* 13(3): 283–309.

See, Sarita Eschavez. 2009. *The Decolonized Eye: Filipino American Art and Performance*. Minneapolis: University of Minnesota Press.

Seneca, R. 1995. "DeLima's Jokes Perpetuate Filipino Stereotypes." *Hawaii Filipino Chronicle*, January 1.

Shapiro, Michael. 1999. *Cinematic Political Thought*. Minnesota: University of Minnesota Press.

Sharma, Miriam. 1984. "Labor Migration and Class Formation among the Filipinos in Hawaii, 1906–1946." In Lucie Cheng and Edna Bonacich, eds., *Labor Immigration Under Capitalism: Asian Workers in the United States Before World War II*, 579–616. Berkeley: University of California Press.

Sherzer, Joel. 2002. *Speech Play and Verbal Art*. Austin: University of Texas Press.

Simonson, Douglas, Ken Sakata, and Pat Sasaki. 1981. *Pidgin to da max*. Honolulu: Bess Press.

Smith, Pam. 1977. "Booga Booga: Three Mokes with Different Strokes." *Hawaii Observer* 99: 18–23.

Sodetani, Naomi. 2001. "Local Humor and the New World Order." *Honolulu Weekly*, May 30–June 5.

Spivak, Gayatri C. 1988. *In Other Worlds*. New York: Routledge.

Sterling, Elspeth P. and Catherine C. Summers, eds. 1978. *Sites of Oahu*. Honolulu: Bernice P. Pauahi Bishop Museum.

Strobel, Leny M. 1996. " 'Born-again Filipino': Filipino American Identity and Asian Panethnicity." *Amerasia Journal* 22(2): 31–53.

Takaki, Ronald. 1983. *Pau hana: Plantation Life and Labor in Hawaii, 1835–1920*. Honolulu: University of Hawaii Press.

———. 1993. *Raising Cane: The World of Plantation Hawaii*. New York: Chelsea House Publishers.

Talmy, Steven. 2009. "Forever FOB? Reproducing and Resisting the Other in High School ESL." In Angela Reyes and Adrienne Lo, eds., *Beyond Yellow English: Toward a Linguistic Anthropology of Asian Pacific America*, 347–65. New York: Oxford University Press.

Teodoro, Luis, ed. 1981. *Out of This Struggle: The Filipinos in Hawaii*. Honolulu: University Press of Hawaii.

Tintiangco-Cubales, Allyson. 2009. "Building a Community Center: Filipinas/os in San Francisco's Excelsior Neighborhood." In *Asian America: Forming New*

Communities, Expanding Boundaries, ed. Huping Ling, 104–25. New Brunswick, N.J.: Rutgers University Press.

Tiongson, Antonio T., Jr. 2013. *Filipinos Represent: DJs, Racial Authenticity, and the Hip-hop Nation*. Minneapolis: University of Minnesota Press.

Tiongson, Antonio T., Jr., Ricardo Gutierrez, and Edgardo Gutierrez, eds. 2006. *Positively No Filipinos Allowed: Building Communities and Discourse*. Philadelphia: Temple University Press.

Tonouchi, Lee. 1999. "No Laugh Brah, Serious: Pidgin's Association Wit Local Comedy." *Hybolics* 1:22–33.

Torres-Kitamura, Maria. 1993. "A Generation Lost?" *Fil-Am Courier*, October, 6–7.

Trask, Haunani-Kay. 2000. "Settlers of Color and 'Immigrant' Hegemony: 'Locals' in Hawai'i." *Amerasia* 26(2): 1–24.

Vergara, Benito. 2008. *Pinoy Capital: The Filipino Nation in Daly City*. Philadelphia: Temple University Press.

Ward, Ethel A. 1994. *Filipino Culture: Reclaiming a Heritage*. Honolulu: University of Hawai'i at Mānoa Summer Session.

Wolf, Eric R. 1984. *Europe and the People Without History*. Berkeley: University of California Press.

Woolard, Kathryn A. 1998. "Language Ideology as a Field of Inquiry." In B. Schieffelin, K. Woolard, and P. Kroskrity, eds., *Language Ideologies: Practice and Theory*, 3–47. New York: Oxford University Press.

Yamamoto, Eric. 1979. "The Significance of Local." *Social Process in Hawaii* 27: 102–15.

Yamamoto, Michael T., Nina Yuriko (Ota) Sylva, and Karen N. Yamamoto. 2005. *Waipahu . . . Recollections from a Sugar Plantation Community in Hawaii*. Albuquerque: Innoventions.

INDEX

Note: An *f* following a page number indicates a figure; an *n* following a page number indicates a note.

Abercrombie, Neil, 99–100, 120, 134
absolutism, ethnic, 95–96
Aguinaldo, Emilio, 85
ahupua'a (land division), 34, 141n9, 141n11
Alcantara, Ruben, 29, 36
Alconcel, Lito, 109, 110
Alconcel, Soledad, 109
aloha, 35, 54, 141n14
American Dream, 12, 25, 102, 118, 127, 134
Americanization, 13–14, 134
AmFac/JMB Hawai'i, 111, 112
Amianan Studies (Philippines), 77, 146n2
Andaya, Leonard, 12–13
Anderson, Robert, 41, 142n23
annexation: Hawai'i, 38, 41, 42; Philippines, 37, 38, 42
Aquino, Belinda, 122–23, 124
architecture: *bahay kuba*, 107–8f, 140nn2&5; *bahay na bato*, 28, 140n2; Filipino Community Center, 28–29f, 30–31f, 32f–33, 48f, 140n6; Spanish mission–style, 31–32, 140n5; Waipahu, 27–28
Asian Americans, 4, 53
Asian Pacific American identity, 53, 55
Asian settler colonialism, 47, 125, 134–35
assimilation, 13, 14; blending process, 54; ideology, 102–4; linguistic, 83; narratives, 30

Austronesian language family, 80

bachelor societies: Hawai'i, 45, 60, 144n24; U.S. West Coast, 142n21
bahay kubo (nipa hut), 107–8f, 140n2, 140n5
bahay na bato (stone house), 28, 140n2
Baldoz, Rick, 21
bayanihan (cooperation), 35, 107, 108
Beechert, Edward, 38, 40
Benton, James, 56, 143n4
"Big Five," 40, 112
Bonifacio, Andres, 78, 84, 90, 92
Bonus, Rick, 22, 101–2
Booga Booga, 56–57, 143n4
"born-again" Filipinos, 91, 93–94
boundary construction, 84, 133
Buckaloose: Shmall Keed Time (Small Kid Time; Da Braddahs), 51–52, 60–68. *See also* ethnic humor
"building," double meaning of, 23
buk buk identity, 52, 73; characteristics, 59, 60, 61–62, 64–65, 79; derivation, 143n23–144n23; otherness, 139n20

Canseco, George, 90
capitalism, 4, 33–34, 38–40, 140n3
Cariaga, Roman, 57
Casamina, Roland, 35, 110, 113, 117, 118–20, 122, 123, 131

Roderick Labrador is an assistant professor of ethnic studies at the University of Hawai'i at Mānoa. He is the coauthor of *Filipinos in Hawai'i* and coeditor of *Empire of Funk: Hip Hop and Representation in Filipina/o America.*

THE ASIAN AMERICAN EXPERIENCE